WELFAR_
& SOCIAL
POLICY IN
AUSTRALIA

the distribution of advantage

edited by

MICHAEL WEARING
ROSEMARY BERREEN

School of Social Work
University of New South Wales

HARCOURT
BRACE

Sydney   Fort Worth   London   Orlando   Toronto

Senior Editor: Nick Kent
Acquisitions Editor: Louise Ewan
Manager, Editorial and
Production: Rema Gnanadickam
Designer: Pamela Horsnell
Senior Production Editor: Fiona Julian

Production Editor: Rema Gnanadickam
Cover and page design: Pamela Horsnell

Harcourt Brace & Company, Australia
30–52 Smidmore Street
Marrickville NSW 2204

Harcourt Brace & Company
24–28 Oval Road, London NWI 7DX

Harcourt Brace & Company
Orlando, Florida 32887

National Library of Australia Catalogue-in-Publication data

Welfare and social policy in Australia: the distribution of advantage.

Includes index.
ISBN 0 7295 1315 7
1. Welfare economics. 2. Public welfare — Australia.
3. Australia — Social policy. I. Wearing, Michael, date–.
II. Berreen, Rosemary, date–.

361.610994

Cover illustration by Judi Kuepper
Index compiled by Garry Cousins
Typeset in 11/13 pt Goudy Old Style by Essay Composition, Sydney
Printed in Australia by Star Printery

CONTENTS

PART TWO Distribution and redistribution

LIST OF TABLES

CONTRIBUTORS

ROSEMARY BERREEN lectures in social welfare history and social policy in the School of Social Work, University of New South Wales. Her research interests are in institutional and general welfare history, classificatory processes in social policy, and the construction of ideas about welfare.

JAN BRECKENRIDGE lectures in the School of Social Work, University of New South Wales. She has co-edited *Crimes of Violence*, a text on sexual violence in Australia and her main research area is the construction of knowledge in child sexual assault.

LOIS BRYSON is Professor of Sociology at the University of Newcastle. She wrote (with Faith Thompson) Australia's first urban community study, *An Australian Newtown*, and has published widely on poverty, family, work, gender, sport, the welfare state and public sector management. Her most recent book is *Welfare and The State: Who Benefits?*

STEPHEN GARTON lectures in history at the University of Sydney and is the author of *Medicine and Madness* and *Out of Luck: Poor Australians and Social Welfare*.

DAMIAN GRACE is a senior lecturer in social philosophy in the School of Social Work, University of New South Wales. His main areas of research and teaching are professional and business ethics.

ADAM JAMROZIK currently lectures in social work at the University of South Australia. He is co-author of *How Australians Live* and author of *Class, Inequality and the State*.

MARTIN MOWBRAY is Professor of Social Work at the Royal Melbourne Institute of Technology. He has published extensively on community work, local government and urban planning.

ELIM PAPADAKIS is Professor of Sociology at University of New England, Armidale, New South Wales. He is co-author of *The Private Provision of Public Welfare* and has also published in the areas of social movements and public opinion about the Australian welfare state.

RODNEY SMITH lectures in the School of Political Science at the University of New South Wales. He has edited an introductory text *Politics in Australia* and writes in the areas of electoral politics and political theory, unemployment, and the welfare state

PAUL SMYTH is Senior Researcher at Uniya Centre for Social Research and Action, Sydney. His main area of writing is on economic thought and social policy in Australia in the 1950s.

FRANK STILWELL is Associate Professor of Economics at the University of Sydney. He is the author of a number of publications in the area of political economy and his most recent book is entitled *Reshaping Australia: Urban Problems and Policies*.

MICHAEL WEARING is a sociologist and lectures in the School of Social Work, University of New South Wales. He has published in the areas of welfare administration, the social control of marginalised groups and public attitudes towards social welfare.

ACKNOWLEDGMENTS

The task of putting together an edited collection depends very much on the goodwill of those approached to participate in the venture. We wish to thank the authors of the various chapters for their contributions and their forbearance with deadlines and editorial requests. The research assistance by Megan Edwards for chapter two and the comments offered by Anya Moore on chapter seven are appreciated. Support offered from within the University of New South Wales in the form of secretarial assistance, research funding and study leave has facilitated the process of submitting the manuscript of this book.

We are grateful to Harcourt Brace & Company for accepting this text: to Louise Ewan, Social Science Editor, Rema Gnanadickam, a most meticulous production editor, and Pamela Horsnell for the cover design and layout. Lastly, the constant challenge presented by students in social welfare and social policy courses offered in the School of Social Work, University of New South Wales has convinced us of the need for this type of text — we thank them.

Michael Wearing
Rosemary Berreen

The authors and the publishers wish to thank the following for permission to reproduce copyright material. J. Lang for extracts pp. 190, 191, from *Urban Development and Social Justice*, New South Wales Council of Social Services, 1991, pp. 3–9.

While every effort has been made to contact copyright holders or their agents, a few have remained untraceable. The publisher would be interested to hear from any copyright holders who have not already been acknowledged.

INTRODUCTION
Redefining welfare

MICHAEL WEARING AND
ROSEMARY BERREEN

This book brings together a collection of writings on some of the key social and political concepts, actors and institutions which have and will influence discourse on welfare in Australia in the 1990s and beyond. The contributions do not attempt to cover the multiplicity of factors which influence the construction and distribution of welfare; rather they present for debate, reflections on a diverse range of influences which impinge on the ongoing construction of Australia's welfare state. The contributors have approached their topics from a variety of theoretical and ideological perspectives in the hope of keeping to the forefront concerns about the nature of the production, distribution and redistribution of material and social resources in Australia and the implications of inequitable distribution for the experience of life in Australian society.

In analysing the philosophy of the Australian Liberal Party following their 1993 election defeat, Brett (1993:43) contends that the emphasis on competition and rewarding winners by the Coalition Parties left people wondering as to what would hold the fabric of Australian society together and what would happen to the losers. This collection of essays entitled *Welfare and social policy in Australia: the distribution of advantage*, looks at the factors which shape the distribution of advantage and disadvantage — the allocation of winning and losing in Australian society. The need for this type of collection has arisen out of the contributors' teaching involvement in a range of courses on social policy and welfare over the last decade. Being confronted by student perceptions of social policy and its outcome, social welfare, as primarily concerned with 'the poor' rather than how and why advantage and disadvantage is produced and distributed in a society, challenged us to collect together a range of writings which demonstrate that who wins as well as who loses is central to explanations about the pattern of welfare in Australian society.

The dangers in studying disadvantage in isolation from its distributional context was evident in a series of articles in a major Australian newspaper on the 'arrival' of Australia's so called 'underclass'. The series constructed a discourse about disadvantage, accepted the validity of the concept 'underclass', and in so doing created a classificatory system of belonging or not belonging to this class.

> ... no work, no hope, no escape... this is the prospect facing a growing number of Australians. Call it a welfare society, a workless class or an underclass, it is the same: a group of people excluded from the mainstream working society.
>
> (Sydney Morning Herald [SMH], 1993: 17)

To concentrate on this excluded 'group' provides a convenient label and focus of analysis which, in the very process, isolates the analysis of disadvantage from a necessary consideration of the interrelationship of advantage and disadvantage. Discourses on welfare are discourses about production, distribution and redistribution across the whole society and not about constructing images of the 'poor' such as:

> Robbery, arson, child abuse and yes, even murder — the price of the recession has yet to be paid in terms of crime. The sad link between crime rates and disadvantage, unemployment and inequality is obvious in the United States. Now it is Australia's turn.
>
> (SMH, 1993: 20)

Definitions

The organising rubric around which this collection has been gathered together is the analysis of the production and distribution of welfare throughout Australian society with international comparisons. The term 'welfare' is a contentious one open to a variety of interpretations. The Macquarie Dictionary definition of welfare as 'the state of faring well' or 'well-being' (1991:1981) fails to specify the parameters of wellbeing. However, if this meaning is expanded to take in the production and distribution of income and assets, status and power in a society (see Walker, 1983:141) then welfare or wellbeing is defined in a manner which includes both material and social dimensions and demands that any analysis of welfare involves looking at distributional patterns across the entire society.

The term 'welfare state' can be defined narrowly according to Pierson (1991) as state measures for the provision of key welfare services or more broadly as a particular form of state, a distinctive form of polity, or a specific type of society, such as the welfare state under capitalism in which the state 'intervenes within the processes of economic production and distribution to reallocate life chances between individuals and/or classes' (Pierson, 1991:7). The nature of state intervention is a political question which includes contest over the scope and extent of state responsibility for reallocating life chances.

The debates in this collection take up the range of factors which have and will influence the reallocation of life chances within the operations of the Australian welfare state. This reallocation or shaping of advantage will depend on the outcomes of decisions of a wide range of social institutions and groups (Walker, 1983:141) and pattern to what extent the individual has an equitable share of resources including, among others, income, employment, education, housing, health care, civil and political rights and leisure. Access to, and a share in these resources will be influenced by the person's socioeconomic position, gender, racial and ethnic background, whether the person lives in an urban or rural environment, his or her age and ability. The market, the non-government and informal sectors as well as the state will constantly influence the nature and scope of distribution of welfare; and judgments about an adequate standard and the preferred patterns of distribution will be mediated continually by political processes and economic structures. A broad understanding of what creates and influences patterns of welfare in Australian society takes debate about welfare from a limited discussion of the 'poor' as a separate object of analysis, to a consideration of the factors that shape advantage and disadvantage for the entire population.

The need for a broadly conceived discourse on welfare is further exemplified when considering the wellbeing of Aboriginal (Koori) Australians. The issue which preoccupied many Australians in 1993 was the Mabo decision on Australian Aboriginal native title, which followed from the 1992 High Court ruling rejecting the doctrine of 'terra nullius' (empty unowned land), as Australia was defined at the time of British settlement (see Gregory, 1992:157). It is now recognised in common law that Aboriginal and Torres Strait Islanders' rights of ownership existed before non-Aboriginal settlement and may still exist 'where the connection with the land has been maintained and title has not been extinguished' (Dodson, 1993:7). Yet, as Aboriginal activist Gary Foley argues, for Aboriginal (Koori) Australians to shape advantage requires an understanding by non-Aboriginal Australians of what that dispossession has meant for Kooris:

> *It is vital and urgent for the non-Koori community to gain some insight into the effects its society, institutions and attitudes have on Koories as people and communities . . . this country will then stand on . . . the edge of a new era born of a just, honourable, equitable and mutually beneficial resolution of the oldest historical dispute that exists in this country today.*

> (Foley 1993:15)

While the implications of the decision are outside the scope of this book, the issue demonstrates that reversing disadvantage often involves claiming territory and power from those with advantage gained as a result of inequitable distribution.

Contents

The book is set out in two parts. Part one on themes and definitions begins by considering the development of welfare discourse in Australia following white settlement and at the turn of the nineteenth century. Chapter one, 'And thereby to discountenance mendicity', suggests that welfare practices in early nineteenth century Australia, as documented in the foundation colony in New South Wales, were informed by the needs of the developing free enterprise system and emphasis on wage labour. Those who were unable to compete and sought help were classified as 'deserving' or 'undeserving' based on criteria related to willingness to work if able, and acceptable moral behaviour. Those who offended against the norms of self-help and self-sufficiency were institutionalised in order to discourage begging and imposition, and the poor who 'outraged public decency' were removed from the streets of Sydney. The role of the British and colonial governments was to be one of strong support of voluntary charitable organisations rather than direct state intervention, so as to avoid any semblance of an English Poor Law system of welfare. Yet while statutory poor law intervention was avoided, the pattern of welfare which emerged contained its philosophies and practices.

In chapter two on 'Rights and duties: Arguing charity and welfare 1880–1920', the author contends that new welfare discourses emerged in Australia in late nineteenth and early twentieth century Australia with, for example, the introduction of aged pensions and the Harvester Judgment of a 'living wage' for workers. These new arguments, based on rights and duties, had to compete with the older arguments of benevolence, obligations, deference and self-help. The outcome was a compromise which is still reflected in Australia's residualist welfare state. Yet, despite its limitations, the author argues that the modern welfare state is worth reforming to retain the hard-won principles of early twentieth century Australian initiatives which emphasised the duty of the state to ensure the right to welfare.

The centrality of the living wage and the role of full employment as the keystone of the Australian welfare state as it emerged in the legislation of the 1940s raises questions about the relationship of economic to social policy in the early postwar history of social policy and is taken up as the theme of chapter three, on 'The macro-economic foundations of the welfare state'. Two stages in the development of the idea of an Australian welfare state are considered, the first being the period from the Great Depression of the thirties to the onset of the Cold War and the planning of the economy in order to ensure economic and political stability. The second stage begins in the late 1950s when Keynesian stabilisation measures began to create expectations of an affluent society and the concern was to produce a better quality of life. These stages are related to the development of economic thought and social policy as subjects of intellectual inquiry and extend the debates about the role of economic policy in social policy initiatives. The author of this chapter argues that the political arithmetic of the mixed economy which emerged in the mid 1950s marked the end of a vision of social policy in which social goals would direct the economy. By this time the demand for social security had been satisfied; the economy was stabilised at full employment without extension of public ownership; and the role of the state was to be one of management of the economy — a technical task which spelt the end of utopian thinking and emphasised an elaboration of the arithmetic of the existing system. Economic policy of full employment and stability emphasised the centrality of employment as a major tenet of the welfare state.

Chapter four on 'The major party competition: Social welfare since 1972' examines the relationship between the major political parties and state welfare since Gough Whitlam's Labor government came to power. The chapter contends that the two major political parties have envisaged the scope of state welfare as dependent upon economic growth. As a result, they have pursued similar welfare rhetorics. Chapter four thus continues the arguments put forward in chapter three, about the role of economic thinking in the determination of social policy. The Whitlam government initially defended an expansionary welfare vision precisely because it assumed that the economy called for welfare growth. In the relatively stable economic context of the late 1960s and the early 1970s, there was little dispute between the parties that welfare was a corrective to capitalism's failures. Since the mid 1970s, the author contends that the parties' rhetorics of welfare contraction have been shaped by their competition to build support in the electorate and among key groups in uncertain economic circumstances.

Part one concludes with the chapter on 'Social justice' which examines the idea of a just society and the concept 'justice', noting that 'social justice' is a product of market societies and is about changing social institutions and attitudes to achieve a fairer society. The use of the concept is central in providing the ground rules for equitable distribution of welfare but, as the author warns, social justice is only part of the answer to deprivation. It must be combined with a shared system of social values; people must care about each other and translate that care into social policies which pursue equity. This analysis of social justice links the first and second parts of the book in that it spells out ways of looking at the nature of distribution and redistribution of welfare, the focus of part two. To shape advantage implies that judgments are made about what is a fair outcome for individuals and groups while also having regard for their quality of life.

In part two on 'Distribution and redistribution', a number of areas are examined for the influences that shape distribution. In chapter six, 'Social class and community services', the author contends that the contemporary welfare state functions in an uneasy alliance with the capitalist system, seeking to enable the market economy to function and providing the means of survival for individuals and groups who do not obtain sufficient means through the market. Given that resource availability and allocation in the market is inherently unequal, it follows that if availability of access to resources provided by the state is also unequal the state actually creates and maintains inequality. Because of the tendency in policy analysis to concentrate on the visible poor or marginalised it is possible that advantage is bestowed on certain population strata who are hidden from public view because they are not seen as 'the poor', Three types of resources are examined: education, employment and child care. The author argues that the welfare state has created new inequalities and community services have become paths to advantage for the middle class and especially for a new middle class who are both the providers and consumers of these services. Advantages accumulate because these resources are interdependent: a good education increases the chances of gaining a well-paid job which is facilitated by access to quality child care if one can afford it. The name community services suggests services established for the whole community but access to them is unequal. The distribution of assets brings and reinforces status and power yet the welfare state, in some of its operations, creates and maintains the inequalities which it seeks to reverse.

The theme of the distribution and redistribution is taken up in chapter seven on 'Public opinion, redistribution and the welfare state' in which the author analyses the nature of public opinion on state intervention for resource distribution and who are perceived to be the major beneficiaries of this intervention. Opinions on the distribution of two resources, health care and education, are analysed from data collected in Australia in 1988; some comparisons with data from the United Kingdom are also included. Results suggest that the individual's self interest and experience of use of these resources are important in shaping public opinion and that most people recognise the importance of both statutory intervention and private provision. Perceptions about redistribution suggest that politics is the art of compromise as ideas about charity, market forces, social solidarity and altruism may all contribute to opinions about the role of the welfare state.

The shaping of advantage through the equitable distribution of welfare may depend on the appropriate nature of conceptualisation of the policy area in question, as is seen in chapter eight on 'Intervention in child welfare' where the way in which 'child sexual assault' is understood intellectually and in the public arena determines the nature of intervention. Prior to the 1970s, child sexual abuse as an area requiring response within Australia and particularly New South Wales, suffered from either a denial of its existence or a recognition that classified sexual abuse under the more general label of child abuse. The rise of feminist movements within the civil rights campaigns in the 1970s and early 1980s promoted the conceptualisation of child sexual abuse within a feminist framework which recognised its gender and power dimensions and highlighted the inadequacies of class-based explanations. The policy responses which emerged necessitated the engagement of feminists with the state despite the paradox of the state perpetuating patriarchal power relationships. However, the need of the NSW Labor government to be seen as reformist, facilitated policy formulation and implementation allowing for feminist claims to be met and programs instituted, which recognised the gendered nature of child sexual assault.

The distinction between housing the rich and housing the poor and the developments in urban and housing policies in Australia are considered in 'Social justice and the Australian city', chapter nine. The chapter synthesises a cross section of research on current policy and future directions derived from a wide range of government reports compiled in the early 1990s in Australia; findings are related to current economic and political trends. Over the last decade, issues such as: access and affordability of housing; its future supply and distribution; infrastructure support; and appropriate responses to a changing demographical profile have been the focus for analysis and policy initiatives.

However, the degree of overall inequality of housing distribution indicates a lack of fundamental change necessary to achieve strong financial support for the non-home owner. Housing and urban policy reflect a priority on the part of the state towards cost containment and concern about the level of profitability derived from housing investment. Policy is driven by economic and political considerations rather than a commitment to equity as manifest in the nature of development of public housing and infrastructure support which would enhance the social wage and residential conditions of low income recipients.

In chapter ten on citizenship and the welfare state ('Dis/claiming citizenship?'), the author examines the politics of citizenship and notes a shift from social to market citizenship in the 1990s in Australia. He identifies six discourses on social justice which may be seen as organising the way in which professionals and administrators in welfare service delivery think about issues of social justice. These discourses have been instrumental in hastening the transformation of social citizenship into a market-based and individualistic enterprise; in the process, the ability of the marginalised and dispossessed to claim social rights has become limited and access to income and assets, status and power determined by ability to compete in the market place. The ideal of social citizenship, as espoused through priority of social goals in the 1940s, has become lost in the new managerialist administrative systems which economise on social justice imperatives.

Chapter eleven on 'The changing shape of gender dis/advantage in Australia' considers the general pattern of women's access to economic resources, social status and power in Australia particularly in the last decade and then concentrates on the nexus between the key areas of social policy, the labour market and the family. The findings demonstrate significant changes in women's labour force participation and equalisation in the formal characteristics of the social security system which remove, to a large extent, the duality of a different welfare state for men and women. On the ground, however, there has been far less change, for while a range of policies have recognised the particular disadvantages suffered by women in the areas of violence, disability, race and ethnicity, the gendered perception of caring has reinforced the traditional sexual division of labour. The picture of formal equality is superimposed by the traditional notions of male and female tasks which reinforce gender disadvantage.

In the final chapter of part two, 'The economic context of social policy', the recurring theme of the relationship between social and economic policy is taken up and attention is drawn to the structural, economic changes, economic ideologies and economic policies which need to be considered if social policy is to be progressive and relevant in the contemporary Australian context. In order to shape advantage in an equitable manner, social policies need to be integrated with an alternative economic strategy and a program of political change. In the Conclusion, 'Reinventing welfare?', prospects for the future of the Australian welfare state are considered in the light of the major themes reflected in the preceding chapters. In the face of conservatism within the political mainstream and a transition to market-based welfare provision there is need for a repoliticisation of welfare to achieve greater equality and social justice for excluded citizens.

REFERENCES

Brett, J. (1993), 'The Headless Chooks Party', *The Sydney Morning Herald*, 31 July, p. 43.
Cleary, P. (1993), 'Locked Out', *The Sydney Morning Herald* , 17 July, pp. 39,42.
Dodson, P. (1993), 'Reconciliation', *Aboriginal Law Bulletin*, 3(61), pp. 6–9.
Foley, G. (1993), 'The Barriers to a White/Black Accord' *The Sydney Morning Herald*, 21 July, p. 15.
Gregory, M. (1992),'Rewriting history 1, Mabo v Queensland : the decision', *Aboriginal Law Bulletin*, 17(4), pp. 157–161.
Pierson, C. (1991), *Beyond the Welfare State*, Polity Press, Cambridge.
Steketee, M (1993), 'The Symptoms of Poverty', *The Sydney Morning Herald*, 20 July, p. 9.
The Macquarie Dictionary (1991), Second edition, Revision, Macquarie Library, Sydney.
Walker, A. (1983) 'Social policy, administration and the construction of welfare' in M. Loney, D. Boswell, and J. Clarke (eds), *Social Policy and Social Welfare*, Open University Press, Milton Keynes, pp. 127–150.

PART ONE
Themes and definitions

CHAPTER ONE

'AND THEREBY TO DISCOUNTENANCE MENDICITY'

Practices of charity in early nineteenth century Australia

ROSEMARY BERREEN

INTRODUCTION

In Sydney, in 1821, an Asylum for 'the aged and impotent true poor' was opened under the auspices of a voluntary organisation, the Benevolent Society of New South Wales. The significance of that occasion, for the practice of charity in the emerging capitalist society of New South Wales, lay in the nature of the debates which surrounded the decision to intervene and provide institutional care for those judged unable to provide for themselves. The debates contained three major themes and it is intended in this chapter to examine each theme and its contribution to the general discourse on practices of charity in early nineteenth century Australia.

The first theme, as to who should intervene to reverse disadvantage for those members of society lacking basic subsistence is examined to clarify why, in New South Wales, the pattern which emerged was one of voluntary organisations, heavily subsidised by the state, as the major dispenser of charity. Second, the debates about who ought to be the recipients of care are considered in terms of the criteria used to classify deserving and undeserving poor. The virtues of thrift, self-help and self-reliance dominated both in entry criteria and institutional management and suggest an ethic-linked value being placed on work and industrious habits as the preferred means of distributing advantage in the colony. Finally, the theme of charity provision as a means of social control is considered in the light of a Benevolent Society Annual Report (BSAR) statement that a role for the Asylum was to remove from the streets of Sydney 'those most unhappily depraved persons who outrage public decency by their intemperance, contaminate the young by their profanity and obscenity and aid every species of fraud and dishonesty' (BSAR, 1830:160).

John Smart was admitted to the Sydney Benevolent Asylum in 1821 after three years in the penal colony of New South Wales. While little is known of what transpired between his arrival as a convict aged in his mid-fifties in 1821 and his admission to the Asylum in 1825, the Asylum House Book (BS AHB:1825) describes him as 'an imposing mendicant'. The judgment classified John Smart as one who begged, perhaps with a tendency to manufacture or embellish his needs as he attempted to gain help from others, a suggestion too that he exploited this goodwill of others towards his misfortune. The category 'imposing beggar' sounded a warning to all who might help John Smart that he was not to be trusted and should only be aided in a manner which might discourage his begging behaviour. While the House Book entry notes his infirmities as 'deafness and a bad leg' it is unlikely that such conditions excused his imposition. His presence at the Asylum suggests that the Benevolent Society thought it better that he reside out of sight of the general public in the hope that better habits might be instilled in him. The classification of John Smart raises questions about the practices of charity which evolved in the early colony of New South Wales, a colony intent on self sufficiency and avoidance of the English poor law system of state intervention with poor relief and a poor law levy. The transition from convict depot to free enterprise economy is examined to determine if the administration of charity was one in which the receipt of poor relief was determined by the needs and values of a free enterprise economy.

The early colony

The question of what happens to those unable to secure life for themselves and who ought to take responsibility is a perennial one. Advantage and disadvantage and the reasons for that distribution, the 'who gets what and why' in a society depend to a large extent on the nature of the social, economic and political systems as instituted and mediated by the state. In the context of the white occupation of Australia, the reasons for settlement would appear to render the question of responsibility for wellbeing for inhabitants as unambiguous in the short term.[1] The early colony, established on the shores of Port Jackson in 1788, was essentially a penal institution consisting of jailer and jailed. The state assumed responsibility for securing for these inhabitants the basics of life: food, clothing and shelter (Dickey, 1987:1). Yet, the challenge to establish a self-sufficient colony had already been given to Governor Phillip for 'his instructions were concerned first with survival, with shaping all the convicts, without gender distinction, into a self supporting workforce' (Aveling, 1992:2).

The mercantile value of Australia was a prime reason for its use as a convict depot and transportation provided a sentence which ensured long-term availability of workers (Ignatieff, 1978: 91–92; Powell, 1989:76). Transportation to the colonies can be seen not only as a solution to the problems generated by rapid social change in Britain but additionally as a 'bridge for the expansion of capitalism into Australia' (McMichael, 1988:72). Despite some attempts at public prison farms, the pattern which emerged by the turn of the century was the assignment of convicts to emancipist farmers who sold their produce to the government and the private market; wage labour was becoming the central feature of the colony's pattern of commerce (Aveling, 1992:8). Unlike the previous practice of the British government in selling convicts to private contractors, the pattern followed in the colonies of New South Wales was one of the state maintaining responsibility for convicts regardless of whether they were assigned to free settlers or to government works. However, while retaining authority over convicts, the British government assigned them in such a way as to encourage free enterprise rather than subsistence production. Conditions of their employment and release were predicated on contribution to the private enterprise economy. Essentially, the way in which convicts were treated was shaped by commercial development (McMichael, 1988:57–59).

Free enterprise and wage labour became the dominant means of attaining well-being and 'by 1800 a majority of freed men and many of the serving convicts worked for wages' (Aveling, 1992:8). Two decades later, the results of a general muster of the inhabitants of New South Wales show that, of the total population of 17 265 persons, less than one-third (31.2 per cent) were victualled by the colonial government while more than two-thirds (68.8 per cent) looked after their own basic needs. The number victualled from government stores was composed predominantly of the civil and military staff and prisoners with the number of free persons victualled less than one-third (26.3 per cent) of all persons in receipt of rations.[2] In the thirty years which had elapsed since the arrival of the First Fleet wage labour and self-sufficiency had became established principles.

The centrality of work as the means by which life was earned had different meanings for men and women. Alford (1984: 1) comments that 'from the onset of European settlement in Australia, women played an important economic role'. While in the early years the emphasis in work was on male physical labour, the dominant female occupation was domestic service and few women became self-employed. The stereotyping of what was acceptable women's labour not only restricted their ability to become self-employed but also underlined the essential role in the economy of women as wives and mothers (Alford 1984:8–9). When in 1800 Governor King introduced the weaving of flax and wool by women convicts as public labour, women were not valued for doing it; rather it was seen as a punishment or an unsatisfactory alternative to marriage or domestic service (Aveling and Damousi, 1991:1). The role of women in the charitable enterprises which emerged in the first few years of the nineteenth century was also prescribed by the traditional division of labour — male-directed charities with women performing roles derived from their familial roles in colonial society (Windschuttle, 1980:59). Although the idealised role conflicted strongly with the situation of many colonial women it served to encourage marriage and proscribe other types of relationships and highlighted the subservience of social policy to economic policy (Alford, 1984:7–9).

The dominant role of economic activity and the wage relationship in the colony underlined the importance of work and its use as a criterion for judging whether or not a person wished to be self-reliant. Given that 'the greatest "social control" available to capitalism is the wage relationship itself — the fact that in order to live and reproduce, the worker must perpetually resell his or her labour' (Stedman Jones, 1985: 48), the individual needed to justify why he/she was asking others to supply the means of living. Classification as 'deserving of help' was linked to relationship with the labour market and whether one was actively looking for work but could not find it or was unable to work because of ill-health, age or other socially accepted reasons for dependency. Persons such as John Smart who preferred to try and live off the labour of others were seen as offending against the norm of self-sufficiency and considered undeserving unless willing to be institutionalised and re-educated. Willingness to work if able, thrift, self-help and acceptable moral behaviour including a degree of temperance were seen as compatible with the values of the free enterprise colony where wage labour was the main means of survival.

The poor law legacy

The question which then arose was what happened to those early settlers and emancipists who in the first three decades of the nineteenth century in the colony of New South Wales were unable to earn a living for themselves. While the British government retained some responsibility for freed convicts who needed help, state intervention as the established way of assisting those in need suggested the dreaded presence of a poor law system under review in England (Golding and Middleton, 1982:15; Dean, 1991: Ch 9). Governor Macquarie made some attempts to introduce small-scale poor law type arrangements in outlying districts of Sydney (Garton, 1990:21), but in general the colony was to take on private benevolence rather than statutory intervention. The avoidance of a Poor Law in the colonies has been discussed by a number of writers (e.g. Dare, 1992; Dickey, 1987: 17–18; Kewley, 1973: 7–13; Garton, 1990:20–21; also Garton, Ch. 2 in this book). Kewley argues that New South Wales had no equivalent of the English poor law and that a different approach was preferred by the colonists who appear 'to have brought with them an abhorrence of the English Poor Law' (1973: 8); the hope was that help through voluntary organisations would obviate the need for such a system.

Midwinter describes the role of the Elizabethan poor laws in the following terms:

> *The poor laws influenced the lives of everyone in that they affected the nation's economy and its administration … they controlled the only thoroughgoing social service that existed, covering all the ground that the myriad welfare facilities of today cover.*
>
> (1968: 9)

Embedded in these laws was the understanding that the state had a duty to intervene to relieve the poor. However the system was perceived as causing dependence on the state, of exacerbating poverty and of using a set of institutions feared by all, the chief amongst them the workhouse, which combined 'the function of schools, asylums, hospitals and old people's homes as well as being the last refuge for the homeless and unemployed' (Crowther, 1981:3). While in some circumstances the workhouse provided a place of refuge for the poor, the image was one of a mixture of all kinds of paupers in dreadful and depraved living conditions under strong discipline, an institutional answer by the state to the question of how to care for, yet deter the poor or, as Dean describes them, 'a condensed solution to a multi-faceted problem of transforming the idle into the industrious' (1991:41).

The notions of 'less eligibility' and the 'workhouse test', principles to underscore the 1834 English Poor Law Amendment Act, relied on the deterrent effects of the workhouse to ensure that the condition of those who worked was always preferable to those who would not work. Poverty was seen as a problem resulting from the attitudes of the poor to work, rather than as an outcome of maturing capitalism. Thus, the poor law amendment principles were at the heart of a moral theory which emphasised the remoralisation of the poor by first, eliminating laziness, intemperance and excessive breeding; second, countering the tendency of the poor to fraud and exploit the good intentions of others; third, deterrence; and finally, classification into categories of poor to separate the deserving and blameless from the undeserving who brought on poverty by their own behaviour (Golding and Middleton, 1983: 15–17). The colonists who wished to avoid a poor law in the new colony had experienced the outcry against the old Elizabethan Poor Laws and the groundswell for a new moral theory to improve the attitudes of the poor. The question which needs to be asked is whether the arrangements which came into practice in early nineteenth-century New South Wales were markedly different in philosophy and outcome from the enactments in the new English Poor Law Amendment Act of 1834.

In the early 1800s, in New South Wales, there was little attempt to meet the needs of the general poor — persons who were unable to participate in wage labour because of age, chronic infirmity, lack of family support or inability to find work. Specialised groups such as neglected children and the sick poor were seen as being catered for through the provision of orphanages, schools and hospitals heavily funded by the British government (see Garton 1990:19–20; Dickey 1987; Cleverley 1971; Snow 1991; Ramsland 1986); the needs of more troublesome or less reputable groups were met by the jails, lunatic asylum and the Parramatta Female Factory. The establishment of the colony's first lunatic asylum at Castle Hill in 1810 avoided sending to jail those causing a public disturbance and thought to be of unsound mind (Best 1992:1). The Parramatta Female Factory, opened in 1821 to replace the older Factory set up in 1802 by Governor King, was used to house: female convicts recently arrived in the colony and not assigned to positions; female convicts returned as unsuitable or pregnant; and those women convicted of secondary offences (Robinson, 1979:8). In Macquarie's view, the lack of seemingly useful labour for women made them a drain on the economy though usefulness tended to be measured in ability to be a wife and mother (Salt, 1984:37). One of the major problems for the all-male Board of Management at the Factory was the difficulty of finding employment for the women 'that was profitable, time-consuming and in harmony with the economic requirements of the colony' (Daniels and Murnane, 1980:15). The warehousing of female convicts in the Factory became a means of regulating and controlling their use in conditions which made the institution assume, among others, the functions of workhouse, jail, hospital, labour bureau and asylum (Salt, 1984:44). Like the Sydney Benevolent Asylum, the Female Factory provided a response in the early colony to the problem of those who did not ascribe to the behaviour patterns necessary for the maintenance of a free enterprise society.

The coming of benevolence

The colony's response to the emerging problem of the general poor was the dispensation of charity which, on first appearances, depended on the benevolence of colonists towards those less fortunate than themselves rather than state-administered charity. The Benevolent Society of New South Wales, established in 1818, was an amalgam of two voluntary organisations, the New South Wales Society for Promoting Christian Knowledge and Benevolence in these Territories and Neighbouring Islands (SPCK) and the Colonial Auxiliary Bible Society. The former Society, founded in 1813, was intent on relieving distress in the colony by outdoor relief and, when its financial position made viability doubtful, the Bible Society, formed partly to distribute Bibles to the poor, was considered a more stable base from which to offer both benevolence and Christian instruction (Cummins, 1971:2).

While the actual formation of the Benevolent Society was more complex than this simple description suggests and is discussed in detail elsewhere (Dickey, 1987:12–20; Mayes, 1964; Cage, 1980,1992; Currey, 1962; Cummins, 1971; Garton, 1990), a number of factors emerged in the debates about its formation which underline the nature of charity discourse. The SPCK in its early attempts to stimulate the idea of community self-help, drew attention to its current list of subscribers (Friends of the Poor) to demonstrate:

> ... that even in this distant and obscure corner of the world, the British character does not degenerate; but that Englishmen, in every clime and on every shore, cease not to remember the characteristic benevolence of their native land; and which benevolence is not the least cause of her present exalted greatness.
>
> (SPCK, 1814:14)

However the SPCK was willing to recognise the dangers of imposition on such benevolence due to the dispensers of charity being unaware of 'the characters of the applicants for their bounty; and their goodness is thereby converted rather into the gratification of vice than the alleviation of real distress' (SPCK, 1814:13). The solution to such imposition was to thoroughly investigate all applicants to make sure that every precaution was taken and charity given only to those who could no longer care for themselves by work. Dispensation of advantage needed to be seen as discriminating charity which upheld values of self-help rather than encourage people not to work, a theme to be enthusiastically espoused by the Benevolent Society. By 1818, the SPCK had floundered because of the lack of strong support from the Governor, an essential factor in attracting potential subscribers in the settlement. However, the amalgamated organisation, the Benevolent Society, was to gain both moral and financial support from the Governor and the British government in encouraging voluntary effort rather than state provision and control of welfare (Cummins, 1971:2).

The formation of the Benevolent Society established outdoor relief for four groups: the poor, the distressed, the aged and the infirm. These interrelated categories covered a range of life circumstances where persons were unable to work and care for themselves either permanently as in old age and chronic infirmity, or in situations of a more temporary and critical nature. The care offered was 'thereby to discountenance, as much as possible, mendicity and vagrancy and encourage industrious habits among the indigent poor,' (BSAR, 1820:8) as well offering religious instruction and consolation. The Society now considered that its presence gave the community the means to prevent that great evil, 'an idle subsistence by mendicity'(BSAR, 1820:10). The colonists were enjoined to make the Society 'the Almoner of their Bounty' so that 'the deserving poor would not be suffered to languish ... nor the bold imposter furnished with the means of idle dissipation' (cited in Peyser, 1939:108). The meeting of the needs of the poor, per se, was not the reason for the Society's existence but rather the relief of poverty administered in such a way as to discourage begging, get the poor to work and simultaneously afford religious instruction. Help was conditional and part of the re-education and remoralisation of the poor.

The institutionalisation of benevolence

A number of the aged or infirm poor had received rations from government stores because some responsibility was felt for ex-convicts who were sick or aged and had no family support. However, these rations did not solve the problem of having somewhere to live and the poor often found it necessary to barter with their rations to obtain lodging and then beg for food until the next ration day. To alleviate this problem the Benevolent Society, in its early years, expended nearly £60 per annum to provide lodgings in an attempt to eliminate the need for begging. This method of relief was seen as unsatisfactory because the outdoor pensioners were miserable and it was inconvenient for Society members to visit them (BS Minutes, May 1825). Surveillance of the poor required containment in a single building where all might be observed by staff rather than in scattered lodgings which necessitated individual visitation.

The decision to ask the Governor for help to build an Asylum fulfilled a primary reason for the Benevolent Society's formation as provision of institutional care was seen as an essential adjunct to outdoor relief. The arguments presented for indoor care were mainly economic and religious in nature, enabling a number of functions of the Society to be carried out as conveniently and cheaply as possible:

> an application as made to the late Governor with the suggestion of the importance of some building to answer the same end as an almshouse in England, principally for the purpose of economy, ready visitation and affording opportunity for imparting religious instruction.

> (BS Minutes, May 1825)

The realisation of an asylum was expedited by the support of Governor Macquarie who agreed to fund 'a suitable plain building … for the accommodation of fifty to sixty persons' (BS Minutes, May 1825). The reference to an almshouse type structure was a further indication of the avoidance of poor law structures such as the workhouse. English almshouses were institutions for the genteel poor usually funded by benefactors who wished to support occupational groups or local citizens. Far from the dreaded poor law workhouses the almshouse was often a building of elegance and substance prided by locals as evidence of their benevolent spirit, for example, the Almshouse of Noble Poverty at Winchester, or Morden College at Blackheath founded for 'decayed Turkey merchants' and described as a 'fine classical building in landscaped grounds' (Bailey, 1988:135). The almshouse was the epitome of voluntary giving, in which 'people blessed with riches have felt a social challenge to hold out a helping hand to less fortunate people' (Tonypandy in Berridge, 1987:vii). Berridge comments that 'the almshouses of London must have seemed like palaces because they provided one of the few alternatives to the horrors of the workhouse'(1988:x).

The type of institution preferred for the Benevolent Asylum emphasised how charity ought to be seen in the colony, the voluntary distribution of advantage to those in need rather than state intervention and poor law institutions. Subscribers were encouraged to increase their donations to the building of the Asylum in the hope that:

> … *public liberality will be further excited; and that the spirit of British Benevolence will animate the Inhabitants of this Colony to increase liberality on this important and interesting occasion; namely for the maintenance of the first charitable asylum erected in New South Wales to be supported by voluntary contribution; and they hope this will provide the seed of a glorious harvest to be reaped in these colonies.*
>
> (BSAR, 1820:14–15)

Governor Macquarie was firmly of the opinion that 'the Colonists themselves should maintain their own free, poor and decayed settlers' (Kewley, 1973:9) yet when the Benevolent Asylum was erected it was furnished at government expense and the salaries of the Master and Matron provided by the Governor (BS AR, 1822:5). By 1828, although Governor Darling's requests to the British government for funding of extensions to the Asylum were not granted, an annual subsidy to the Society from the Convict vote was established (Horsburgh, 1977:78). The Secretary of State for the Colonies was anxious to leave the affairs of the Benevolent Society to private benevolence rather than 'rendering the Society principally dependant upon the assistance of government' (Historical Records of

Australia [HRA], 1828–29:415). Darling agreed, for two reasons, that funding from government for the Asylum should not be increased to the extent that it might appear a venture principally provided by government. First, the inhabitants of the Colony would lose interest in financially supporting the Asylum if it were seen to be substantially supported by the Treasury. Second, and of far greater importance to Darling, was the fear that government funding 'would induce a greater Number of the Poor to seek for support from the Asylum, instead of restraining them as they now find it in their interest to do so' (HRA, 1828–9:39).

Yet, by 1829, support by regular government subsidy was necessary because of the serious decline in the number of subscriptions and donations, and the pressing demands for both indoor and outdoor relief (BSAR, 1829:13–15). The Benevolent Asylum, as an institution operated by a voluntary organisation, was needed as a visible symbol of community self-help even if its continued existence relied on government subsidy.

In the first ten years of the Asylum's operation, the number of inmates doubled and the Asylum became the ultimate destination for the aged poor and chronically ill with nowhere else to go, a general workhouse for a colony without a poor law rather than an almshouse for the genteel poor. By the middle of the nineteenth century, the Asylum accommodated nearly 500 persons who 'were drawn from all classes of the needy ... only the convicted prisoners, the declared lunatics and the genuinely orphaned children were accommodated elsewhere (Horsburgh, 1977:78). The essence of the debates about the nature of intervention and provision of institutional care was that responsibility for care of the poor should not be seen as a duty of the state but rely on the benevolence of the individual and facilitate the upholding of values which reinforced the colony's economic free enterprise system. The fact that the Sydney Benevolent Asylum was heavily subsided but not administered by the British and then Colonial Governments was a subtle way of maintaining the facade of the abundance of voluntary spirit. The duty of care was seen to lie with and be fulfilled by the community not the state even if the NSW Benevolent Society was, with its administration of outdoor relief and provision of an asylum for the poor, 'the acknowledged colonial substitute for the Poor Law and a major instrument of government policy' (Horsburgh, 1977:77).

Destitution and desert

The debates about who ought to be the recipients of care at the Asylum emphasised the dominance of virtues of thrift, self-help and self-reliance in the practice of charity. Entry criteria and institutional management suggest that while it was difficult to enforce a work test, the charity discourse which informed the management of the

Asylum was based on the centrality of work as the preferred means of distributing advantage in the colony. Dickey (1983:247) argues that for most of the nineteenth century the criteria for deciding who among the aged were to be assisted were economic and moral. People were categorised as acceptable recipients of community help only if they were both destitute and deserving. In terms of these conditions it is useful to examine the criteria used for admission to the Benevolent Asylum.

The Benevolent Asylum was opened in October 1821, a two-storey building located at the southern end of the settlement. Admission was gained by applying to the Acting Committee of the Benevolent Society, a committee derived from the management committee with power to co-opt other subscribers who were able to assist in visitation. All applicants required recommendation from a subscriber of the Society who needed to furnish details of the applicant's present residence, family circumstances and the cause or nature of the applicant's distress. In the first six months of operation, sixty-three men, eighteen women and two children were admitted and the main reasons for admission were cited as 'being aged, infirm, and otherwise incapable of wholly supporting themselves' (BSAR, 1822:6). Attempts to enforce a work rule were difficult because of the poor health of these inmates (BSAR, 1822:6). The nature of the inquiry process was under constant scrutiny to ensure that the persons seeking help had no other means of supporting themselves. Inquiry was a necessary first step in the classification process providing the details needed for categorisation of the poor as deserving or undeserving of help. The Acting Committee even sought to change its membership rules so as to be able to enlist the assistance of those 'moving in the lower rank of life' (BSAR, 1821:10) who might be able to more readily detect imposition as well as give advice on the best way of meeting the needs of the poor. The danger of imposition were ever present and prompted the Committee to consider the regulation 'that all who receive relief from the Society, should wear a distinctive garment' (BSAR, 1821:12). While this suggestion was not adopted, parallels can be drawn with the English practices of 'badging' the poor in receipt of relief and the wearing of the workhouse uniform outside the workhouse, means by which those on poor relief could be clearly identified (Crowther, 1981:195). Such identification was disciplinary and prevented imposition while at the same time extending surveillance of the poor outside the institution.

Many of these first inhabitants of the Asylum had been in receipt of outdoor relief from the Benevolent Society. If outdoor relief became inadequate, the individual was required to enter the Asylum for any continued assistance, a regulation similar to the poor law amendment principle of being willing to enter the workhouse in order to receive relief. Out pensions given by the Society were no longer available if the recipients refused admission (Cage, 1980:167). More emphasis was placed on indoor relief for the individual, with outdoor relief being restricted to families. In the years 1821 to 1831, a total of 1152 persons were admitted to the Asylum. While one-third of these inmates were eventually permitted to leave the Asylum, presumably able to live by their own means, almost one quarter died and one-fifth absconded or were dismissed (BSARs,1821–31). The function of the Asylum had became one of providing 'sustenance and shelter for those persons who were vocationally and socially indigent and pauperised' (BSAR, 1828:11). Yet part of the reason for this function was one of public order and remoralisation with a reminder to the settlement that the proper way to help the poor was to refer them to the Asylum rather than encourage individuals such as beggars and vagrants who were a visible evidence of the lack of self-help. The Benevolent Society's Annual Reports constantly restated that beggars and vagrants were not to be helped but sent to the Asylum because 'by far the greatest number come to want and wretchedness through their own immoralities' (BSAR, 1828:11). The consequence of allowing such beggars (described in one Society Annual Report as 'moral pestilence') to remain on the streets of Sydney was the danger of the example of their vagrant ways to the young and to servants who might be tempted to copy this means of maintaining an existence without working (BSAR, 1828: 11).

To be deserving of care within the Benevolent Asylum, in the first decade of its existence, the person needed to be destitute and willing to be institutionalised. Those who begged and were willing to enter the Asylum were seen as deserving because they accepted help to change their ways in an institution intent on promoting 'habits of economy, industry, morality and religion' (BSAR, 1823:11). The label undeserving was for those who would not submit to the rules and regulations of the Asylum. Admission of beggars and vagrants educated the new settlement that self-help, self-sufficiency and hard work were important values and those who did not practice it should be removed from the public gaze. In 1828, the Benevolent Society claimed that the only common beggars still on the streets of Sydney 'are such as should not be relieved, being idle and dissolute imposters, who will not submit to the constraints of the Asylum' (BSAR, 1828:10). The Society then published the names of four men whom they exhorted the public not to assist for they had been in the Asylum but preferred 'a life of idleness, dissipation, and imposture, and ought not receive the least relief, except through this Society' (BSAR, 1828:10–11). Dickey's claim that the main criteria for help were destitution and desert can only be sustained in relation to the Benevolent Asylum if desert is understood as being willing to change one's dissolute ways within the institution designed as an almshouse but fulfilling the tenets of the workhouse gospel of remoralisation of the poor. The undeserving poor were the destitute unwilling to be deterred.

The regulated life

In 1822, the Benevolent Society pleaded with potential supporters that if only they would investigate the nature and objects of the Asylum 'they would be convinced of the necessity, importance and usefulness of the New South Wales Benevolent Society' (BSAR, 1822:11). In asking about the nature of its usefulness and importance in the 1820s in Sydney, the poor relief offered was:

> ... *only to supply that which is indispensable as well to preserve them in health, and to protect the community at large from the importunities of nearly one hundred and forty miserable human beings, living as mendicants and common beggars* ...
>
> (BSAR, 1831 :14)

This statement suggests that a social control function was exercised by the Society, both in its institutional role of providing a well-disciplined Asylum with its 'necessary restraints', and in its public role in colonial Sydney of keeping out of sight those who offended against the ethic of work.

The restraints of the Asylum provided deterrence and regulation to ensure that the poor did not seek admission as a preference or view it as a right. If a person seeking indoor relief was not willing to work and conform to certain norms of behaviour then the Asylum would either limit or cease assistance. In 1826, the Society resolved that its maintenance by voluntary means was the best option for relieving the distressed poor because this arrangement did not suggest a right to help or a duty of the state to provide for:

> ... *those who bring themselves to poverty and want by idleness and intemperance, as none can have a legal claim, and all who are relieved are subject to dismissal for misconduct, or if considered able by this Committee to provide for themselves.*
>
> (BSAR, 1826: 5)

The poor laws in England had aimed to 'duplicate an ideal moral-political order within the walls of the workhouse' (Dean, 1991:63), and within the Benevolent Asylum, the nature of the rules and the manner of rewarding work demonstrated a determination to eradicate laziness and inculcate temperance and religious observance as part of the attempt to change the behaviour of the poor. The general public were invited to visit the Asylum to witness 'the comfort enjoyed, in temperance, frugality and general good order by the inmates' (BSAR, 1829: 20). The rules regulated every aspect of the daily life of the inmates, prescribing hours of rising and retiring; attendance at prayers morning and evening; personal hygiene; care of sleeping quarters, furniture and eating utensils; the weekly allowance of food and the nature of clothing to be worn (BSAR, 1822 Rules of Conduct: 18–19). 'Well conducted men and women' were given a general permission to attend Sunday Divine Service outside the Asylum but otherwise permission to leave at any time needed to be sought. To obtain a discharge from the Asylum it was necessary to ask and be granted permission. The minutes of the Asylum House Committee recorded that when permission to be discharged was given, the inmates 'returned thanks' for their stay, presumably in humble recognition of the debt owed to their benefactors.

The requirement of willingness to work was clearly stipulated in the Benevolent Asylum Rules:

The people admitted shall be variously employed, according to the ages
and peculiar infirmities of the individuals; and they shall be allowed certain
small indulgences or premiums, on account of work done to be settled by
the Committee.

(BSAR, 1822: 18)

The House Committee Minutes (HCM), in the period 1821–1831, contained numerous entries recording not only the rewards for good behaviour but the punishments for disorderly behaviour and intemperance. Included were the cases of: John Murphy, who whitewashed the House throughout and was allowed an extra ration of tea, sugar and tobacco for a month (HCM, March 1829) and Maurice Quinlan — allowed extra tea and sugar for working in the garden and digging the graves of Catholics (HCM, August 1830). This practice of rewards or 'indulgences' was a common institutional device to reward the 'good' inmate who worked hard, and was used by English Poor Law Guardians to get special work done. Conversely the removal of food and tobacco as punishment was an essential feature of workhouse discipline (Crowther, 1981:197, 214) and was common at the Benevolent Asylum. Profane swearing brought a removal of indulgences as did bringing alcohol into the Institution. One inmate who was 'grossly impertinent to the Master' and wished to leave the Asylum, was granted permission to go on the condition that readmission be refused unless he was 'truly contrite' for his behaviour (HCM, Nov. 1827). Another inmate had his indulgences stopped for giving tea to an inmate under punishment for a misdemeanour. The infringements appear petty but they demonstrate that the life of 'retirement and comfort' was carefully regulated, observed and controlled.

In 1825, concern was expressed in the Annual Report that because of the crowded nature of the Asylum it was difficult to provide work for those who were able. A visit to the Asylum by the Governor Darling and his wife in 1826 brought comment about the lack of employment for the inhabitants and a recommendation that workshops be provided 'so that, as far as possible, it may be a House of Industry, as well as an Asylum for the Aged, Blind, Paralytic and Destitute' (BSAR, 1826:11). Mrs Darling, concerned about the welfare of the women inmates, sent some 'coarse work' for the women to do '… and there has been a two-fold advantage, the occupation of their time usefully, and the satisfaction of providing for themselves some additional comforts' (BSAR, 1826: 1112). Inmates were sometimes admitted on condition that they used the skills of their former occupation within the Asylum as in the case of John Brown, a barber, who was admitted in July 1830, on condition that he used his hair-cutting skills for the inhabitants. Alternatively, Robert Williams was dismissed from the Asylum on the grounds of his refusal to pick oakum (BSAR, 24:11). Within the Asylum work not only contributed to its management but maintained discipline, taught the value of labour and self-sufficiency and ensured a regime which the poor would not choose as a preferred way of life. As with the English workhouse, the idle were taught 'an industrious mode of life' (Dean, 1991:46).

The problem of intoxication was a constantly recurring theme especially when inmates managed to imbibe on their weekly outings to Divine Service. In January 1824 the House Committee Minutes recorded that four male inmates, who had permission to go out to Divine Service, became intoxicated. One returned to the Asylum and was of particular concern because he would not express sorrow for his behaviour while 'the other three were brought Home by the order of the Superintendent who sent a wheelbarrow for Edward Roach' (HCM: January 1824). These and similar instances of intemperance were usually punished by withdrawal of indulgences and not being allowed to go out for a number of months as in the case of Mary Devoy who returned to the Asylum intoxicated and was refused permission to go out again for twelve months. The ongoing ability of inmates to obtain alcohol on their way to and from church on Sundays demonstrated a resourcefulness not appreciated by the Master of the Asylum, and eventually, in 1830, led to a recommendation that Church services be organised inside the Asylum. Apart from imbibing, the other public misdemeanour was begging and a number of inmates observed and reported for begging in Sydney streets were not allowed to go out again on the Sabbath. Watts (1988:92) argues that the Benevolent Society was able to discreetly watch over the lives of the poor and yet, while using the language of benevolence, exert social control.

By June 1831 the Benevolent Asylum accommodated 107 men and 34 women with an average age of 66 years (BSAR, 1831:15). More than half the inmates were over the age of seventy years and the need for medical facilities was evident. In contrast, only seven persons were receiving outdoor relief emphasising that the acceptance of indoor relief was the condition of receiving charity. The Society drew attention to the fifty-five acts of absconding in the previous year and the 'unwillingness of many of the inmates to submit to the restraints of the Asylum ... many would no doubt prefer the precarious life of a vagrant for the sake of liberty, to the regular and orderly habits of the Asylum' (BSAR, 1831:13). This statement was followed by the usual exhortation to the people of Sydney to send the vagrant to the Asylum for help and not encourage his or her mendicity. In the new colony the person in need was to be removed from the streets and contained in a regulated regime within the Asylum so as not to offend against the dictum that work was the means of obtaining advantage in the colony. In so doing the Asylum fulfilled a similar function to that of workhouses which were founded ' to counter the threat to public security posed by both the unemployed and unemployable' (De Swann, 1988: 46).

CONCLUSION

Currey argues that:

> *When the Benevolent Society was formed, and for some fifty years thereafter, the principle of self-help dominated the social philosophy of Governments in Great Britain and Australia.*
>
> (1962:2)

Within the other Australian colonies this principle of self help was reflected in a variety of administrative systems developed to render charity to those in need. A number of writers (Brown, 1972: Cage, 1992: Ch 6; Garton, 1990: Ch 3; Dickey, 1986:xix–xx; 1987:Ch 1) compare the local variations in charity administration in the different colonies and the diverse roles taken up by government and voluntary organisations. Garton notes that 'despite the high priority given to private benevolence as a safeguard against pauperism, colonial governments played a large and often direct role in the distribution of poor relief' (1990: 47). Voluntary organisations such as the NSW Benevolent Society showed that self-help rather than state dependence needed to be seen as the dominant theme in charity discourse. Poor laws did not appear on the statute books but their principles permeated arrangements for those unable to compete for wages and a century later it could be argued that 'the legislative vehicle which now constitutes the Australian welfare state carries an amount of intellectual baggage of the Poor Law' (Carney and Hanks, 1986:21).

In this chapter, the nature of charity provision in the early Australian settlement of New South Wales has been considered as an introduction to underlying discourses about the nature of distribution of advantage and disadvantage in Australia. While the state maintained some responsibility for convicts transported to set up a self-sufficient colony and commercial base, the major discourses which gave meaning to the practices of charity were those which supported a covert but substantial role for the state while encouraging private benevolence through voluntary organisations. A poor law system was avoided but the practices of charity, in the first three decades of the nineteenth century in the colony of New South Wales, spoke the language of the principles and moral theory which was to characterise the 1834 English Poor Law Amendment Act.

The emphasis in the new colony on self-sufficiency and the wage relationship saw social policy as a means of reinforcing the centrality of work in a free enterprise society. The Benevolent Asylum, as operated by the NSW Benevolent Society, was founded as an economical and convenient way to dispense charity within this philosophy. Like many nineteenth century charity workers and organisations the Society defined the problem with the poor as the way they behaved (Watts, 1988: 92), and sought to remoralise them by deterrence, discipline, classification of the deserving and undeserving, less eligibility and a de facto workhouse test which saw those unwilling to undergo the Asylum regime undeserving of help. The intention of the Benevolent Society was to be the manifestation of the new settlement's intention to avoid a poor law system of dependence on the state by the poor. The nature of charity provision, to maintain self-help, was to be at a level which would not encourage people to seek it as a preference. The financial and moral support given by the British and Colonial governments suggest that while the administration of charity was in the hands of a voluntary organisation, the Benevolent Society was in effect 'Government Almoner' (Kewley, 1973:8) and the poor law was evident in practice if not in statute to complement and sustain the emerging capitalist economy. The nature of welfare provision for the destitute poor and infirm of the colony needed to demonstrate to the wider community its role in institutionalising those who offended against the norms of self-help and self-sufficiency. The production and distribution of advantage and disadvantage in early colonial Australia was informed by the dominance of wage labour and the free enterprise system.

---

[1] This chapter does not explore the question of treatment of Australian Aborigines which is considered in detail in Saunders and Evans (eds.) (1992: Chs1–3) and Brook and Kohen (1991).

[2] Derived from figures presented in Historical Records of Australia (1828: 722–23).

REFERENCES

Alford, K. (1984), *Reproduction or Production?: an economic history of women in Australia 1788–1950*, Oxford University Press, Melbourne.

Aveling, M. (1992), 'Imagining New South Wales as a gendered society, 1783–1821,' *Australian Historical Studies*, 25(98), pp. 1–12.

Aveling, M., and Damousi, J. (eds) (1991), *Stepping Out of History: Documents of Women at Work in Australia*, Allen and Unwin, Sydney.

Bailey, B. (1988), *Almshouses*, Robert Hale, London.

Benevolent Society of NSW (1820–30), *Annual Reports*, Mitchell Library, Sydney.

Benevolent Society of NSW (1825), Asylum House Book, MSS, Mitchell Library, Sydney.

Benevolent Society of NSW (1821–31), House Committee Minutes, MSS, Mitchell Library, Sydney.

Benevolent Society of NSW (1830), Acting Committee Minutes, July, MSS, Mitchell Library, Sydney.

Benevolent Society of NSW (1825), General Committee Minutes, MSS, Mitchell Library, Sydney.

Berridge, C. (1987), *The Almshouses of London*, Ashford Press, Southhampton.

Best, R. (1992), 'The Castle Hill Lunatic Asylum 1811–1826', *Journal of the Royal Australian Historical Society* 78 (3/4), pp.1–18.

Brook, J and Kohen, J. L. (1991), *The Parramatta Native Institution and the Black Town: A History*, NSW University Press, Kensington.

Brown, J. (1972), *Poverty is not a Crime: The Development of Social Services in Tasmania 1803–1900*, Tasmanian Historical Research Association, Hobart.

Cage, R. (1980). 'The origins of poor relief in New South Wales: An Account of the Benevolent Society 1809–1862', *Australian Economic History Review*, (20), pp. 153–169.

Cage, R. (1992), *Poverty Abounding, Charity Aplenty: The Charity Network in Colonial Victoria*, Hale and Iremonger, Sydney.

Carney, T., and Hanks, P. (1986), *Australian Social Security Law, Policy and Administration*, Oxford University Press, Melbourne.

Cleverley, J. (1971), *The First Generation: School and Society in Early Australia*, Sydney University Press, Sydney.

Crowther, A. (1981), *The Workhouse System 1834–1929: The History of An English Social Institution*, London, Metheun.

Cummins, C. (1971), *The Development of the Benevolent (Sydney) Asylum 1788–1855*, NSW Department of Health, Sydney.

Currey, C. (1962), 'The foundation of the Benevolent Society of New South Wales', *Journal of the Royal Australian Historical Society*, 48(1), pp. 1–17.

Daniels, K., and Murnane, M. (1980), *Uphill All The Way: A Documentary History of Women in Australia*, University of Queensland Press, St Lucia.

Dare, R. (1992), 'Paupers rights: Governor Grey and the poor law in South Australia', *Australian Historical Studies* 25(99), pp. 220–243.

Dean, M. (1991), *The Constitution of Poverty*, Routledge, London.

Dickey, B. (1983), 'Care for the Aged Poor in Australia 1788–1914,' *Community Health Studies* 7(3), pp. 247–255.

Dickey, B. (1986), *Rations, Residences, Resources: A History of Social Welfare in South Australia since 1836*, Wakefield, Adelaide.

Dickey, B. (1987), *No Charity There*, Allen and Unwin, Sydney.

Garton, S. (1990), *Out of Luck: Poor Australians and Social Welfare*, Allen and Unwin, Sydney.

Golding, P., and Middleton, S. (1982), *Images of Welfare: Press and Public Attitudes to Poverty*, Martin Robertson, Oxford.

Historical Records of Australia, (1828–9), Series 1, Vols 11,15.

Horsburgh, M. (1977), 'Government Policy and the Benevolent Asylum', *Journal of the Royal Australian Historical Society*, 63(2), pp. 77–93.

Ignatieff, M. (1978), *A Just Measure of Pain: the Penitentiary in the Industrial Revolution 1750–1850*, Penguin, London.

Kewley, T. (1973), *Social Security in Australia 1900–1972*, Sydney University Press, Sydney.

Mayes, B. (1964), 'Benevolence and Beneficence', *The Medical Journal of Australia*, 50(10), pp. 341–348.

McMichael, P. (1988), 'Brutalised, beggared and bought' in V. Bergmann and J. Lee (eds), *A Most Valuable Acquisition*, McPhee Gribble and Penguin, Fitzroy, Victoria, pp. 57–72.

Midwinter, E. C. (1968), *Victorian Social Reform*, Longman, London.

NSW Society for Promoting Christian Knowledge and Benevolence (1814), *Annual Report*, Mitchell Library, Sydney.

Peyser, D. (1939), 'A study of welfare work in Sydney from 1788 till about 1900 (Part 1)', *Journal of the Royal Australian Historical Society* 25(2), pp. 89–128.

Powell, F. W. (1989), 'Vagrancy and deterrence', *Social Policy and Administration*, 23(1), pp. 72–83.

Ramsland, J. (1986), *Children of the Backlanes: Destitute and neglected children in colonial NSW*, NSW University Press, Kensington .

Robinson, P.(1979), 'The first forty years; punishment of convict women' in J. Mackinolty and H. Radi (eds), *In Pursuit of Justice: Australian Women and the Law 1788–1979*, Hale and Iremonger, Sydney, pp. 1–17.

Salt, A. (1984). *These Outcast Women: The Parramatta Female Factory 1821–1848*, Sydney.

Saunders, K. and Evans, R. (eds) (1992), *Gender Relations in Australia: Domination and Negotiation*, Harcourt Brace Jovanovich, Sydney.

Snow, D. (1991). 'Family policy and orphan schools in early colonial Australia', *Journal of Interdisciplinary History* 22(2), pp. 255–284.

Watts, R. (1988), 'As Cold as Charity' in V. Bergmann and J. Lee (eds), *Making A Life: A People's History of Australia since 1788*, McPhee Gribble and Penguin, Fitzroy ,Victoria, pp. 85–100.

Windschuttle, E. (1980), 'Feeding the poor and sapping their strength: the public role of ruling class women in eastern Australia, 1788–1850' in E. Windschuttle (ed.)(1980), *Women Class and History: Feminist Perspectives on Australia 1788–1988*, Fontana/Collins, Melbourne, pp. 53–80.

CHAPTER TWO

RIGHTS AND DUTIES
Arguing charity and welfare 1880–1920

STEPHEN GARTON

INTRODUCTION

The bold 'state experiments' that earned Australia an international reputation as a 'social laboratory' at the turn of the century have long been a source of debate and argument. The object of praise, fascination, condemnation or disappointment they remain a major theme in the writing of Australian history. Early accounts such as those of Pember-Reeves (1902) up to postwar accounts, such as those of Greenwood (1955) and Gollan (1960), had little trouble in seeing the turn of the century as a time of innovative change, when the foundations for Australian social democracy and social policy innovation were laid. But more recent historians have been more cautious and ambivalent. Both J. Roe (1976) and M. A. Jones (1983) qualify their characterisations of this period with question marks — 'pioneers?' and 'leading the world?' — suggesting difficulties and ambiguities in any character-isation of these developments. Others have, instead, shifted the foundations of the welfare state to the 1940s (Watts, 1987).

These ambivalences arise from the troublesome questions that historians have begun to pose. Were these state experiments the beginning of a new system of 'universalist' welfare policies based on rights and needs or a reordering of older charitable priorities in a new guise? Were they humanitarian efforts to alleviate poverty or concessions from the state to blunt labour radicalism? Were these experiments 'meagre' or substantial foundations for a modern welfare state? And probably most importantly, did these experiments alleviate or perpetuate poverty? Perhaps these contrasts and points of debate are too stark. Depending on one's focus or angle of vision, and even on which state experiments are examined, it is possible to find arguments in support of all of the above positions. The issues, imperatives and desires involved in the creation of the old age and invalid pension for instance do not necessarily correspond to those involved in the creation of the 'living wage'. Finding a link between such diverse developments has tested the historical imagination.

So what should be taken as the key sign of this period of welfare history or is the search for a key or a dominant characteristic failing to represent the conflicts and contradictions within welfare culture at the turn of the century? J. Docker's (1991) picture of the 'nervous nineties' as a time of immense cultural flux and a profusion of discourses stands as an adequate warning for any attempt to provide a summary characterisation of welfare policy in this period. Moreover, much of the historical analysis so far has focused on the development of the Commonwealth social security and industrial relations systems but this ignores what Beilharz, Considine and Watts (1992) have called 'the other state' — the vast system of State government and voluntary agency systems of welfare that continued to grow even after the establishment of the present social security systems. Were the initiatives pursued by 'the other state' consonant with those pursued by the Commonwealth or did they signify different welfare and charity strategies and paths, and if so, what were their consequences and effects? Any attempt to conceptualise welfare practice at the turn of the century not only has to investigate a range of policies but also developments at different levels of welfare provision — Commonwealth, State, local and voluntary initiatives. Added to this are the treacherous waters of definition. So far, the term welfare has been used in a rather general and unproblematic sense but is there a valid analytic distinction to be drawn between charity and welfare? It is the distinction used frequently and most often to distinguish voluntary, selective provision from state, universalist provision. It certainly has its uses but on closer examination the distinction is often blurred in practice and policy. Moreover, where does a system of conciliation and arbitration fit into such schemes? Is it part of an overall welfare system as Roe (1976) and Castles (1985) suggest, or a separate system for social and economic management? This makes the argument for any sharp historical break difficult and any such argument needs to be tentative and aware of the artificial categorisations involved in such representations. Nonetheless, some distinctions need to be drawn, and while the lines between charity and welfare are somewhat blurred a clearer point of demarcation might be the concepts of 'state experiments' so preferred by the participants involved in these processes of change. It is these experiments which will form the basis of this chapter.

This chapter sets out to contribute to some of these questions and debates. It works from the premise that state, voluntary agency and Commonwealth initiatives need to be considered and that these policies have to be placed in their historical context not assessed by anachronistic criteria of modern welfare practice. The conclusion reached in doing so is that the turn-of-the-century developments marked a point of emergence for many welfare discourses and practices and provided the foundation for contemporary policies (for good or ill). And while some marked the beginnings of heightened practices of surveillance and state intervention into everyday life, others had a limited but positive impact on the material life of the poor. The latter argument in particular is perhaps a controversial and unpopular one. Not least, given the poverty of reliable sources on the life of the poor and the problems in interpreting the few that do exist, it is a difficult argument to sustain. But at a time when we have faced a decade or more of calls to wind back the welfare state it is perhaps timely to shift focus to a time when there were many calls to establish a welfare system and expand state intervention for 'the public good'.

The charity system

If we are to explore the possibilities of a break with past practice at the turn of the century what then was the mould that was broken? Charity and philanthropy have been seen as the characteristic features of colonial provision for the poor. Historians have long asserted that the Australian colonies, unlike Britain and America, had no poor law (Dickey, 1992). This system of parish relief for the poor which had evolved since Elizabethan times established a right for people to seek assistance from local parish authorities. Supplementing this system of local provision was a vast system of private charitable provision, increasingly necessary as people left their local parishes in search of work and were thus unable to seek parish relief in times of distress (Owen, 1964). In the late eighteenth century the poor law came under increasing attack from evangelicals, who believed it undermined the ethic of self-help, and laissez-faire political economists, who believed that it disrupted market forces thus creating unemployment and poverty rather than alleviating it. Both groups disputed the efficacy and morality of a system based on a right to relief and were prominent in the campaigns to abolish the poor law. The consequence of these campaigns, the New Poor Law of 1834, introduced philanthropic criteria of 'the deserving' into relief decisions and made assistance significantly more difficult to obtain, especially for able-bodied men (Williams, 1981). This is a familiar story but its significance for Australia lies in the impact of the New Poor Law on poor relief in the colonies. The Australian colonies were established at the height of these debates about poor relief and those officials and colonists inspired by evangelicalism and liberal political economy were anxious not to repeat the mistakes of Britain in the new world. They opposed efforts to institute a poor law system in the colonies. Equally, the colonial working classes, migrating from a context of harsh workhouses and intrusive work tests to determine eligibility for relief, were anxious to avoid such 'horrors', obviously buoyed by the confidence many had in their capacity to 'make it' in the new world. As a consequence Australia lacked a poor law system, although more recently Garton (1990) has noted Macquarie's early, failed efforts to establish a poor law system and Dare (1992) has forcefully argued that many elements of the new poor law influenced the provision of charitable relief in colonial Australia (especially South Australia).

Poor relief in the Australian colonies was largely the responsibility of philanthropists and private charities. There was a bewildering array of private charities, especially after the gold rushes. Melbourne alone was reputed to have 400 charities in the late nineteenth century. They varied both in size and scope: from small rural benevolent societies of three or four people and a few pounds to distribute to the extensive operations of the New South Wales Benevolent Society which assisted over 600 people a week from the 1860s, from hospitals, soup-kitchens, orphanages, lying-in homes and asylums for the aged to organisations for the relief of distressed mothers, neglected children, the ill and new migrants. There were two general forms of relief – outdoor relief, in the form of food or clothing, and indoor relief, involving some form of hospital or asylum care. The practices and impact of different charities also varied enormously but there were some central tenets to charity practice, at least, in the rhetoric they espoused.

Fundamental to charity was the belief that there were two types of poor — the deserving and the undeserving. The former were those whose poverty was a result of circumstances beyond their control — old age, desertion of a family by a male breadwinner, orphans, the sick and the injured. The latter were those who brought on their own misfortune through 'moral depravity' — the drunken, criminal and dissolute and those who were capable of fending for themselves in the colonial labour market — able-bodied men. This latter group did not warrant assistance. These categories, however, were less clear-cut in practice. Philanthropists were uneasy in making the diagnosis of deserving, clearly suspicious of the claims to moral worth of many applicants. The major fear of philanthropists was that they would confuse the two categories by assisting the undeserving, thus encouraging pauperism — undeserved dependence on charitable relief. The figure that haunted the philanthropic imagination were the imposters, the persons who lied about their circumstances, representing themselves as deserving when they were not or those who received assistance from more than one charity (double-dippers), and thus undermined the aim of self-help. The avowed aim of the philanthropists was less to relieve the poor than to discourage pauperism wherever possible. Thus it was seen as essential to investigate applicants for relief to ensure that they were not imposters. Most charities interviewed applicants for eligibility and suitability and some had volunteer visitors, often respectable women, who paid periodic visits to recipients to ensure that they had not lied about their circumstances and were genuine in their claims for relief. Equally, it was essential that any relief provided should be less than the lowest that could be obtained in the labour market (the less-eligibility principle) to further encourage recipients to re-enter the labour market in preference to dependence on charity (Dickey, 1987:21–47; O'Brien, 1988).

Underpinning these principles and fears was the belief that most poverty was a consequence of moral laxness and that the poor should be encouraged to be self-reliant and practise the virtues of thrift, sobriety and hard labour. The denial of relief to the able-bodied was a stimulus to self-help. But in other institutions, such as orphanages, ragged schools, homes for neglected and delinquent children, inebriate asylums and homes for fallen women, or the 'morally depraved', there was an effort to isolate those, such as children, from these corrupting environments and train them in moral virtues. Within this domain of charity discourse and practice, moral reform became a central concept and combating imposture a major concern. Thus the key to successful philanthropy became its administration by the morally upright. Only they had the ethical capacity to be able to identify the imposters and distinguish the deserving from the undeserving and thus provide assistance to those who would benefit from it. Only they could administer institutions and thus subject the morally weak to their own moral strength, bringing about improvement. If this was the case then charity had to be in the hands of proper philanthropists. Relief was only provided after a recommendation from a respectable subscriber to a charity or member of the clergy, guaranteeing their deserved character, or after interview. In this delicately poised ethical universe of moral good and evil the function of public provision was seen as undermining philanthropic efforts. Government officials did not have the moral capacity or desire to diagnose imposters and were thus more likely to resort to indiscriminate giving, encouraging imposture (Garton, 1990:43–61).

Historians have pointed to the assumptions based on class, gender and race informing these discourses (Dickey, 1987; Kennedy, 1985; Rowley, 1972; Godden, 1982). Middle-class philanthropists seemed to have little understanding of the broader circumstances underlying the plight of the poor or Aboriginal and Torres Strait Islander inmates of missions and reserves, preferring to see the problem in the poor themselves rather than the culture and economy which produced poverty. At best, their attitude to the poor and Aborigines was patronising and paternalist, at worse it was harsh, moralist, unsympathetic and condemning. Some such as Dickey (1987) have attempted to see philanthropy as worthy humanitarian intentions betrayed by middle-class prejudices, allowing for some much-needed assistance but insufficient to alleviate the problems of the poor. Others such as Kennedy (1985) have developed a sustained critique of charity as a means of ruling-class oppression. This account has some penetrating insights into the pervasive moralism of philanthropists and their singular blindness to the plight of the poor but it is itself blind to the complexities and contradictions in charity practice. This blindness, and neglect of the agency of the poor, makes it an interpretation incapable of explaining historical change. It is the complexities and contradictions of charity that made it vulnerable to the development of state welfare alternatives.

The provision of minimal assistance without encouraging imposture was the charity ideal but the practice was more ambiguous and complex. Philanthropists stoutly resisted incursions of the state into poor relief for fear of encouraging imposture but they themselves were dependent on government assistance. The number of colonists with the inclination or resources to finance charities was small and as a consequence many charities were reliant on government subsidies, for up to three-quarters of their income, to continue their operations. The return for governments were their entitlements (as subscribers) to recommend people for assistance (those seeking assistance could usually apply to the Colonial Secretary's Department), undermining the careful safeguards of philanthropists. Equally there were many areas of poor relief that found few philanthropists willing to assist and in these instances governments were required to step in, most notably in the care of the insane but increasingly in the care of the aged. More significantly, there were some areas of relief considered too important to be left to private efforts, most notably the care of neglected and delinquent children. Likewise, in many rural areas the majors distributors of relief were the local police (Garton, 1990:43–61; Ramsland, 1986:111–58).

The idea of charity was itself more complex and ambiguous than the above account suggests. Further, there were divisions within the ranks of philanthropists. There were those who cherished the basic Christian virtue to give, believing that it was better to give generously even at the risk of encouraging imposters than to possibly deny assistance to the genuinely needy. And there were others, who stressed the absolute importance of strictly enforcing investigation procedures at the risk of denying assistance to the deserving for the sake of preventing imposture. Moreover, the scale of the poor relief problem was often too enormous to police. Charities found themselves with too many applicants and no time or resources to interview and visit recipients properly. In many instances they gave indiscriminately, sometimes even generously by their standards, undermining their own ideals (Garton, 1990:43–61).

The charity crisis

Perhaps crisis is too strong a word to describe the various reassessments of the efficacy of charity in the late nineteenth century. But it is possible to argue that increasingly the standard practices of colonial charities were found wanting, by philanthropists themselves but also by governments, women social reformers and liberals and radicals who questioned the basis of charity practice. Out of these challenges came the space for thinking of new ways to tackle the problem of poverty. Historians have usually seen the 1890s depression, widespread poverty, and the mobilisation of labour, as the key factors in explaining the shift from a charity to a welfare system (Dickey, 1987:72–5) but indeed the crisis began much earlier and arose out of contradictions and ambiguities in charity practice itself. This broader crisis provided the context for the failure of charity in the 1890s and the rapid adoption of alternative solutions.

By the 1870s it was becoming apparent to many reformers that charity was not as effective as philanthropists had hoped. In this decade many colonies held large-scale inquiries into the operation of charity and in these and other sources the symptoms of concern can be diagnosed. One of the most significant reassessments was in the domain of institutional care. Since the early nineteenth century there had been two types of asylums; those for the care and comfort of the aged, infirm and invalid and asylums for 'moral therapy' where vulnerable populations amenable to moral improvement might be restored to moral health. By the 1870s, however, the confident moral environmentalism that inspired the belief in moral therapy was undermined by increasing admission and readmission rates, overcrowding and no decline in the incidence of such problems in the community. Moreover, many juveniles in asylums later appeared in the prison population, many of the insane remained incurable and inebriates (alcoholics) continually lapsed into their old ways. Far from being reformative these institutions were becoming repositories for the incurable or universities for later 'moral depravity' (Garton, 1988 and 1990). This tendency was of particular concern for the reform of children, the hope for the future. In the famous phrase of New South Wales Public Charities Commission (1873, 4:40) 'the barracks system bred the barracks child', perfectly adapted to the demands of institutional life but incapable of leading a productive life in the wider community. The preferred solution, gradually adopted in many colonies in the 1870s and 1880s, was boarding-out; the placement of children with foster families where they could be raised in the moral environment of the nuclear family (Ritter, 1978; Ramsland, 1974 and 1986; Dickey, 1979). In one sense this was a reaffirmation of the moral environmentalism of traditional philanthropy, refined to combat shortcomings in method, but the increasing role of the state in organising boarding-out betrayed a growing sense that private charities lacked the capacity for systematic administration of important strategies of moral reform.

The sense of concern amongst some philanthropists was even more apparent in their dissatisfaction at the distribution of outdoor relief. In their view there were too many charities giving indiscriminately, failing to adequately interview or regularly visit recipients and working in an uncoordinated fashion, thus allowing imposters to slip through the net of investigation. Instead of charity being a stimulus to reform and self-help it was becoming an encouragement to pauperism. In the 1880s and 1890s philanthropic reformers, particularly those involved in the Charity Organisation Society, urged the implementation of 'scientific charity' to combat this evil. This approach involved the establishment of a central coordinating society to prevent duplication of services, a register of recipients from all societies to prevent double-dipping, closer monitoring and regular visiting of recipients to prevent imposture, and the introduction of the case-work method where philanthropists would be trained to take each case individually and develop a strategy for reducing their dependence on charity (Kennedy, 1985; Garton, 1990:84–7). Most charities refused to cooperate with this scheme, fearing the decline of their own power, but the widespread discussion of the ills of charity and the need for improved procedures put into discourse the idea of charity as an inefficient and flawed practice.

Concern was also apparent in the drift of some reformers away from charity work. Some people, particularly middle-class women, traditionally involved with and sympathetic to philanthropy, began to divert their energies into other reform movements; notably temperance and feminism. Formed in the 1880s, the Women's Christian Temperance Union was the largest social reform movement of the nineteenth century. Many of its adherents had been involved in philanthropic work but their experience there led them to the conclusion that intemperance in drink and other vices was the root of much poverty. Their support for social purity and temperance was an effort to combat poverty more effectively than charity (Hyslop, 1976). To assist their campaign they did not rely just on the older strategies of moral suasion and individual reform but increasingly turned to the state for legislation to prevent intemperance. They sought a greater cooperation between public and private efforts than had traditionally been the case in philanthropy (Bollen, 1972:99–155; Garton, 1987). Some went even further to diagnose the problem not just as intemperance but male intemperance. These women saw the solution in legislation to protect women and children from 'the animal in man' and measures to increase the ability of women to live independently of men. To facilitate these aims they sought womanhood suffrage as a means of forcing parliaments to legislate in the interests of women (Allen, 1988). Feminists also sought to harness the capacities of public authorities to private ends, marking a significant break within the philanthropic suspicion of government action.

One final symptom of crisis for charity is evident in the rise of labour, liberal and radical critiques of the individualising moralism of charity. Such a shift was particularly significant within liberalism. There was nothing intrinsically antithetical between individualism and liberalism, quite the contrary, but the emergence of labour opposition to the inadequacy of charity relief, lead many to consider that the market was not always a perfect instrument for the allocation of labour and other resources and if this was the case, poverty was not always the result of individual moral failing. Despite the generally favourable economic climate of the late nineteenth century there were short but serious recessions in 1860, 1866, 1872 and 1884. On each of those occasions unemployed workers marched claiming the right to work and lobbied governments for work relief rather than 'demeaning' charity. Government investigations of these claims often found that the men were genuinely unemployed due to broader economic circumstances and this became the basis for the organisation of government work relief schemes, providing small wages for labour on public works (Macintyre, 1985:59–63; Garton, 1990:33–6). In the 1880s, governments also established labour bureaus to find work for the urban unemployed in rural areas (O'Brien, 1988:204-5; Garton, 1990:76-7). These government efforts were a significant rebuttal of the charity strategy of denying assistance to the able-bodied poor. Liberal legislatures grudgingly admitted that the market created some forms of poverty and that the government had a responsibility to alleviate its worst effects. This established an important principle that shaped government intervention in subsequent years.

The emergence of welfare

These symptoms of crisis in charity and the emergence of movements critical of its central tenets and methods laid the foundations for the more fundamental reassessments of poverty and welfare in the cauldron of the 1890s. The depth of the 1890s Depression, probably Australia's worst, the consequent unemployment, possibly as high as a third of the workforce, the collapse of financial institutions, especially in Victoria, and the bitter struggles between capital and labour (to the detriment of labour) have all marked the decade as a watershed in Australian history. Its significance for charity lay in the ample evidence of its incapacity to deal with large-scale destitution. The earlier fear that poverty was increasing and that charity was failing to arrest its increase was replaced by the stark realisation that charity, even with increased government subsidy, was hopelessly inadequate. At least, that was a realisation for some. Many philanthropists obstinately maintained the relevance of their practice, continuing to insist on investigation, maintaining the poor on the most meagre of rations, insisting on refusing aid to the able-bodied or forcing them into demeaning labour camps to work for relief (Kennedy, 1968). Charity did not collapse as a practice but the pre-Depression discontent with poor relief crystallised in the 1890s into an earnest search for alternatives.

Other factors favoured the emergence of new strategies. The cultural ferment of the period, where utopian, socialist, radical, millenarian, nationalist, republican and liberal ideas jostled for space, created a climate for new approaches to old problems (Docker, 1991). The federation movement provided another context in the search for new political arrangements (de Garis, 1974). Additionally, the political landscape of colonial politics was being charted by new forces, most notably the rise of Labor as a parliamentary party (Rickard, 1976). Labor may not have governed in its own right at this time but it was an increasingly influential voice in colonial politics and was able to win concessions to their social democratic ethos from the free trade and protectionist parties that controlled the parliaments.

The most significant challenge was for the colonial liberals who had dominated Australian politics since the 1850s. Colonial liberalism was a complex political beast. While espousing much of the political rhetoric of classical liberalism, colonial liberals adapted these ideas to colonial circumstances, embracing free trade in some colonies but protectionism in others, notably Victoria (Macintyre, 1991). Moreover they demonstrated none of the classical reserve in interfering in the market, prompting Noel Butlin (1959) to argue that they pursued 'colonial socialism'. But this was a particular style of intervention. Although some used tariffs to protect the domestic market, their main concern was to prime the market through large-scale public works financed by considerable overseas borrowings, and having done so, the market could then operate to the benefit of all. By the 1890s this confidence in the market was eroding. Evidence of continuing poverty, the exploitation of female and juvenile labour, unemployment and the significant confrontations between capital and labour convinced many liberals that the social order was in danger and that a new social contract had to be forged to ensure Australia's progress towards higher stages of civilisation (Campbell, 1976). This 'new liberalism' meant intervening in the relationships of the market (capital and labour) to ensure greater equity and justice for all parties. This also meant a new conception of the role of the state. No longer was it an entirely neutral force guarding existing relationships; increasingly it had to be an active shaper of social arrangements. The state had to experiment and from these experiments came some of the major social welfare institutions of modern Australia — old age and invalid pensions, maternity allowances, the living wage, workers' compensation, and factory and shop legislation. The following is a brief discussion of two of the most significant experiments — old age pensions and the living wage.

In the 1890s the idea of old age pensions was raised by a number of reformers, such as J.C. Neild, William Lyne and J.H. Howe. The idea of pensions themselves was not new. The British poor law prior to 1834 contained provisions for parishes to grant pensions to the needy and a number of countries had military pension schemes (Fraser, 1984:31-6). But, in the Australian colonies, care for the aged, infirm and invalid was an individual and family responsibility and only when these systems failed did charities provide asylum care. By the late nineteenth century, however, the increasing proportion of people aged over 65 in the population, almost a third of whom had no property or income, was placing an considerable burden on scarce charity resources. Governments were forced to increase their subsidies to asylums for the aged or in some instances take over direct responsibility for their administration and maintenance. This was a costly burden. But a series of inquiries into the operation of such asylums in the late nineteenth century also revealed widespread ill-treatment of inmates. Married couples were separated on admission, patients beaten or locked in rooms for long periods, forced to stand in the sun during the day, denied food and generally treated as prisoners (Garton, 1990:95–9; Kewley, 1973:5–13). These concerns provided the context for the introduction of pensions.

The advocates of pensions stressed that they would bring a considerable saving to governments, enabling the abolition of costly charitable institutions for the aged and allowing the aged and infirm to live in greater dignity in their declining years. But these advocates also resorted to a new language to push their reforms – a language of rights. For politicians, such as Sir William Lyne, William Morris Hughes and King O'Malley, pensions were to give people 'rights' to prevent them from being paupers. They gained these rights from having contributed to the general well-being throughout their working lives. Tied to the notion of 'rights' was that of citizenship, whereby it was the duty of people to show their allegiance to the state and the duty of the state to make good laws to ensure the well-being of their citizens (Commonwealth Parliamentary Debates, 1901–2: 3475–87; NSW Parliamentary Debates, 1900: 4941–57). In the framework of T.H. Marshall (1950) citizenship now involved not just political rights but also social rights. The politicians urging this new social contract argued forcefully against the many philanthropist critics who suggested that pensions would undermine thrift and the desire for self-help.

The emphasis on inalienable rights was reinforced by the type of pension scheme adopted in Australia, first in Victoria (1901) and New South Wales (1901) and then in the Commonwealth (1908). These pensions were funded from consolidated revenue, and were thus non-contributory as distinct from the insurance scheme being developed in Germany, and which was later adopted in Britain and America. Advocates of the non-contributory system argued that it was a fairer system, providing for the large number of workers unable to make regular contributions to insurance funds and more particularly women who contributed greatly to the national good but did not always earn wages for their efforts. The non-contributory system became the hallmark of Australia's distinctive social security system. The consequence of such a system, however, were elaborate residence, race, income and means tests to reduce the burden on consolidated revenue. Historians have tended to concentrate on the limitations to the pension system, seeing them largely as a pragmatic measure to solve a social problem (Kewley, 1973:28–42). This may be the case but the fact that they saw it as appropriate to advocate this scheme with a language of citizenship, rights and duties points to an important break with philanthropic arguments that relief was a benevolent gift not a right.

This new role for the state was even more apparent in the desire to regulate wages and labour. In the 1880s and 1890s the first efforts to reduce the exploitation of labour were evident in the Factory and Shop Acts which addressed 'sweating' (low wages and long hours) and attempted to regulate the employment of female and juvenile labour (Lynzaat, 1979). In the new Commonwealth, liberal politicians attempted to go further in cementing a secure and peaceful relationship between capital and labour. The mechanism for achieving this was Australia's unique system of industrial relations — conciliation and arbitration. Advocates of arbitration argued that through this mechanism the state could intervene in the labour market to 'forbid tyranny' and ensure 'justice'. The framework for achieving this was 'white Australia' and 'new protection'. The first would eradicate competition from cheap foreign labour, maintaining wage rates at an acceptable level. The second would provide tariff protection to manufacturers provided they undertook to pay 'fair and reasonable wages'. In 1907 Mr Justice Higgins of the Federal Conciliation and Arbitration Court, in the famous Harvester Judgment, attempted to create a mechanism for 'fair and reasonable' wages by setting a minimum standard of wages, for 'frugal comfort' for a family of five, at seven shillings a day. His ruling was disputed but the principle of a 'living wage' was firmly established in industrial awards by the 1920s (Macintyre, 1985:40–58).

The 'living wage' was a major plank of Australian social security. It attempted to ensure social justice in the labour market, although subsequent investigations of the cost of living suggested that it fell short of this aim. Nonetheless it was a major support for workers. But it also attempted to bolster other social arrangements. Higgins determined that the wage was a male wage to assist men in supporting their families. Women were not seen as breadwinners and were generally awarded only half the male wage rate (Ryan and Conlon, 1975:50–111). Thus, the thrust of living wage determination was to cement the ideal of the male breadwinner and the female dependent, despite evidence which suggested that women with dependents were the bulk of the poor and the efforts of feminists to ensure the capacity of women to live independently of men (Roe, 1983). A key feature of Australian social policy became the market as the guarantee of an adequate income, and pensions when the worker was no longer able to work — the safety net — a structure that has marked Australian social policy ever since. But such a structure is largely a (male) wage earners' welfare state (Castles, 1985), those falling outside the wage/safety-net relationship having fewer benefits and facilities. Ironically, as Roe (1987) has argued, at the very moment when women achieved political citizenship new policies disenfranchised them from social citizenship, a trend exacerbated by the new definitions of citizenship occasioned by Australia's participation in the First World War.

These developments did not go uncontested. Each step of the way, there was fierce opposition from those who maintained that philanthropy should remain the basis of welfare: from employers who resented any interference in their operations; from conservatives who believed that deference and paternalism should be the basis of society; and from workers who feared that state regulation was a mask for more ruthless exploitation of labour. Philanthropists were sufficiently concerned at the potential of state experiments to undermine self-help, that far from charity being replaced by social welfare, it actually expanded its operations in the twentieth century (O'Brien, 1988:200–24). Social welfare legislation itself bore the marks of compromise, on the one hand registering the right to welfare and on the other, qualifying that right with conditions which betrayed the older fears of pauperisation and imposture.

Although social security has come to achieve a significant place in Australian welfare policy, at the turn of the century these Federal initiatives were by no means the only, or necessarily the most significant state experiments. The bulk of poor relief and welfare continued to be subsidised or directly provided by State governments. They played a major role in the provision of general and mental health services, education, child welfare, maternal and infant welfare services and Aboriginal welfare. In each of these fields, State governments assumed a larger role in the early twentieth century. But it was not just a matter of the increased scale of state involvement, the character of some of these services also changed in significant ways. Space does not permit an extended discussion of all the developments relevant here but new policies in the field of Aboriginal and child welfare point to some more general trends. Both these fields were characterised by increased state intervention. For Aborigines the punitive protectionist Acts marked out further restrictions on Aboriginal freedom, compelled many to incarceration on reserves and missions, and legitimised the forced removal of Aboriginal children (Rowley, 1972; Read, 1983). In the field of child welfare, the state expanded the system of surveillance over families through the introduction of the children's court. Here 'neglectful' parents could be admonished for their failure and their children removed if they failed to improve the home environment. Expanded facilities for the boarding-out, fostering, adoption and institutionalisation of 'problem' children marked the greater willingness of the state to 'police' families (van Krieken, 1992; Garton, 1986). In both Aboriginal and child welfare the state was displacing the authority of the family (particularly the father) and positioning itself in *loco parentis*, to ensure that children (Aboriginal and non-Aboriginal) were fitted to the needs of (white) civilisation.

CONCLUSION

The late nineteenth and early twentieth centuries marked a point of emergence for new welfare discourses of significance for the growth of Australia's welfare state of later years. Despite their limitations, for their time and in comparison to welfare developments elsewhere, as Roe (1976) has suggested, they represented an advance. Nonetheless, these new discourses of rights and duties had to negotiate with older discourses of benevolence, obligations, deference and self-help and the resulting policies have all the marks of compromise. The legacy of these compromises can be seen in Australia's residualist welfare system, its tests and exclusions and the prevailing sense that recipients are 'unworthy'. Australia's modern welfare state is far from perfect in its niggardly provisions, reliance on a labour market/safety-net system, its intrusive forms of welfare surveillance and its denial of local initiative.

These failings have lead to more recent calls for a 'retreat from the welfare state' (Graycar, 1983) but a historical perspective points to the problems in such a call. The history of the poor is notoriously elusive. The evidence is patchy, and usually only found in the records of those who policed the poor. However, reading against the grain of such sources for the presences, absences and hidden voices suggests that the plight of the poor has improved, marginally, since the introduction of the turn-of-the-century state experiments. Elsewhere, this evidence is marshalled in detail (Garton, 1990), but it seems reasonable to suggest that some of the poor in nineteenth century Australia lived in conditions of absolute destitution. The effect of twentieth-century welfare has been to produce 'poverty', in the sense of relative disadvantage. And while the proportion of the population living in 'permanent poverty' may not have changed (Roe, 1975) the nature of their circumstances is improved on that of their counterparts in the nineteenth century. The modern welfare state may be in need of significant improvement but it is worth defending and reforming nonetheless. Attempts to wind back benefits, rely on voluntary agencies and encourage greater self-reliance exist in profound historical ignorance of the reasons why liberal, labour, feminist and radical reformers sought to use the state to alleviate the chronic destitution that private charity and the ethics of self-help perpetuated.

REFERENCES

Allen, J. (1988), 'Our Deeply Degraded Sex' and 'The Animal in Man: Rose Scott, feminism and sexuality 1890–1925', *Australian Feminist Studies*, (7/8), pp. 65–91.

Beilharz, P., Considine, M., and Watts, R. (1992), *Arguing About the Welfare State: The Australian Experience*, Allen and Unwin, Sydney.

Bollen, J. D. (1972), *Protestantism and Social Reform in New South Wales 1890-1910*, Melbourne University Press, Melbourne.

Butlin, N. G. (1959), 'Colonial socialism in Australia 1860-1900' in H. Aitken (ed.), *The State and Economic Growth*, Social Science Research Council, New York, pp. 35–53.

Campbell, C. (1976), 'Liberalism in Australian history' in J. Roe (ed.), *Social Policy in Australia: Some Perspectives 1901–75*, Cassell, Sydney, pp. 24–33.

Castles, F. (1985), *The Working Class and Welfare: Reflections on the Political Development of the Welfare State in Australia and New Zealand 1890–1980*, Allen and Unwin, Sydney.

Commonwealth of Australia. (1901–2), *Parliamentary Debates*.

Dare, R. (1992), 'Paupers' rights: Governor Grey and the poor law in South Australia', *Australian Historical Studies* 25(99), pp. 220–43.

de Garis, B. (1974), '1890–1900' in F. K. Crowley (ed.), *A New History of Australia*, William Heinemann, Melbourne, pp. 216–59.

Dickey, B. (1979), 'Evolution of care for destitute children in New South Wales 1875–1901', *Journal of Australian Studies* (4), pp. 38–57.

Dickey, B. (1987), *No Charity There: A Short History of Social Welfare in Australia*, 2nd edn, Allen and Unwin, Sydney.

Dickey, B. (1992), 'Why were there no Poor Laws in Australia?', *Journal of Policy History* 4(2), pp. 111–33.

Docker, J. (1991), *The Nervous Nineties: Australian Cultural Life in the 1890s*, Oxford University Press, Melbourne.

Fraser, D. (1984), *The Evolution of the British Welfare State*, 2nd edn, Macmillan, London.

Garton, S. (1986), 'Sir Charles Mackellar: psychiatry, eugenics and child welfare in New South Wales 1900–1914', *Historical Studies* 22(86), pp. 21–34.

Garton, S. (1987), 'Once a drunkard always a drunkard: social reform and the problem of habitual drunkenness in Australia 1880–1914', *Labour History*, (53), pp. 38–53.

Garton, S. (1988), *Medicine and Madness: A Social History of Insanity in New South Wales 1880–1940*, NSW University Press, Kensington.

Garton, S. (1990), *Out of Luck: Poor Australians and Social Welfare 1788–1988*, Allen and Unwin, Sydney.

Godden, J. (1982), 'The work for them and the glory for us! Sydney women's philanthropy 1880–1900' in R. Kennedy (ed.), *Australian Welfare History: Critical Essays*, Macmillan, Melbourne, pp. 84–102.

Gollan, R. A. (1960), *Radical and Working Class Politics: A Study of Eastern Australia 1850–1910*, Melbourne University Press, Melbourne.

Graycar, A. (1983), 'Retreat from the welfare state' in A. Graycar (ed.), *Retreat from the Welfare State: Australian Social Policy in the 1980s*, Allen and Unwin, Sydney, pp. 1–12.

Greenwood, G. (1955), 'National development and social experimentation 1901–1914' in G. Greenwood (ed.), *Australia: A Social and Political History*, Angus and Robertson, Sydney, pp. 196–257.

Hyslop, A. (1976), 'Temperance, Christianity and Feminism: the Women's Christian Temperance Union of Victoria 1887-97', *Historical Studies*, 17(66), pp. 27–49.

Jones, M. A. (1983), *The Australian Welfare State: Growth, Crisis and Change*, 2nd edn, Allen and Unwin, Sydney.

Kennedy, R. (1968), 'The Leongatha Labour Colony: founding an anti-utopia', *Labour History*, 14, pp. 54–8.

Kennedy, R. (1985), *Charity Warfare: The Charity Organisation Society in Colonial Melbourne*, Hyland House, Melbourne.

Kewley, T. H. (1973), *Social Security in Australia 1900–72*, 2nd edn, Sydney University Press, Sydney.

Lynzaat, A. (1979), 'Respectability and the outworker: Victorian Factory Acts 1885-1903' in J. Mackinolty and H. Radi (eds), *In Pursuit of Justice: Australian Women and the Law 1788–1979*, Hale and Iremonger, Sydney, pp. 85–94.

Macintyre, S. (1985), *Winners and Losers: The Pursuit of Social Justice in Australian History*, Allen and Unwin, Sydney.

Macintyre, S. (1991), *Colonial Liberalism: The Lost World of Three Victorian Visionaries*, Oxford University Press, Melbourne.

Marshall, T. H. (1950), *Citizenship and Social Class and Other Essays*, Cambridge University Press, Cambridge.

New South Wales. (1900), *Parliamentary Debates*.

O'Brien, A. (1988), *Poverty's Prison: The Poor in New South Wales 1880–1918*, Melbourne University Press, Melbourne.

Owen, D. (1964), *English Philanthropy 1660–1960*, Harvard University Press, Cambridge, Mass.

Pember-Reeves, W. (1902), *State Experiments in Australia and New Zealand* Vols.1 and 2, Grant Ritchards, London.

Royal Commission on Public Charities (1873–4), *NSW Legislative Assembly Votes and Proceedings 1873–4*.

Ramsland, J. (1974), 'The development of boarding-out systems in Australia: a series of welfare experiments in child care 1860–1910', *Journal of the Royal Australian Historical Society* 60(3), pp. 186–98.

Ramsland, J. (1986), *Children of the Backlanes: Destitute and Neglected Children in Colonial New South Wales*, NSW University Press, Kensington.

Read, P. (1983), *The Stolen Generations: The Removal of Aboriginal Children in NSW 1883–1969*, NSW Ministry of Aboriginal Affairs, Sydney.

Rickard, J. (1976), *Class and Politics: New South Wales, Victoria and the Early Commonwealth 1890–1910*, ANU Press, Canberra.

Ritter, L. (1978), 'Boarding-out in New South Wales and South Australia: adoption, adaptation or innovation', *Journal of the Royal Australian Historical Society*, 64(2), pp. 104–26.

Roe, J. (1975), 'Social policy and the permanent poor' in E. L. Wheelwright and K. Buckley (eds), *Essays in the Political Economy of Australian Capitalism*, Vol 1, Australian and New Zealand Publishing Company, Sydney, pp. 130–52.

Roe, J. (1976), 'Leading the world 1901-14?', in J. Roe (ed.), *Social Policy in Australia: Some Perspectives 1901–75*, Cassell, Sydney, pp. 1–23.

Roe, J. (1983), 'The end is where we start from: women and welfare since 1901' in B. Cass and C. Baldock (eds),*Women, Social Welfare and the State*, Allen and Unwin, Sydney, pp. 1–20.

Roe, J. (1987), 'Chivalry and social policy in the Antipodes', *Historical Studies*, 22(88), pp. 395–410.

Rowley, C.D. (1972), *The Destruction of Aboriginal Society*, Penguin, Ringwood(Vic.)

Ryan, E., and Conlon, A. (1975), *Gentle Invaders: Australian Women at Work 1788–1974*, Nelson, Melbourne.

van Krieken, R. (1992), *Children and the State: Social Control and the Formation of Child Welfare*, Allen and Unwin, Sydney.

Watts, R. (1987), *Foundations of the National Welfare State*, Allen and Unwin, Sydney.

Williams, K. (1981), *From Pauperism to Poverty*, Routledge and Kegan Paul, London.

CHAPTER THREE

THE MACRO-ECONOMIC FOUNDATIONS OF THE WELFARE STATE

1950 to 1960

PAUL SMYTH

INTRODUCTION

Earlier definitions of social policy in terms of income support and social services proved less serviceable in the 1980s under the impact first of the 'fiscal crisis of the state' and then, 'economic rationalism'. A return to basics brought the recognition that 'Social policy ... is essentially concerned with the question: what is the appropriate scope for social, as distinct from individualist, action?' At the same time it became clear that the answer to this question involved economic as much as welfare policy (Mishra, 1984; Bulmer et al., 1989; Esping-Andersen, 1990; Smyth, 1991). This widening of the scope of our subject is a matter of no small importance in a book focusing on the distribution of welfare, because, as Mishra (1984:169) pointed out, one of the effects of the earlier, narrower approach was that 'the importance of full employment and economic growth for the general welfare of the masses was disguised by the emphasis on social welfare and distribution.'

This chapter explores some aspects of the history of social policy after the Second World War which led to the later neglect of its economic dimension.

Assumptions

The chapter makes some broad contextual assumptions which are not all found in the published literature but cannot be argued in any detail here (see Smyth 1991). To begin with, it assumes that there were two stages in the development of the central idea in postwar social policy, the welfare state. The first spans the period from the Great Depression to the onset of the Cold War and centered on the issue of how to plan the economy in order to ensure social security through the provision of full employment. Especially through the ideas of the British economist John Maynard Keynes it became accepted that free markets left to themselves might not generate enough demand to create full employment. Governments therefore needed to take on a role of demand management if full employment was to be achieved and maintained. The second begins in the late 1950s when the unanticipated achievement of social security through these Keynesian measures began to create expectations of an affluent society. Then, as Tierney (1965:128 ff) wrote in the mid-1960s, the purpose of social policy began to shift from 'the defeat of mass poverty' through full employment, to the improvement of the quality of life through higher welfare benefits, attention to specific groups neglected by the normal safety net, greater participation of welfare state clients and the expansion of state intervention into new policy areas such as the family and leisure. In Australia the social policy emphasis to which Mishra refers belongs to the phase of the affluent society. Only with the erosion of its economic base have the social policy implications of the Keynesian policies for full employment and growth returned to view.

The second set of assumptions concern the postwar social policy as a subject of intellectual inquiry. As a distinct academic subject social policy in Australia only began to emerge in the early 1960s, an affluent society origin which explains much of the distinctive preoccupation with welfare and distribution. Its prehistory in the postwar period was centered primarily in economics, specifically in the policy debates surrounding the Keynesian revolution. In the pre-Keynesian order, of course, debate about the appropriate scope for social action was sharply defined by the importance accorded the activity of individuals in the market. When the Keynesian revolution broke this mould and — at least in its early stages — opened the prospect of collective economic planning in order to achieve socially agreed goals, the very distinction between economic and social policy was blurred. This intellectual confusion continued in economics until the early 1950s when the idea of the welfare state emerged, locking in place the respective roles of state and market. However, for reasons which will be explained in this chapter, the social policy foundations of the new mixed economy slipped from view in mainstream economics. Until the break up of the Keynesian welfare state consensus, the social policy dimension of full employment and growth remained as disguised in economics as was the economic dimension in social policy.

We have become so used to the differentiated approach to economic and social policy analysis established in the 1950s that it is not easy for us to re-enter an intellectual world where social policy, far from being an adjunct to the economy

— expansive in periods of economic growth, contracting in recessions — was thought to provide the foundations of economic policy. A full account of that world would need to establish the social context of the Great Depression and Second World War in which Western nations saw notions as diverse as Roosevelt's America, Hitler's Germany and Staliin's USSR involved in a variety of forms of economic planning in order to restore economic and social progress. In economics the era is associated with the Keynesian revolution when the central issue in policy was whether the new mechanism of government economic planning was destined to supplant the free market altogether, or whether the two methods could be reconciled or synthesised. This chapter follows the transition in Australian economic thought from the period of revolution to the synthesis which resulted. First, we see the ways in which the revolutionary social approach to the economy was thought to be incompatible with traditional market economics; then, the way in which the two were brought together in a synthesis; and how this synthesis concealed its ideological foundations.

The 'Keynesian' revolution

The body of writing with which this account begins is representative of the last phase of the 'Keynesian' revolutionary period in Australian economic thought. In that period, beginning in the 1930s, the free market model of the neoclassical system had been widely seen as too hypothetical and remote from the real world, a poor guide to policy in what was called a dynamic world. Economists were seeking a 'general theory' which would take more account of the sociological and political factors operating in economies in a world of rapid change, as it was thought the classical tradition had done. Taking account of the new planning roles of government was a central concern and obviously a matter of profound ideological disagreement. The writings which follow indicate the ways in which the sought-after 'general theory' would have inscribed social policy implications into a new framework of economic analysis.

At the beginning of the 1950s, the major inflationary crisis which greeted the new decade seemed to underline the necessity for a continuation of the revolutionary trends in economics. This was evident in the public lectures of the Canadian, Benjamin Higgins (1951), then visiting Melbourne University as Ritchie Professor of Research in Economics. The book shows the impact of the Cold War on economics, thus it is subtitled, 'Economics in the Crisis of Democracy', and refers to the 'threat of World War Three' arising from the 'clash of two rival economic ideologies'. Higgins shows that there were four schools of international economic thought, each offering a very different vision of society: Marxists, Keynesians,

Institutionalists, and the 'School of Latter-day Laissez-faire' (by which he meant the Chicago economists — Higgins, 1951:109–110, ch 2).

Australian economic thought

The Australian economic writing is too slight to arrange in terms of such schools of thought. In his presidential address to the ANZAAS Conference of 1952 significantly entitled 'Authority and Control in a Free Society', D. B. Copland (1952:1–3, 19–21) considered the ethical responsibilities of the social scientist in what he called, this ' totalitarian age'. Rejecting the dominant pre-Keynesian tendency to identify the methods of economics with those of physical scientists, he indicated the reasons why economists had not 'acquired the mana of the physical and biological scientists'. The latter, according to Copland, were properly concerned with the 'explanation and production of happenings ... with ideas and things, while the former studied "men in their community relationships" ' . Such a study, he continued, necessitated moral judgments together with the need to take responsibility for the 'social consequences of new techniques'. Copland thought that modern education had been so overtaken by the scientific method that questions relating to values were being ignored. Acknowledging that such issues were subject to the 'play of prejudice, emotion and basic political belief' he nevertheless believed them to be unavoidable. Confronting in particular the view that economics concerned means not ends, Copland roundly endorsed the words of his British contemporary Sir Alexander Gray :

> Unless we are prepared to regard ourselves merely as a company of
> irresponsible idiots dancing in the void, we must frame for ourselves, if only
> as a working hypothesis, some sort of view of the kind of cosmos which we
> inhabit and the manner of its governance.

To this end Copland urged that the economist work in cooperation with other social scientists in order to be clear about 'the basic social structure he thinks desirable or enduring'. This 'reorientation of our ideas', he hoped, would be furthered by the new School of Social Sciences at the Australian National University.

The most prominent advocate of such a reorientation and arguably the profession's most distinguished theoretician was E. R. Walker. He was especially concerned with the relation of economic theory to public opinion. The former concern appears to reflect the cold war context. 'It must be admitted,' he said, 'that they (economists) are subject to social pressures to produce findings that lend quasiscientific justification to what is politically popular'. However, he believed Economics was in some sense a science with a 'logic of its own' though one which differed from the physical sciences because of the impossibility of ethical neutrality. It should be recognised, he continued, that economic thought developed both in response to the 'play of scientific imagination' and 'under the pressure of dominant currents in the vulgar version'. Instead of attempting to purify their views of 'popular opinion' in the interests of objectivity, Walker continued, economists should recognise first that popular beliefs placed limits on the understanding and implementation of policy proposals; and second that popular economics might well reveal inadequacies in the scientific analysis. As example of the latter he suggested that Keynesianism had brought 'scientific respectability (to) certain popular ideas previously considered as having their origin in the intellectual confusion of untutored minds' (here he is probably referring to the popular demands in the 1930s for cheap money and expansionary fiscal policy).

More generally, Walker (1951:65–69) believed that the growing application of economic theory to public policy was increasing the pressure 'to transform economic theory into a branch of sociology'. Walker suggested that historically, economic theory had been the doctrine of free enterprise and it was therefore:

> bound to be reabsorbed into a more comprehensive and complete structure of social science as the system of free enterprise is itself transformed into a more centralised structure of economic society.

> (1951:65–69)

Still engaged in the construction of a theory of the mixed economy, Walker referred to the difficult problems involved in the attempt to 'combine in the one system, principles of organisation that appear, at least superficially, to be in conflict'. Traditional theory was proving increasingly inadequate, he thought, in policy areas such as social services, industrial relations and productivity, which were clearly fields of 'political activity and struggle'. Future research in such areas, he thought would 'blur the limits of economic theory and promote the development of economic sociology'.

Walker's confidence in this opinion was based in part on his experience with United Nations organisations concerned with world development. Early attempts to distinguish between economic and social development, he said, had resulted in proposals for a joint 'Economic and Social Council', or alternatively, a 'Social and Economic Council'. Initially the two tasks had been assigned to separate institutions but in 1949 they were united with the aim of integrating economic factors of development such as capital and production skills with social factors such as education, health, changes in societal organisation, 'political morality and conventional attitudes of mind'. This perception of the interdependence of economic and social factors would, Walker believed, hasten the development of economic sociology, a project he commended to 'the rising generation of economists'.

Walker's methodological concerns were shared by Colin Clark, then attached to the Bureau of Industry in Queensland. He introduced his second edition of 'The Conditions of Economic Progress' with a warning against the dangers of an over concentration on what he called 'factual economics' to the neglect of theoretical work (Clark, 1951:vii–ix, 2–4). This reversal of priorities since the pre-war period had left current economic theory with certain fundamental weaknesses. Their source he located in the narrow definitions of nineteenth century liberal economic theory whereby the scope of the discipline was confined to the purely economic. It had now been shown, Clark argued, that a 'laissez-faire system is not self-regulating' and economies required a degree of government intervention. Further, even 'a community in which the economic results of laissez-faire are perfectly satisfactory may still have good political or social reasons for interfering with the unimpeded workings of laissez-faire'.

Reviewing the history of economic conceptions of welfare, Clark noted that what he called the nineteenth century 'Liberal error of claiming absolute validity for economic conclusions' had not been followed by Marshall or Pigou. The latter's welfare economics, he continued, had supplied an alternative framework for the previous generation whereby economics was made subordinate to ethics. However, Clark thought the earlier conception of welfare was now inadequate. Other criteria of human happiness needed inclusion, among which he listed, the desire for security, the ability to choose the work one liked, and the need for the great majority 'to own their means of production'. Finally, he thought the criteria lacked any reference to the political framework of economic life. 'In the light of grim experience he proposed, 'the existence of a just, ordered and stable political system must … be specifically considered rather than tacitly assumed'.

Like Copland and Walker, Clark looked for the reconstruction of economic theory in an interdisciplinary setting. He believed this reconstruction ought to recognise a 'hierarchy of arts and sciences' in which economics would acknowledge the higher authority of political science; political science, ethics; ethics, philosophy; and philosophy, religion. While Clark's emphasis is on the ultimate priority of religion, and the scholastic, philosophical scheme of the hierarchy of knowledge sets his analysis apart from his contemporaries, his writing indicates that the wide-ranging methodological concerns typical of the Keynesianism in the 1940s persisted into the Cold War, at least among the senior economists.

These writings of Copland, Walker and Clark were to represent the end of the quest for a new theoretical model for a dynamic world, rather than a renewed advance. The political turmoil of the 1930s and 1940s had introduced a new logic into the play of the economic imagination, one which would address the seemingly inevitable trend to an increasingly centralised economy. The older mainstream theory of the textbooks had come to be seen as an ideology of free enterprise and linked to an inappropriate nineteenth century liberal political philosophy. The need to address institutional change and associated conflicts over values had created the theoretical space in which a revolution in the idea of social policy had occurred. In such circumstances, it had been argued, it was irresponsible for an economist to adopt the stance of a mere technician, silent on the question of the type of society we ought to have.

The end of the Keynesian 'revolution'

The new generation of academics brought a very different set of intellectual practices to their craft than that which had been proposed by Walker (the economic historian J. F. Cairns was a notable exception). Their approach would be aggressively value-free and agnostic about the political framework of the economy. They assumed a stable not a dynamic world in which the tendency to centralise economic structures had ceased. In policy, debate about social goals gave way to specification of the mix of policies necessary to maintain stability. Their theoretical tools were a mix of Keynes and the neoclassical tradition and it expressed not a philosophy of the mixed economy but a new technocratic ideology.

The new intellectual context reflected in the break up of the synthetic approach to social inquiry showed itself in economics in the abandonment of the endeavour to explore the dynamic world. Success of that endeavour had been predicated on the creation of a new general theory to supplant the previous static, equilibrium model. Its demise was evident in a review of recent trends in economic theory in 1955 by H. Kolsen:

> The craze of 'General Theories' (he wrote) carried with it the seeds of its
> own decline; nothing can be devised in the way of theoretical models which
> is applicable to all situations under all circumstances, unless the model is
> couched in such general terms as to have little real content.

(1955:4)

Kolsen continued that whereas approaches to the analysis of the economy in general and to its partial aspects had become antagonistic in the previous decades, now it was dawning on economists that they could be complementary. The new complementarity observed by Kolsen can be taken as evidence of the end of the revolutionary phase of Keynesianism through its reincorporation in the neoclassical tradition.

The end of the Keynesian revolution and its synthesis with neoclassical theory reversed all those theoretical trends which had tried to bring some account of social and political factors into economic analysis. We cannot pursue all these complicated theoretical developments here but it is important to identify the main features which led to economists' diminishing concern with social policy.

The point of neoclassical synthesis which followed the so-called Keynesian revolution has been summarised by Whitewell. 'Once Keynesian demand management techniques had been used to establish full employment, neoclassical theory could come into its own.'(1986:172).

The synthesis reinstated the fundamental validity of the traditional axioms of market theory. The Keynesian ingredient allowed that because the real world did not usually measure up to the theoretical premises of the market model, there would, at least in the short-term foreseeable future, be the need for governments to 'steer' the markets towards the 'full employment' equilibrium.

With the emergence of the neoclassical synthesis there was a loss of interest in the complexity of social causes influencing economic behaviour. As Baumol (1970) writes, the new orthodoxy marked the end of the era of 'magnificient dynamics' reported by Marx and Schumpeter whose writings had had a major impact in the preceding decades. It was replaced by a 'comparitive statics' which looked at change over time but in a system whose basic framework was assumed not to change.

The other key feature which hastened the exit of social policy from economics was the reconstruction of welfare economics. The old welfare economics associated with A. C. Pigou had incorporated a value commitment to greater equality but it had assumed that the free market was the optimum vehicle for economic welfare. It offered no way of evaluating the ends or means of the new mechanism of state economic planning. With the reinstatement of the fundamental premises of market theory in the neoclassical synthesis came a revival of welfare economics.

In the long-term separation of social policy from economics in this period, welfare economics was of minor importance. It was a child of neoclassical theory and of more importance is the question of whether particular theoretical systems have some necessary association with particular world-views. The whole subsequent history of social policy and economic thought has been profoundly influenced by the participation of all the social sciences at this time in an attempt, as Giddens (1987:183–187) writes, to construct 'social science as a science'. In this reconstruction the idea was deeply implanted in economic thought, that as a science, economic theory need not correspond to reality, let alone make judgments about the social structure. It was thought to be primarily a science of prediction concerned with a distinct range of purely economic phenomena.

Friedman and positivism

A close reading of the Australian literature shows that the reconstitution of economics as a science in the 1950s was subject to significant theoretical variations (Smyth, 1991). For the purpose of this chapter, the approach with which it became most popularly associated in the international literature, that developed by Milton Friedman (1953: 3-5, 41) will be illustrated. His *Essays in Positive Economics* have, of course, generated a large critical literature but it is not a purpose of this chapter to enter into analytical detail (see Caldwell, 1982, for a detailed discussion). What needs to be noted is what Giddens (1987:187–189) indicates as the influence of logical positivism on Friedman's interpretation. Primarily through this influence Friedman was led to present economics as a science of 'prediction' not 'realism'. The argument is made to rest on J. M. Keynes's distinction between economics as a 'positive science ... a body of systematised knowledge concerning what is; and as a normative science... a body of systematised knowledge discussing criteria of what ought to be'. For Friedman, positive economics could be objective in precisely the same way as the physical sciences. While agreeing that the subject matter of the human sciences and the involvement of the investigator in that subject matter raised special problems of objectivity, he saw no reason to make a fundamental distinction between the social and the physical sciences.

Considering the relationship of positive to normative economics, Friedman accepted that there could be no 'one to one' relation because of the possibility of conflicts of values. Nevertheless, he ventured that:

> ... *the judgement ... that currently in the Western World, and especially in the United States, differences about economic policy among disinterested citizens derive predominantly from different predictions about the economic consequences of taking action — differences that in principle can be eliminated by the progress of positive economics — rather than from fundamental differences in basic values, differences about which men can ultimately only fight.*
>
> (1953:3–5, 41)

Friedman then offered a number of examples to show that given what he saw as an 'underlying consensus' on policy objectives, differences of opinion were related to the means of attaining these objectives and thus best decided by the findings of positive economics.

The remainder of his essay concerned the criticism that the assumptions of mainstream theory lacked realism; for example, the assumption of rational economic man. Here, Friedman found attack the best form of defence, challenging the critics to formulate a set of assumptions which could capture all the complex social and political influences on economic behaviour. Instead of pursuing an impossible realism he proposed that economists be concerned with 'prediction' i.e. with generating empirically testable hypotheses concerning economic phenomena which 'yield predictions that are good enough for the purpose in hand or that are better than predictions from alternative theories'.

Given that Friedman's understanding of positive economics conveys the most widely accepted methodological assumptions of the new orthodoxy, the steps by which the critique of positivism, in the early Keynesian period, was overcome in the new orthodoxy, are clear. The difficulties raised by claims to ethical neutrality were evaded by the assertion that value conflict had become insignificant in a society characterised by an underlying consensus. The argument against economics as a science uncovering universal laws of human behaviour could be accommodated by the lesser claim to predictability. The demand for realism involving the development of a comprehensive social science was easily represented as grandiose in an intellectual climate permeated by a new empiricism. If economic thought develops, as Walker believed, both in response to the 'play of scientific imagination' and 'under the pressure of dominant currents' of popular thought, the new assumptions were clearly related to shifts in the social context. The questioning of claims to objectivity and the demand to take account of the social and political framework reflected a world when capitalism and democracy were seen to be in crisis. The synthesis rested on the assumption of a new consensus concerning social objectives. If the ends could be assumed why should economics not focus on the means and once again be concerned with neither more nor less than its own technique?

Political arithmetic

The new theoretical ground rules impacted radically on the relation between social policy and economic thought. The disharmony between economic theory and the dynamic world (which had produced the social approach to the economy in the 1940s) having been largely resolved through the synthesis of static equilibrium economics with Keynesian macro theory, there was a resurgence of the economic approach to social policy. Now that it was safe to assume an underlying consensus on the economic role of the state, economists could pursue a scientific account of what was thought to be rational behaviour within the system. Indeed T. W. Swan (c. 1953) was emboldened to describe the result as 'iron laws of political arithmetic' forming the 'rules of conduct of a … workable system'.

Identifying the place of social policy in the new orthodox writings is a complex task. First, the new ground rules meant that the subject of social policy was no longer identified as such in the mainstream literature. Social policy largely became economic policy. Second, there was no longer a single policy objective to provide the focus of debate as was the case with full employment in the 1940s. To simplify our task, this account followed the transition from the idea of government economic planning in order to achieve social security to the idea of economic management in order to attain a range of related economic objectives.[1] The latter was expressed in a particular form of macro-economic policy analysis which became characteristic of the postwar period and indicates the essentials of the new economic approach to social policy.

Histories of Australian economic policy do not record this change in the way economists considered their subject but they do show relevant features of the economic context. Most importantly, the overriding concern of the 1940s with security became less important as overall economic demand remained strong. According to Maddock (1987:79) the causes of the boom 'remain something of a mystery', but as various historians have commented, it was the luck of the conservative government to arrive with this economic wave which was sustained through to the 1970s. Lack of adequate demand, with which the planners of the 1940s had been primarily concerned, turned to an abundance. Maddock and McLean (1987:89–90) indicate that, by the measure of nominal GDP, demand grew by 3 per cent per year from 1920 to 1940, by 6 per cent to 1947, and then by 9 per cent from 1947 to 1967. The most important factor in this growth, given the emphasis on public expenditure in the social policy planning of the 1940s, was the strength of the private sector after 1947. Boosted to nearly 40 per cent in the war and early postwar years, the leading role of public sector demand was displaced thereafter.

While the boom clearly facilitated the dominant position of the private sector in the post-war mixed economy, reaction to its early excess upon the outbreak of the Korean War helped settle the questions regarding the appropriate measures of social control. The crisis — general prices rose by 26 per cent in 1950–51 — produced a considerable controversy. For some, Australia's exposure to international market forces argued a return to market oriented policies and a curtailment of extravagant Keynesian social and economic policies. Others urged the reimposition of more direct controls at least for the period of the emergency. In the event through a combination of the first anti-cyclical budget, the so called 'Horror Budget', the imposition of import controls in 1952 and a revival of export earnings, the crisis passed and the efficacy of the indirect techniques of demand management came to be accepted. Whitwell has nicely summarised the impact of these early experiments in management on the Treasury officials. In addition to a shift of concern from unemployment to inflation, the period:

... saw the department learning to rely more or less solely on Keynesian techniques of demand management and to forsake wartime controls. It saw the department coming to grips with the link between internal and external balance. While there was a continuing concern with boom collapsing into severe slump, the period saw a growing realisation that the timing and severity of such a slump depended not simply on the state either of the United States or British economies but on the structural characteristics of the Australian economy and on the extent to which domestic demand pressures were permitted to expand.

(1986:109)

Thus by the mid 1950s the major social policy issues raised in earlier economic debate were settled. The economy would be predominantly privately owned but the social responsibility of government was enlarged. No longer, as Kaldor (1983:169) writes in relation to the British experience, was its role simply to maintain 'a framework of laws and institutions which provided the best environment for the operation of market forces' but it was to manipulate those forces in order to achieve certain 'national economic objectives'. To the overriding objective of full employment, circumstances had added several related goals, namely, the curtailment of inflation and the maintenance of internal with external balance.[2] Responsibility for the attainment of these goals was to be exercised through indirect means of demand management.

The new economic approach to social policy emerged in Australia towards the middle of the 1950s. Its formal structure was introduced in several important papers by Swan and it was given popular explanation in writings by Arndt, Downing and Karmel. The papers by Swan and by Karmel offer sufficient illustration of the new approach (e.g. Arndt ,1954, 1955; Downing, 1954). The new style of policy analysis followed the international pattern, one which took its form from the work of the Dutch econometrician, Jan Tinbergen. The 'Tinbergen rule' indicated that in order to achieve a given number of objectives government must operate at least an equal number of different policy instruments (for further discussion see Kaldor, 1983; Thompson, 1985). Its operation was given early expression in Australia by Swan. His 'Economic Control in a Dependent Economy', introduced with an excerpt from a dialogue by James Mill concerning the usefulness of political economy, considers the relationship between policy objectives and policy instruments (Swan:1960:51–52, 60). Focussing on the objectives of internal balance, external balance and internal price stability, Swan explores the gamut of related choices of policy instruments involved in the regulation of demand, the money wage level and the external price level. To achieve the objectives, he shows the logically necessary combination of policy instruments which must be put in place. Swan thought of this essentially mathematical modelling of economic behaviour as an 'essay in political algebra'. It showed he said 'the iron law of political arithmetic' which says 'that we can't both have our cake and eat it too'. Revelation of this law, he said, gave 'rules of conduct (which) form(ed) the basis of a workable system'. Rules, which if they were not followed by the 'ignorant', 'greedy', or 'ambitious', he warned, would lead the offenders to what Croce had called 'economic remorse'.

Swan's extraordinary ability to elaborate mathematically the different policy permutations to which the economic relationships within the postwar mixed economy could give rise, achieved most recognition through his study of the 'Longer Run Problems of the Balance of Payments' (Swan, 1963:384–5). The paper makes clear the fundamental dilemmas of macro policy which had arisen in the early 1950s. As he explained, in the 1940s it had been well-recognised :

(a) that incomes and employment depend on the level of spending; and
(b) that there is no automatic mechanism to keep spending near its full employment level, without conscious action by economic and financial authorities.

The program which had resulted 'did not recognise the possibility of balance of payments deficits arising from Australian over-spending'. It had to be recognised, he said, that the balance of payments depended as much on the level of spending as did full employment and he posed the question:

Must it be only a happy chance if the 'internal balance' and the 'external balance' levels of spending coincide? Is there an automatic mechanism to ensure this, or what kind of conscious action by the authorities is required ?

The resulting 'Swan Diagrams' set out in mathematical form the different sets of relationships which could occur and indicated their corresponding policy implications.

Swan's notion of political arithmetic was of course quite opposite to the type of political economy much discussed in the preceding years. The difference had been observed in 1948 by the American economist D. M. Wright (1948:452 ff.) in his review of writings on the future of capitalism. He considered three main schools of economic thought, the socialist, laissez-faire and a third who were sociologically oriented but more conservative than the socialist. All three had emphasised what he called the 'ethical' dimension in their prognostications. In addition, he adverted to the recent emergence of 'the Keynesian "political arithmetic"... which display(ed) an apparent rigid "scientific" neutrality' in these matters. This introduction of the scientific method into social study he believed to be of limited use because 'unfortunately life is not so simple'; and proceeded to indicate various cultural, ethical and political factors influential on economic behaviour and of which the political arithmetic took no account.

For the Australian economist, G. R. Mountain (1955:10), the new approach brought to mind the 'equilibrium' economics of the prewar period. Citing the challenge to explore the dynamic world — an approach he thought best represented in the work of Copland — he criticised the 'use of models or similar theoretical simplifications' based on the postulate of equilibrium conditions. Referring to the work of Swan in this respect, he argued that such analyses produced equilibrium only on paper and omitted the dynamic factors at work in the economy.

That it was an essentially apolitical analysis was evident to Swan himself. In a brief reflection entitled, 'Why Economists Don't Know' (c.1953), he indicated that, in general, economists' policy judgments were not only limited by the difficulty of 'finding empirical regularities that are useful for forecasting purposes' but by the fact that questions of economic policy involve 'issues of social justice and other political alternatives', as well as the lack of political certainty about the future decisions of government. However, he believed these difficulties were not always insurmountable:

> Nevertheless, the political and social climate of a particular place and time often very greatly narrows the range of alternatives which the economist needs to consider in practice, if he is to be concerned with real possibilities rather than with hypothetical questions which might arise in some utopia of his own devising.

The ascetic logic of Swan's analysis was given more popular form by P. H. Karmel (1954:4–10, 27) in his G. L. Wood memorial lecture. Karmel, then a very youthful professor of economics at the University of Adelaide, indicated that 'the general approach of much of the paper and the analytical framework owes a great deal to Professor T. W. Swan'. Karmel's commentary indicates the way in which the social policy framework came to be assumed. Introducing his audience to the role of government in the economy, Karmel found no cause to turn to the old debates about planning and freedom, simply noting the 'remarkable change' in the previous twenty years whereby people had 'come to accept the view that conscious governmental action in economic matters is necessary'. Apparently for Karmel this change had little to do with politics but with advances in economic science: 'the result', he said, 'of our improved knowledge of the workings of the economy'. Ethical and political considerations in his statement of economic objectives were minimal because he saw point in a democracy in raising only those ends about which there was 'substantial agreement' The existence of an underlying consensus was as patent to Karmel as to Friedman. Thus he expected no quibble on the desirability of full employment, balance of payments equilibrium and a stable internal price level. As much consensus appeared as to the means as to the ends — means he saw determined by the fact that:

> *Australia is a free-market economy … There are, at present no serious suggestions that the free-market mechanism as a whole should be abandoned. For, in spite of all its imperfections, the free-market mechanism does achieve an allocation of resources which is far less arbitrary and more impersonal than any allocation by government fiat could be.*

Given these assumptions the major areas of government economic policy — the budget, money, wages and external economic policy were not fundamentally controversial.

Disagreement could occur among economists, Karmel pointed out, in two more marginal areas of policy. It was difficult, he argued, to find unanimity on what constituted equitable distribution; and the necessary direction of investment into areas of greater productivity caused difficulties because of its differential impact on other sectors of the economy. In these areas would reside the future discourse of social policy in economics in the period of the welfare state. About the key objectives and instruments of economic policy however, there was no fundamental conflict in Karmel's Australia of the mid 1950s. In such a world the tasks of economists were primarily technical achieving the given objectives kept the economy 'delicately balanced on a knife edge', requiring economists always to be 'on their toes' and alert to the 'key variables' influencing the 'overall pattern'. There was no point, he concluded, in economists concerning themselves with 'Utopia', which he thought 'foolish to expect' and 'even more foolish to desire'; rather should they expand that scientific knowledge which could lead to greater 'control over our economic destiny'. The end of utopia was the same message which Arndt took to the labour movement in the same year (Arndt, 1954).

CONCLUSION

The new political arithmetic of the mixed economy represented by the writings of Swan and Karmel brings to an end the revolution in the idea of social policy in economics initiated in the 1930s and 1940s. The demand for social security toward which the latter had been directed appeared to have been satisfied. However through the unanticipated strength of private sector demand the economy had been stabilised at full employment without the extensions of public ownership and control many had thought would be necessary. The idea of planning, of setting social goals and directing the economy accordingly had given way to the lesser aims of management — assisting a largely autonomous market to reach equilibrium. Management may have been a less than anticipated social role for the state but nevertheless it inscribed in economic policy the objectives of full employment and stability, together with instruments of control, albeit indirect , unknown in the prewar period.

While this narrowing of the scope of social policy was clearly facilitated by the buoyancy of the economy this does not itself entirely explain the end of the revolution. Most economists in the previous decade had thought the achievement of minimum social goals would introduce a dynamic for change leading to more not less social planning. To understand why economists such as Karmel and Arndt now proclaimed the end of utopian thinking and turned to elaborating the arithmetic of the existing system, it is necessary to unravel the underlying consensus on which the new political arithmetic was based. Popular economic debate shows that the politics of the Cold War produced less a consensus than what might be termed a first class ideological muddle.

Finally, the transition from the social approach to the economy to the new economic approach to social policy had an intellectual history quite apart from these contextual influences. This was the purging from economic analysis of those ideological elements which had accompanied the innovations of the Keynesian revolution. Although a forgotten chapter in the history of Australian economic thought, it is difficult to over-emphasise the importance of the aborted political economy movement for the future history of social policy and economic thought. While all the social sciences were to embrace the new positivism, as Giddens (1987:185) writes, its subsequent dissolution 'pronounced' and 'complete' among sister disciplines, did not proceed apace in economics. Attempts to remarry the languages of economic and social policy now stumble at this divided heritage. The economic literature of the Keynesian Revolution and the Cold War opens up a historical moment in economic thought when the boundaries of the discipline were first blurred and then redefined, resulting in ground rules for the 'play of the scientific imagination' about social policy which were to hold at least for the term of the welfare state.

---

[1] For the difference between planning and management, see Cairncross (1971: 28). He writes, 'those who think of planning as something different from management usually have a longer time-dimension in mind. They are thinking of... a transformation of the economy...of direct intervention to influence production...and ...have in mind a system of tighter central control'.

[2] The evolution of these goals lies outside the scope of this chapter, but it should be emphasised that, as Dow (1964: 178 ff) writes in relation to Britain, that their development in the postwar years was 'gradual and only half-conscious'.

REFERENCES

Arndt, H.W. (1954), 'Economic policy-stability and progress', in A.F. Davies and G. Serle (eds), *Policies for Progress*, Longman Cheshire, Melbourne, pp. 35–39.

Arndt. H.W. (1955), 'The State of the Australian Economy: 1955', Australian Canning Convention Proceedings, pp. 21-29.

Baumol, W.J. (1970), *Economic Dynamics*, 3rd edn, Macmillan, London.

Bulmer, M., Lewis, J., and Piachaud, D.(eds) (1989), *The Goals of Social Policy*, Unwin Hyman, London.

Cairncross, A. (1971), *Essays in Economic Management*, Allen and Unwin, London.

Caldwell, B. J. (1982), *Beyond Positivism: Economic Methodology in the Twentieth Century*, Allen and Unwin, London.

Castles, F.C. (1989), *Australian Public Policy and Economic Vulnerability*, Allen and Unwin, Sydney.

Clark, C. (1951), *The Conditions of Economic Progress*, 2nd edn, Macmillan, London.

Copland, D. B. (1952).'Autonomy and control in a free society', ANZAAS Proceedings, Sydney, pp. 1–24.

Deane, P. (1989), *The State and the Economic System*, Oxford University Press, Oxford.

Dow, J. C. R. (1964), *The Management of the British Economy*, Cambridge University Press, Cambridge.

Downing, R. I. (1954), 'Budgeting between inflation and deflation', *The Sydney Morning Herald* (Financial Supplement), 21 September, p. 2.

Esping-Andersen, G. (1990), *The Three Worlds of Welfare Capitalism*, Polity Press, Cambridge.

Friedman, M. (1953), *Essays in Positive Economics*, University of Chicago Press, Chicago.

Galbraith, J. K. (1987), *Economics in Perspective*, Houghton Mifflin, Boston.

Gerrard, B. (1988), 'Keynesian economics: the road to nowhere?', in J. Hillard (ed.), *J M Keynes in Retrospect*, Edward Elgar, Aldershot, pp. 125–152.

Giddens, A. (1987), *Social Theory and Modern Sociology*, Polity Press, Cambridge.

Groenewegen, P. D., and McFarlane, B. (1990), *A History of Australian Economic Thought*, Routledge, London.

Hebert, R.F., and Ekelund, R.B. (1984), 'Welfare economics', in J. Creedy and D.P. O'Brien (eds), *Economic Analysis in Historical Perspective*, Butterworths, Southampton, pp. 46–81.

Higgins, B . (1951), *What Do Economists Know ?*, Melbourne University Press, Melbourne.

Kaldor, N. (1983), 'Conflicts in national economic goals', in C. Feinstein (ed.), *The Managed Economy*, Oxford University Press, Oxford, pp.169–83.

Karmel, P.H. (1951), *The Australian Economy From Federation to Jubilee and Beyond*, Adelaide Chamber of Commerce, Adelaide.

Karmel, P.H. (1954), 'Economic policy in Australia — ends and means', G. L. Wood Memorial Lecture, Melbourne University Press, Melbourne.

Kolsen, H. (1955), 'Some current trends in economic theory', *Economic Monograph*, (183), 1955, p.4.

Kemp, M.C. (1954), 'Welfare economics : a stocktaking', *Economic Record*, (30), 1954, pp. 245–251.

Maddock, R. (1987),'The Long Boom 1940-1970', in R. Maddock and I. McLean, *The Australian Economy in the Long Run*, Cambridge University Press, Melbourne, pp. 79–105.

Maddock, R., and Stilwell, F. (1987), 'Boom and Recession', in *Australians From 1939*, Fairfax, Syme and Weldon, Sydney, pp. 225–71.

McCord Wright, D. (1948), 'The prospects for capitalism', in H. Ellis and B. Haley (eds.), *Survey of Contemporary Economics*, vol.2, Irwin, Homewood, pp. 449–76.

Mishra, R. (1984), *The Welfare State in Crisis*, Wheatsheaf, Brighton.

Mountain, G. R. (1955), 'A new look at the mechanisms of the Australian Economy' ANZAAS. roneo.

Smithies, A. (1948), 'Federal budgeting and fiscal policy', in H. Ellis and B. Haley (eds), *Survey of Contemporary Economics*, vol 1, Irwin, Homewood, 1948, pp. 174–209.

Smyth, P. (1991), 'T Bones and Television: Social Policy and Australian Economic Thought 1956–1960', PhD, University of New South Wales.

Swan, T.W. (1950), 'Progress Report on the Trade Cycle', *Economic Record*, (26), pp. 186–200.

Swan, T.W. (c.1953), 'Economic control in a dependent economy', (composed c.1953, published 1960), *Economic Record*, (36), pp. 51–66.

Swan, T.W. (c.1953), 'Social Control', paper presented to Seminar on Social Control, Research School of Social Sciences, Australian National University (the paper is a draft in transcript form, available in the National Library of Australia).

Swan, T.W. (1963), 'Longer-run problems in the balance of payments', Section G ANZAAS, 1955, reprint in H.W. Arndt and W.M. Corden, *The Australian Economy*, Cheshire, Melbourne, pp. 384–95.

Thompson, G. (1985), 'Objectives and instruments of economic management', in G. Thompson et al., (eds), *Managing the U K Economy*, Polity Press, Oxford, pp. 1–37.

Tierney, L. (1965). 'The pattern of social welfare', in A.F. Davies and S. Encel (eds), *Australian Society*, Cheshire, Melbourne, pp. 200-223

Walker, E.R. (1951), 'Economic science and public policy', ANZAAS, Sydney, pp. 13-70 (roneo).

Whitwell, G. (1986), *The Treasury Line*, Allen and Unwin, Sydney.

Winch, D. (1969), *Economics and Policy*, Hodder and Stoughton, London.

CHAPTER FOUR

THE MAJOR PARTY COMPETITION

Social welfare since 1972

RODNEY SMITH

INTRODUCTION

The Labor Party under Bob Hawke and Paul Keating represents something of a puzzle to many observers of the Australian welfare state. Its predecessors in power — Malcolm Fraser's Coalition Government and Gough Whitlam's Labor Government — appeared to fit a traditionally held pattern of Labor as the party of expanded state welfare and the Coalition as the parties of state welfare contraction (see, for example, Elliott and Graycar, 1979). On this model, however, welfare policy under Hawke and Keating has been like that of a Coalition government rather than a Labor government, more an extension of Fraser than a return to Whitlam (see the views summarised in Gibson, 1990:183–191).

In recent years, because both major parties have envisaged the scope of state welfare as contingent on economic growth, they have pursued similar welfare rhetorics since economic growth became uncertain in the 1970s. The expansionist welfare vision of Whitlam Labor and the meaner perspective of Hawke–Keating Labor are merely two expressions of Labor's commitment to this basic argument. Within the Coalition parties, the call for state welfare tightening and targeting fits neatly into the strand of traditional Liberal rhetoric centred on individualism, voluntarism and minimal state intervention. This Coalition rhetoric became increasingly well-developed throughout the 1980s and early 1990s.

Thus the parties' rhetorical contest over state welfare shifted from the broad Whitlam era pattern of 'more versus less' to a pattern of 'less versus less' in which the Coalition had the fullest set of justifying arguments and Labor was left without a coherent conception of the role of state welfare.

These developments in the welfare rhetoric of the two major parties were neither accidental nor inevitable. Instead, they were produced by the parties' competitive attempts to build the necessary support from within the electorate and from key economic and social groups, particularly business and trade unions, that would allow them to govern. It was also spurred by internal party changes. The most important changes in the Australian Labor Party (ALP) were the increasing dominance of the parliamentary Right faction and alterations to the party's structure that gave greater power to the ministry and key ministers. The emergent power of the group known as the 'Dries' was equally important in the Liberal Party.

Limitations of the argument

This chapter covers two periods of ALP government (1972–5 and 1983 onward) and one of Coalition government (1975–83). Its concentration is on the major parties, because they have had the greatest influence on the direction of welfare policy. As the Liberal Party and the National Party (earlier called the Country Party) operated in coalition for almost all of the period under review and have cooperated on a number of major social and economic policy statements (*Future Directions* and *Fightback!*, for example, were both Coalition rather than Liberal documents), they are usually treated as a single actor in the discussion that follows. The Australian Democrats' role in social policy formation is not considered in the chapter. While the Democrats have certainly influenced national welfare policy since they gained the balance of power in the Senate in 1980, the major parties have continued to set the direction of national welfare policy.

This argument focuses entirely on the national party contest. The impact of party competition on welfare policy in the states and territories is too broad a topic to cover here. So is the impact of Australia's federal arrangements on the parties' approaches to welfare. This chapter does not examine the specific details of national social welfare policy implementation by the Coalition and Labor party governments. That topic is well covered elsewhere (see, for example, Elliott and Graycar, 1979; Watts, 1989; Gibson, 1990). Instead, this chapter focuses on the patterns of rhetorical competition that helped both to guide and to justify those policies. In order to analyse this rhetoric, the major parties' election policy speeches, other policy documents, parliamentary speeches and other speeches and texts relating to social welfare issues since 1972 have been examined.

Major party rhetoric: the primacy of the market

It has long been commonplace to argue that Labor as well as the Coalition is committed to the continuance of capitalism in Australia (see Catley and McFarlane, 1974; Johnson, 1989). Nonetheless, between Whitlam and Hawke, the Labor Party moved to a much less suspicious view of markets and a more sceptical view of government action against market forces (see Maddox, 1989). This acceptance and promotion of markets by both major parties has limited the extent to which they are prepared to push welfare goals.

For the Liberals, the welfare state constitutes an ever present threat to the continued existence of Australian capitalism. As Andrew Peacock put it in a 1983 speech:

Liberals do not want gov to intervene

> ... *although there are excellent social reasons for governments to intervene in the distribution process, it will be counterproductive if this intervention damages the machinery of wealth creation. Government intervention should not undermine the incentives which drive work and creativity.*
>
> (1986:179)

Labor Party rhetoric in the period under review here has not explicitly depicted the welfare state as a danger to capitalism. Rather, it has portrayed state welfare as a corrective adjunct to capitalism. At the end of the postwar economic boom, Gough Whitlam viewed the state's role as correcting capitalism's sins of 'omission' rather than one of challenging its central relations of ownership and control (Johnson, 1989: ch. 6; Beilharz, 1989:144). Despite the tougher economic period since the early 1970s, Labor's position has not altered. Its 1991 'Social Justice' platform , for example, argues that:

> *It is important that government economic policy reflect social justice goals. Economic growth and improvements to the market economy can provide a significant force for social good but do not automatically assure this outcome. This necessarily means that economic policy must be concerned not only with growth and efficiency but also with issues of economic justice and economic democracy. It must be concerned not simply with the output of jobs or wealth, but also the fair distribution of them especially in a labour market that is often discriminatory and segmented.*
>
> (ALP, 1991: 210)

As with Whitlam, the basic task of the state here is correction of the omissions of the market to ensure that it operates fairly. In recent Coalition and Labor rhetoric, the market always precedes social welfare.

The necessity of welfare restraint

An important consequence of the primacy accorded to the economy in Coalition and Labor welfare rhetoric has been that the needs of the economy have determined the parties' commitments to social welfare. This is clearly seen in the parties' treatment of economic growth and taxation since the 1970s.

For both parties, it has been established as a policy, that state welfare programs depend on growth within the economy. Whitlam set the tone in his 1972 election policy speech: 'Our program, particularly in education, welfare, hospitals and cities, can only work successfully within a framework of strong uninterrupted growth'; 'The key to financing Labor's programme must be strong and continuing economic growth ...' (McAllister and Moore, 1991:102, 103). This theme has been repeatedly stressed by Coalition and Labor leaders over the past two decades (see, for example, Fraser 1979:2; Peacock, 1986:177; Liberal Party of Australia and National Party of Australia, 1988:71; McAllister and Moore, 1991:212; Manning, 1992:21).

While Whitlam claimed that Labor's social welfare programme was '... the basis of strong (economic) growth' (McAllister and Moore, 1991:102), later Labor and Coalition leaders have not argued the benefits of social policy for economic growth. Instead, they have presented economic growth as, in Paul Keating's words, 'the main game' on which state welfare is entirely dependent (quoted in Manning, 1992:21). Indeed, for Keating and Coalition leaders like John Howard, economic growth in itself largely replaces and removes the need for state welfare. The Coalition's *Future Directions* statement (Liberal Party of Australia and National Party of Australia, 1988:71), launched by Howard in 1988, argues as follows:

> One of the main reasons we have not been able to do better in providing for the needy as a nation is that our economy has not grown as rapidly as that of other countries and so has not produced additional resources for improving the real standards of community services.
> ... In the long term, the best way to help the needy is to improve economic growth and defeat inflation through the creation of a more productive, competitive economy.

The debate between Coalition and Labor leaders has centred on which party can provide such an economy.

Similarly, both major parties have argued consistently against the extension of taxation since 1972 and have argued for tax reductions for most of that period. In his 1972 election speech, Whitlam argued that taxation on business and 'the wealthier sections of the community' was 'already high enough' and that no further increases in taxation were necessary to carry out his party's program. All that was needed was action against tax avoidance (McAllister and Moore, 1991:102). While Labor produced no defence for increased taxation in the 1970s, Liberal leaders like Malcolm Fraser found it easy to depict Labor as a high-tax party and to present taxation as being against the interests of the economy and, by extension, all Australians. In his 1975 election speech, for example, Fraser stated that:

> *The great strength — the real wealth — of Australia is the creative energies of its people. We will encourage people's initiative and enterprise, not batter them to the ground with punishing taxes.*
>
> (McAllister and Moore, 1991: 211)

What Fraser was asserting here was an opposition between, on the one hand, the 'strength' and 'energy' of individuals and the economy and, on the other, the negative impact of government and taxation. Fraser and later Coalition leaders have often returned to this dichotomy in key speeches and documents, most recently in the *Fightback!* statement (Hewson and Fisher, 1991:53; see also Cook, 1993).

The ALP leadership in the late 1970s, rather than attempting to challenge the logic of this opposition between taxation and the Australian people, itself asserted both the need to reduce taxation and its own ability to achieve this (see McAllister and Moore, 1991:130). After Labor won office in 1993, its taxation rhetoric focused on the reductions it had achieved under successive Hawke and Keating governments. Despite tax debates throughout the 1980s and early 1990s that went into trivial details, the differences between Labor and the Coalition boiled down to who had and would cut taxes most and whose tax reforms could produce a fairer system. Often these issues were seen to be one and the same (see Kelly, 1992, passim, for an account of these debates).

The effects of this agreement between the parties have been substantial. Both parties agree that the needs of the economy precede those of social welfare, that no economic growth would mean no change to welfare and that taxes must be reduced. First, it has provided a rhetorical framework for both parties to restrict welfare expenditure in an era in which they have found it extremely difficult to sustain economic growth. The Coalition from the Fraser period was committed to such restrictions. By accepting the logic of the 'no growth — no welfare growth' equation and failing to counter the Coalition's anti-tax rhetoric, Labor found itself inevitably supporting similar reductions to welfare in the 1970s and 1980s. Second, this agreement meant that much of the welfare debate was conducted on Coalition's ground, since its rhetoric of individualism, the dangers of a welfare culture and the need for a small state sat more comfortably within this agreement than did Labor's traditional rhetoric of equality. These Coalition themes fleshed out the rationale for welfare restraint in a way that Labor's rhetoric did not.

Individualism

Individualism, central to Liberal rhetoric at the Party's formation in the 1940s, has remained a key theme in more recent years (Liberal Party Committee of Review, 1983:51, 52; Peacock, 1986:174; Liberal Party of Australia and National Party of Australia, 1988:1; Hewson and Fisher, 1991:26; McAllister and Moore, 1991:211, 214). In Liberal rhetoric, individualism has several facets. First, the individuals referred to by the Liberal Party are self-reliant. They look after themselves and do not expect other people to take care of them. John Hodges, for example, argued in Parliament in 1985:

> We believe in the philosophy of people primarily looking after themselves.
> We do not believe that they ought to be mollycoddled. We do not believe that
> taxpayers' money should be expended indiscriminately at will by people who
> will tend to take handouts and not fend for themselves

(House of Representatives, 19 April 1985: 1494).

Second, individualism is commonly linked by Liberals to notions of freedom. This means freedom from government interference, as Prime Minister Billy McMahon (1972:3) pointed out while drawing contrasts between Liberals and Labor in his 1972 election policy speech:

> The Liberal way ... seeks to encourage the freedom, the talents, and the
> dignity of the individual, in a society in which the Government is the servant
> not the master. The other (way) is the Labor philosophy of socialism and
> the all-powerful state, in a society where the Government is the master — not
> the servant.

Third, it means freedom in the sense that individuals should always be allowed a choice between different options rather than having a course of action determined for them.

What these uses of individualism mean for state welfare should be fairly clear. They suggest that the welfare state should be kept to a minimum, but that where state welfare is necessary, it should foster self-reliance and choice (see, for example, Chaney, 1984: especially 301–3). Much of the pattern of the Coalition's support for and opposition to welfare legislation since 1972 can be understood in these terms. For example, the Liberals praised those aspects of the 1985 Home and Community Care Bill that fostered self-reliance among the aged (House of Representatives, 13 November 1985:2632, 2633) and condemned the Government's 1990 Superannuation Bill for reducing individual choice over retirement income provision (House of Representatives, 16 May 1990:592).

Government and the dangers of a welfare culture

Why should the Liberal account of individualism be accepted? Because, Liberal leaders suggest, it is drawn from the experience of most Australians. This argument which echoes the 'forgotten people' rhetoric of Liberal leader Robert Menzies in the 1940s (Brett, 1992) is put explicitly in *Fightback!* (Hewson and Fisher, 1991:23; see Cook, 1992), and is found in a number of recent Liberal speeches. Former Fraser Minister Robert Ellicott (1986:187), for example, updates Menzies for the 1980s:

> ... there are literally millions of Australians who ... are the very core of the nation ...

> They come from all walks of life and are found engaged in most occupations. Some are members of unions. By and large they are neither rich nor poor by today's standards. They are culturally and ethnically diverse, and of all ages.

> But different though they be they have one common characteristic. They are strongly independent. They believe that life is what you make of it ...

> Although they believe that everybody should have a fair go, they detest rip-off merchants, tax avoiders, bludgers and government extravagance ...

> In essence they provide the intellectual, spiritual and physical drive of the nation and are potentially as gifted as any other people in the world.

This argument invites people who identify themselves as Australian to define themselves as rugged individuals and to adopt the minimalist attitudes towards state welfare that this requires. Social position is irrelevant to defining this Australian 'core' (even union members can belong); it is a person's outlook which is crucial. This outlook, which drives the nation, must be preserved.

Government is pivotal to Liberal arguments here, since government , and especially the welfare state, undermines this outlook and creates in its place what *Fightback!* calls 'a culture of dependence' (Hewson and Fisher, 1991:19; see also Peacock, 1986:180). Government activity can thus break the culture on which Australia was founded:

> ... *generations of Australians ... came into this land seeking freedom,*
> *opportunities and self-respect for themselves and their families. These are not*
> *the values of some historic past. They are values of enduring importance for*
> *all Australians, and the task of government is to make sure that they can be*
> *given full play.*
>
> (Hewson and Fisher, 1991: 25)

How was Australia's foundation culture undermined and replaced with the new culture of dependence? According to the Liberal account, as more and more Australians came to rely financially on government welfare support, they came to rely intellectually and emotionally on this support. This change has affected everyone: 'Welfare changed from a system of support for the needy to one where everyone believed they were entitled to something' (Liberal Party of Australia and National Party of Australia, 1988:72). While the Coalition is sometimes vague as to when this change occurred, it usually nominates the Whitlam period as the watershed or crucial one (Fraser, 1979:2; Hewson and Fisher, 1991:23).

This Coalition account of a government-induced shift in Australian culture represents an extension of its more commonly expressed argument that Australians will modify their behaviour to qualify for any incentive offered by social policies. Coalition parliamentarians have argued, for example, that pregnant women would join the public service to take advantage of maternity leave provisions, that people would make unnecessary use of health services because of Medicare and that people would stop working to enjoy unemployment benefits (House of Representatives, 29 May 1973:2782; 14 September 1983:738, 739; 8 May 1991:3289; Chaney, 1984:300).

The Labor Party, rather than rejecting this view of Australians eagerly pursuing welfare incentives, has fostered it. It was Labor ministers in the Whitlam Government, for example, who began the public campaign against the unemployed as work-shy bludgers happy to live on the dole (Windschuttle, 1980: ch.9). Much of the Hawke and Keating governments' approach to social security reform has involved examining the minutiae of legislation to eradicate every possible monetary incentive that might change people's behaviour. Social Security Minister Brian Howe's defence of the 1990 Social Security and Veterans' Affairs Amendments Bill, for example, was largely taken up with the way its provisions gave no monetary incentives for people to enter marriages and other relationships, to leave school, to go on the dole, to stop looking for work, or to live with their parents (House of Representatives, 9 May 1990: 171, 172).

While Labor has not extended these concerns about welfare incentives to embrace the notion of a changed Australian culture in the same way as the Coalition, the major parties clearly see the consequences of state welfare on Australians in the same negative terms. The Coalition simply has a fuller image of these consequences, contrasting them with a picture of Australia founded and driven by self-reliant individuals. Labor governments, concentrating on the economic 'main game', have not sustained an alternative rhetoric about the relationship between the Australian people, their culture and state welfare. At the same time, in their periods in office they have actively promoted the logic of incentive-led behaviour that lies behind the Coalition's rhetoric.

Finding the really needy

Given this framework, the major parties view the welfare state as residual. According to the Coalition, the proper objects of state welfare are not all citizens but only the 'genuinely needy', the 'weaker members'of society, those in 'greatest need' (Hewson and Fisher, 1991:19, 24, 29, 53) As Cook (1992:11) argues, in recent Coalition thought the state has two roles: the first is to provide a framework to protect individual freedom; second to '… protect those who, through no volition of their own, are unable to succeed in such a framework.' From this perspective, the market allows most people to care for themselves and their families; the residue of 'genuinely needy' are cared for by the state.

Labor rhetoric, particularly in the period of the Hawke and Keating governments, has also stressed the residual role of state welfare. Adopting a slightly different tone to the Coalition, Labor has argued that in a period of economic 'restraint', state welfare must go to 'the poorest in the community' and those 'in greatest need' (see, e.g. House of Representatives, 6 September 1983: 399; ALP, 1991:57, 58). The Hawke Government used these arguments in 1987 to justify transforming one of the very few universal provisions in Australian state welfare, family allowance, into a selective means-tested benefit (Gibson, 1990:193, 194).

The question of who actually falls into the 'genuine/greatest need' category is never clearly answered in Liberal or Labor rhetoric. According to former NSW Liberal Terry Metherell (1986: 228), it includes '… pensioners, the mentally and physically handicapped, Aborigines, lone parents on low incomes and similar groups'. *Future Directions* (Liberal Party of Australia and National Party of Australia, 1988:72) elaborates a similar list: 'children in need, the old, the disabled, the sick and the poor'. The dividing line here between the 'genuinely' and otherwise needy seems to be whether or not individuals themselves could have taken action to avoid their position or to extricate themselves from it. This dividing line of responsibility is evident in the earliest Liberal rhetoric in the period under review (see, for example, House of Representatives, 3 December 1974:4458). Labor rhetoric on this point refers less to a single moralistic division than to a vague but apparently scientifically determined series of gradations of wealth and need within society, with state welfare applying to those classified as 'the poorest' or as 'in greatest need'.

The clear feature of both the Coalition's dividing line and Labor's gradation definitions of the true objects of state welfare is that they are restrictive rather than expansive. When the Coalition wants to exclude more people from welfare benefits, it simply argues that those people or their families could take steps to help themselves and are therefore no longer among the 'genuinely' needy (Carney, 1991:14). When Labor wants to exclude more people from the welfare ambit, it defines them as falling outside a more narrowly defined group of 'the poorest'.

Targeting and the residual state

To ensure that only those in 'genuine/greatest need' receive state welfare, government policy must, according to Coalition and Labor rhetoric, be carefully targeted (Liberal Party of Australia and National Party of Australia, 1988:72; Hewson and Fisher, 1991:19, 53; ALP, 1991:58). For Labor this was presented throughout the 1980s as a matter of priorities in hard economic times and formed the basic framework for the Hawke Government's Social Security Review (Gibson, 1990: 190, 191). It was accompanied by strong assurances from Ministers that those not eligible for welfare were being excluded from the system. In his 1987 election speech, for example, Hawke claimed that his government had ' ... conducted the most systematic crackdown on tax avoidance and welfare cheating ever attempted' (in McAllister and Moore, 1991:147).

For the Coalition, targeting forms part of a deeper suspicion about government spending. Coalition spokespeople throughout the 1970s and 1980s repeatedly claimed that governments have been guilty of 'throwing' money at social problems to no effect (Missen, 1986:183; Greiner, 1986:200; Chaney, 1986:209). From the mid 1980s, such comments were bolstered by the ascendancy within the Liberal Party leadership of a more general rhetoric about the virtues of less government (Liberal Party of Australia and National Party of Australia, 1988:71; Hewson and Fisher, 1991:11, 23; McAllister and Moore, 1991:241, 246).

Despite the differences between the parties, the result of their common emphasis on targeting has been to reduce much of their welfare debate in recent years to one of claims and counter-claims about which party can best target reduced levels of welfare programmes and payments.

Voluntarism and the family

According to Coalition rhetoric, voluntary organisations and families are the institutions that should take up welfare needs. Labor itself has always seen an important place for voluntary welfare organisations. Speaking of voluntary organisations for people with disabilities in 1974, for example, Social Security Minister Bill Hayden (House of Representatives, 13 November 1974:3442) praised them as having:

> ... an 'individual touch'. They can deal with the person as a whole, helping with not one but perhaps four or five interlocking personal difficulties... And they can be so much more flexible in their approach.

The implicit and favourable comparisons made by Hayden here are with government welfare bureaucracies. Nonetheless, Labor has never developed this argument to the same extent as the Coalition.

Over the last decade in particular, the Coalition has argued that voluntary activity and organisation, rather than government, should be at the heart of welfare. *Fightback!*, for example, contrasts the 'socialist' view that governments 'are the heart of community' with the true centre of community (Hewson and Fisher, 1991:27; see also Liberal Party of Australia and National Party of Australia, 1988:72–74):

> ... there is a whole sphere of private life where relations between people are based on affection, altruism and voluntary association.
>
> It is here — in the families, churches, clubs and local activities of Australians — that the foundations of community are laid down. It is here that the real networks of mutual support, of welfare and sustenance, exist.

This argument both draws on and expands the long-standing Coalition rhetoric regarding 'the family' as central to Australian society by suggesting that the 'sphere of private life' of which families form a central part is really self-sufficient and self-sustaining (see, for example, Liberal Party Committee of Review 1983:33).

There is simply no *need* for government here. Between them, the market and this 'private sphere' can satisfy all needs (Cook, 1992:8–10).

This type of rhetoric informs not only well-established Coalition arguments that people should take more responsibility for their health through voluntary health insurance rather than relying on Medicare (or Medibank in the 1970s), but also more recent Coalition arguments that government social security functions could be taken over by voluntary non-government agencies (*Sydney Morning Herald*, 18 October 1990).

In 1972, Labor had an alternative to this type of Coalition rhetoric. For Whitlam, a large part of the rationale for increased social intervention by government was precisely to build community through increased access to education, child-care health, community centres and other community resources. Voluntary organisations had some place in this scheme, but the driving force had to be government, if only to make up for previous years of government neglect (see Whitlam, 1985: chs. 6–11; McAllister and Moore, 1991:105–8).

By the 1980s, both Whitlam's confidence in government and his view of the dynamics between government and the *community as a whole* had largely disappeared from Labor rhetoric. What remained for Labor was a series of much more specific tasks such as improving the position of women and increasing school retention rates, among others. Behind these tasks lay elements of an alternative view of community, including a broader and less traditional concept of 'the family' and gender relations than that espoused in Coalition policy (Sawer, 1990); however, the possible inter-connections between these various elements remained unclear. While not moving to the Coalition's view of community, Labor in the 1980s and early 1990s failed to articulate a persuasive alternative.

The major party rhetorical contest since 1972: Conclusions

Labor's rhetoric about welfare and equality, although powerful in 1972, lost much of its power throughout the 1970s and 1980s. By the Hawke era, Whitlam's 'doctrine of positive equality', in which government intervened to improve society, was re-placed by a Labor doctrine of 'restraint with equity' in which the governing principle was to ensure that the very worst off did not decline further (Whitlam, 1985:3; Beilharz, 1989:143–6; ALP, 1991:57, 58). While perhaps a plausible argument in the short term, 'restraint with equity' lost its power as the economic difficulties of the 1980s and 1990s dragged on.

The interpretation presented above suggests that this change in Labor's use of equality occurred not because Labor under Whitlam and under Hawke conceived of Australian welfare in very different terms, although in the Whitlam years Labor had a clearer view of the relationship between government, welfare and the community. Rather, the change stemmed precisely from Labor's *consistent* conception, from Whitlam through to Keating, of state welfare as residual and secondary to economic growth and reduced taxation. The scope of Labor's promised equality had to diminish as the economic growth on which it was based became less certain.

The Coalition, on the other hand, developed an increasingly well-defined rhetoric of welfare throughout this period. Much of the form of this rhetoric was not new. It drew on the well-established reactionary themes of perversity (in trying to help the poor, the welfare state hurts them), futility (state welfare can never really change society) and jeopardy (state welfare threatens Australian culture and character) (see Hirschman, 1991); however, by the mid 1980s it pulled these themes together more coherently than it had in the 1970s.

Never as sceptical of the virtues of markets as the ALP, the Coalition built up a rhetoric of individual, family and voluntary welfare provision via the market and community, with governments only intervening in cases of 'genuine need'. During the late 1970s and early 1980s, this rhetoric remained disorganised, although some of its constituent elements (such as individualism and the centrality of the family) were standard parts of Liberal argument. This disorganisation was caused by the Fraser Government's inability to reduce public welfare spending and by competition from voices within the Liberal Party who held views less hostile to state welfare. As economic 'dries' gained ascendancy in the Parliamentary Liberal Party under Howard and Hewson, however, this rhetoric became progressively clarified in policy documents like *Future Directions* and *Fightback!*.

In the 1980s and early 1990s, the rhetorical contest over welfare between the major parties reversed previous assumptions about the parties, with the Coalition now appearing as the more rhetorically assured and ideological party, the new party of 'true believers'. Labor, on the other hand, appeared to be increasingly pragmatic and less rhetorically coherent.

The dynamics behind the major party welfare contest since 1972

The rhetorical contest between the parties over welfare and the course this contest took did not occur in a vacuum. Rather, they were influenced by the way in which the parties attempted to negotiate various social, political and economic forces in order to win and retain government. Since 1972, the major parties have adopted a changing set of strategies to build support from key forces, especially business, unions and sections of the electorate. These strategies have affected the parties' outlooks on welfare (among other policy areas).

Whitlam came to power in 1972 in a context of relative economic stability. Labor managed to win again in 1974, despite growing economic problems (Oakes and Solomon, 1974) but lost the 1975 election to the Coalition in a landslide, largely because of its perceived failure to control the economy. Whitlam's inability to retain office was used years later by Hawke and Keating to denigrate many of his government's policies, including its emphasis on social policy (see Johnson, 1989: 94, 95). Immediately following 1975, however, Labor drew other lessons from Whitlam's loss. As part of these lessons, Labor identified business and the news media as Whitlam's most powerful opponents (see, for example, Sexton, 1979: ch. 3). Poor relations with unions were also seen as crucial to the loss (Whitlam, 1985:743; Singleton, 1990: chs. 3, 4). Not yet convinced of any need to change its *electoral* strategy, Labor fought the Fraser Government's anti-welfare measures and unemployment record at the 1977 election and lost again, increasing its two-party preferred vote by less than one per cent (see Penniman 1979).

The 1977 loss produced crucial changes in Labor's outlook, among them its attitude to social welfare issues and elections. A number of senior Labor strategists opposed the ALP's emphasis on the unemployed in the 1977 campaign, seeing unemployment as a big vote loser (Federal Parliamentary Labor Party, 1978; Goot, 1979:215–217). Labor's Inquiry into the 1977 loss urged the Party to target electoral groups like ethnic communities and women, but significantly said almost nothing about how social welfare policies and recipients might form part of Labor's future strategy (ALP 1979). Now wanting above all else to win office, Labor was defining its new constituency in ways that played down welfare.

In response to this Inquiry, as well as to continued party polling that showed unemployment, welfare and social equality to be electoral drawbacks, particularly among swinging voters, Labor went into the 1980 election promising much less on unemployment and on welfare generally (Goot, 1983:154, 197, 198; Mills, 1986:21–9). For its part, the Coalition was confident voters would view other issues as being more important than unemployment and welfare (Rawlinson, 1983:40, 41). Labor failed to win the election; however, it led in the polls for most of the campaign and managed a big vote swing away from the Coalition (Kelly, 1984: 93–5). Last-minute Coalition advertisements accusing Labor of new taxes were seen, perhaps incorrectly, by Hayden and Labor strategists as crucial to Fraser's win (Goot, 1983:202–5).

By 1983, Labor's outlook had vastly altered from that of 1972. The lesson of 1972 to 1975 seemed to be that the ALP could not govern without business support and union moderation. The contrasting 1977 and 1980 election results suggested that welfare was not electorally popular. Both major parties now saw, rightly or wrongly, Australian voters as unwilling to elect a party committed to expanding government welfare, to maintaining or increasing taxation, and to attempting to mobilise welfare recipients. Electorally successful parties in the late 1970s and early 1980s were those that promised tax cuts, welfare cuts and campaigns against welfare 'bludgers'.

Labor won the 1983 election, making very few welfare commitments beyond the resuscitation of public health care but promising to create jobs through wage restraint and economic growth. In order to stay in power, the Hawke Government openly and assiduously courted big business, pursuing economically 'responsible' policies and involving business in policy decision-making (McEachern, 1991). The union leadership under the Australian Council of Trade Unions (ACTU), accepting the benefits of dealing with a Labor rather than a Coalition government, endorsed a series of Accord agreements that reduced real wages but also involved income tax reductions and workplace superannuation. The ACTU helped the government to control militant worker aspirations (Watts, 1989:115, 116; Singleton, 1990: chs. 7–11). As for the electorate, the Hawke Government took care to avoid welfare policy decisions, such as its favoured Option C at the 1985 Tax Summit, when these were perceived via opinion polling to be electorally unpopular (see Mills,1986: ch.3).

Key parts of the Hawke Government's vaunted commitment to economic responsibility were reducing the deficit, tightly targeting welfare payments and refusing to countenance expansive welfare programmes. Labor's one significant expansion to state welfare after 1983 — Medicare was presented by the Hawke Government as not only a fairer but a cheaper and more economically responsible way to provide health care. As Health Minister Neal Blewett assured the Parliament (House of Representatives, 6th September 1983: 398, 399), Medicare was ' … an essential part of the Government's economic strategy' and would … play its part in economic recovery'. Throughout the 1980s, in contrast to the 1970s, Labor successfully juggled support from the union leadership, business and the electorate. An important part of the way it did so was to constrain state welfare.

The initial Liberal response to its 1983 electoral defeat was to reaffirm the Party's traditional values and to look for ways in which communicating and representing those values might be improved (Liberal Party Committee of Review, 1983). With Labor more and more surely occupying the Liberal's electoral 'middle ground', however, the Liberal Party began a shift towards the 'right', hoping to present a distinct image of itself as the party of greater market and industrial deregulation, privatisation, and a smaller welfare state. The Fraser Government was re-interpreted by the Party leadership as having laid the groundwork for these policies but as not having used its opportunities well or gone far enough (Hewson and Fisher, 1991:23).

Buoyed by 1980s legal successes against unions and by the intellectual support for 'new right' policies and 'economic rationalism' in significant sections of the news media and think-tanks, the Coalition followed this path to the right despite losses in four successive elections between 1984 and 1993 (Kelly, 1992: ch. 5). The Liberals interpreted these election losses primarily as failures of leadership rather than of policy or rhetoric. All the leaders from 1985 onward encouraged the Liberal shift to the right. Howard and Hewson did so from conviction. Peacock, although not by nature an economic rationalist, had acceptance of 'dry' Liberal policies forced upon him as a condition of his re-elevation to the party leadership in 1989 (Kelly, 1992:468, 476).

It is still too early to talk definitively about the impact of the 1993 election on the welfare policies of the major parties. Nonetheless, there are signs that the pattern of the 1980s may be shifting once more. Keating's 1993 election speeches attempted to emphasise Labor as a party of 'community values' in a deliberate contrast with the Coalition's emphasis on individualism (Jones, 1993). Significantly, while Labor retained the support of unions and won a majority of lower house seats in the election, it lost the support of large sections of business (Hooper, 1993). A substantial part of Labor's electoral support seemed to derive not from support for the Hawke-Keating record but from a fear of the Coalition's promises of a Goods and Services Tax, changes to Medicare and a potential reduction in wages (O'Reilly, 1993). Labor, faced with a Coalition that is likely to drop or modify these unpopular policies (Sydney Morning Herald [SMH], 30th March 1993), may attempt to redefine its electoral appeal yet again by expanding its welfare commitment. Within the ACTU and the Parliamentary Labor Party there have been calls since the election for the Government to increase taxation and government spending to meet welfare needs (Sydney Morning Herald, 12 May 1993).

The Coalition's welfare stance may also be changing. Some sections of the Liberal Party have argued since the election for a more pragmatic and flexible approach to policy that stresses social as well as economic imperatives (see, for example, Fraser, 1993; Harley, 1993). The limits of the Coalition's move toward minimalist state welfare were probably reached before the March 1993 election in any case. As Cook (1993:15) points out, Hewson's response to criticism of the original *Fightback!* by welfare, church and community leaders was to reintroduce a positive role for state welfare in his revised *Fightback!* statement of late 1992: 'In *Fightback! 1* government was a nation destroyer, in *Fightback! 2* it is a nation builder'. If the

Coalition leadership believes Fraser's (1993:15) post-election advice that 'Australians will never vote a party believed to be ideological into office', it will probably move further away from its rhetoric of the 1980s over the next few years.

Welfare policy and changes within the parties

To this point in the discussion, the major parties have been largely treated as united monoliths moving with their parliamentary leaderships. This treatment of the parties, while a necessary simplification, underplays the impact of internal party dynamics on the party's welfare policies, performance and rhetoric.

The major party competition over welfare since 1972 has been affected by changes within both major parties. Within the ALP, the Right faction has become very powerful over this period. Equally important, however, have been changes to the Party's decision-making structure which have given Labor's Right-dominated parliamentary leadership greater flexibility to pursue welfare (and other policy) goals largely as it sees fit, without hindrance from other sections of the party. Within the Coalition, the key change was the growing dominance of economic 'dries' in the federal Parliamentary Liberal Party during the 1980s. In contrast to the ALP, this dominance was achieved without changes to the party structure.

The ALP's decision-making structure formally limits the power of Labor parliamentarians and cabinets by establishing a non-parliamentary body, the National Conference, as 'the supreme governing body of the Party'. Policy decisions made by Conference are 'binding upon every member and every section of the Party', including individual parliamentarians, the collective group of Labor parliamentarians (Caucus) and Labor cabinets. Within the Parliamentary Labor Party, Caucus is the body formally responsible for 'taking such action which may be possible to implement the Party's platform and Conference decisions' (ALP, 1991: 253, 254). Caucus is thus meant to keep Labor cabinets from moving outside or against Labor policy as determined by Conference. These structural arrangements were established at the formation of the ALP in order to prevent Labor MPs from losing touch with the party's affiliated union and rank and file membership.

Since the 1960s, these structural arrangements have been undermined by a series of formal and informal changes to Labor's decision-making processes, with the result that Labor governments can effectively determine party policy themselves. They are:

1. The National Conference, traditionally dominated by union leaders and excluding Labor parliamentarians was expanded and redesigned to include the party's parliamentary leadership.

2.   The solidification of Labor's Left, Right and Centre-Left factions in the 1980s meant that Conference decisions were determined by faction leaders, particularly those from the dominant Right faction. These Right faction leaders included key Hawke and Keating ministers, giving the parliamentary Right faction much greater control over formal ALP policy than that enjoyed by previous parliamentary leaderships (Maddox, 1989: ch. 4; Jaensch, 1989:160).

3.   The 1988 Conference effectively accepted it was no longer the 'supreme governing body' by referring important decisions to sub-committees (Jaensch, 1989:166–9).

4.   Labor leaders and cabinets since Whitlam have announced policy decisions which either had not been previously passed by Caucus or were contrary to stated Party policy. Caucus, not wishing publicly to undermine the parliamentary leadership, has increasingly endorsed these decisions with little complaint since 1983 (Maddox, 1989:73–84).

5.   The establishment of an inner and outer ministry under Hawke, with Right ministers dominating the inner ministry, further insulated Hawke's cabinets from the more diverse party views in Caucus (Jaensch, 1989:164, 165; Maddox, 1989:85).

6.   After the 1993 election, Keating successfully imposed his slate of ministerial candidates on Caucus, significantly diminishing Caucus's power to inject a variety of perspectives into the ministry (SMH, 23 March 1993).

7.   Finally and partly because of the above developments, Labor's rank and file membership has shrunk dramatically and become more middle class (Scott, 1991), re-orienting the party away from the working class well-spring of many of its traditional welfare concerns.

These developments have meant that although the Right is by no means numerically dominant throughout all the structures of the ALP, its domination of the prime ministership, cabinet and the ministry since the early 1980s has left it in a position to shape Labor's welfare policies. The minority of cabinet ministers drawn from the Left, such as Brian Howe, have generally shared the Right's approach to welfare reductions and targeting and have been just as insulated from competing views within the ALP (see Stutchbury, 1992:195–9). Voices in the party opposed to Labor's welfare policy over this period have largely been stifled or heard only in forums that no longer count in party policy-making. Labor leaders who defend these policy-making changes argue that a flexible and unencumbered party leadership, especially in government, is necessary to satisfy the electorate, to respond to economic changes and to meet demands from key pressure groups. Many critics from within the ALP and outside it argue that in the pursuit of these goals

Labor leaders have 'hijacked' the party and lost sight of its important traditions (Jaensch, 1989; Maddox, 1989).

The most important change within the Coalition in the period under review was the growth in power of economic 'Dries' within the Liberal Party. Although not factionalised in such a clear-cut way as the ALP, Liberal Party politics have been dominated in recent years by conflict between so-called 'Wets' and 'Dries'. The 'Wets' are either conservatives or liberals who believe in maintaining a Keynesian role for the state within capitalism. They believe that governments should protect industry and regulate the labour market. Although they espouse much of the rhetoric of individualism encountered earlier in this chapter, Wets generally see a moderate role for state welfare as a safety net and to provide 'equality of opportunity' for individuals (see O'Brien, 1985: ch. 2; Thompson et al., 1986). Dries, on the other hand, endorse 'New Right' ideas of minimal government and laissez-faire economics. They see market forces as the primary organising principle of a wide range of social relations including work, education and welfare (O'Brien, 1985: ch. 3). Dry arguments became dominant in the Coalition during the 1980s.

Although the Liberal Party has an extra-parliamentary Federal Council that debates policy, it is the Liberal parliamentary leadership that actually determines party policy. Liberal Prime Ministers also select their own ministers. This freedom of the parliamentary leadership over policy and the cabinet was one of the founding principles of the party. Control of the parliamentary party and its leadership is thus crucial to determining Liberal policy. In the 1970s, Dries like Jim Carlton were frustrated within the Liberal Party by the policy outlook of Prime Minister Fraser. While Fraser spoke some of the language of the New Right and wound back some welfare measures, he was too pragmatic a politician to embark on a full New Right programme (Simms, 1982: ch. 8).

Only in the 1980s under Howard, Peacock and Hewson did the Dries become dominant in the Parliamentary Liberal Party and in Coalition shadow ministries. Telling indications of the extent of this sea change within the Liberal Party were the 1989 pre-selection dumpings of sitting Wet MPs Ian Macphee, Roger Shipton, Ken Aldred and David Hamer in favour of Dry candidates and, in the same year, the organisation of Peacock's leadership challenge against Howard - himself a Dry - by a group dominated by Dry Liberal MPs (Kelly, 1992: ch. 25). The Wets were almost entirely excluded from leadership positions and marginalised in party policy discussions. Hewson's leadership after 1990 continued this trend. After the Coalition's 1993 election loss, many Wets complained that they had never agreed with *Fightback!* and that Hewson had not consulted them on policy questions over the preceding three years (see, for example, *Sydney Morning Herald*, 16 March 1993).

CONCLUSION

The contest between the major political parties is crucial to understanding their approaches to social welfare. Although the broad boundaries of welfare policy are set by wider structural forces in society and the economy, it is political institutions, forces and processes such as the parties and their competition that determine how those structural forces are negotiated to produce welfare outcomes.

This chapter has shown how the ALP's combination of a broad perspective on the relationship between the economy and state welfare with a specific interpretation of its experiences during the Whitlam and Hayden years developed a particular outlook on welfare in the 1980s and 1990s. The Coalition in turn developed its own approach to welfare in the 1980s from traditional Liberal rhetoric, New Right arguments and an attempt to respond to Labor's new-found electoral success. These developments changed the rhetorical contest between the parties from one characterised by 'more versus less welfare' debates to one that involved competing explanations for the necessity of less state welfare.

How does this argument relate to the dominant conceptual accounts of the major party competition in Australia? First, and most obviously, it suggests that if Elliott and Graycar's (1979) 'initiative-resistance' style account of the parties and welfare ever held in Australia (see Watts, 1987 for an opposite view), it certainly no longer held by the 1980s. Labor in the 1980s and 1990s was not an initiator of major welfare expansion and reform. Moreover, the Coalition was less a resister of Labor initiatives than the provider of a set of arguments that matched Labor's welfare policy better than Labor's own rhetoric.

Second, Maddox's (1989) argument that the ALP under Hawke and Keating simply lost sight of Labor traditions cannot entirely explain Labor's welfare changes. As this chapter points out, it was because Labor under Hawke held a traditional Labor view of the relationship between the economy and welfare — the same view as Whitlam — that in the 1980s, Labor Governments promoted welfare restraint, targeting and so on.

Third, Jaensch (1989) gets closer to an adequate explanation with his argument that the ALP has moved from being a party expressing interests of working people via the party's program, structure and trade union nexus, to being a 'catch-all' party responding to as many demands from the electorate as possible. Despite Manning's (1992) claims, the ALP certainly has altered its relationship with the unions to give it greater freedom to construct electoral support. As Jaensch argues, its new internal power relations allow it to compete as a 'catch-all' party almost as easily as the Coalition parties.

Two important elements missing from Jaensch's argument, however, are an adequate account of the *specifics* of Labor's shift to 'electoralism' and a more precise concept than 'catch-all' to describe the outcome. Neither Labor nor the Coalition are literally 'catch-*all*' parties. They do not 'catch' exactly the same groups and opinions and they do not attempt to catch them in the same way. Labor is a 'catch-more' party compared with Labor of the mid 1960s; however, as this chapter shows, the specific groups and opinions Labor has attempted to catch, as well as those it has made no attempt to catch, have been crucial to giving the party its present character. The specific implications of the party's new catches for Labor's welfare rhetoric and policy have been equally important. The same points hold true for the Coalition and welfare.

Finally, with its electoral focus, Jaensch's argument underplays the importance of the parties' attempts to build support from the business community. Johnson's (1989) account, which argues that the limitations on successive ALP governments' welfare and other policies since the 1940s occurred largely because of Labor's repeated attempts to gain business support, is a useful corrective here. Nonetheless, her argument uses this insight rather too mechanically. As a result, her view of continuity in Labor's governing ignores other political considerations that led to important changes in Labor's outlook in the late 1970s and early 1980s. This chapter suggests that a successful account of the parties and welfare since 1972 must marry Johnson's argument regarding business support with a modified and more carefully specified version of Jaensch's shift to the 'catch-all' parties argument.

Marrying these arguments provides the solution to the Hawke-Keating welfare puzzle outlined at the beginning of this chapter. The type of solution it proposes suggests that the present relationships between the major parties and state welfare will not be frozen into a stable pattern during the 1990s and beyond. Precisely because the current party-welfare relationships are built on judgments by the parties about how to build political, social and economic support around welfare policies and policies affecting welfare, because this support shifts over time, and because the parties' judgments are affected by the dynamic of party contest and by internal party developments, these relationships are open to change again.

REFERENCES

Australian Labor Party (ALP), (1979), *National Committee of Inquiry: Report and Recommendations to the National Executive*, ALP, Canberra.

Australian Labor Party (ALP), (1991), *Platform Resolutions and Rules 1991*, R. Hogg, Barton, Canberra.

Beilharz, P. (1989), 'The Labourist tradition and the reforming imagination', in R. Kennedy (ed.), *Australian Welfare; Historical Sociology*, Macmillan, Melbourne, pp. 132–153.

Brett, J. (1992), *Robert Menzies' Forgotten People* , Macmillan, Melbourne.

Carney, S. (1991), 'The liberal face of liberalism', *Australian Left Review* (135), pp. 12–15.

Catley, R. and McFarlane, B. (1974), *From Tweedledum to Tweedledee: The New Labor Government in Australia*, ANZ Book Company, Sydney.

Chaney, F. (1984), 'Welfare and income security', in G. Brandis, T. Harley and D. Markwell (eds), *Liberals Face the Future; Essays on Australian Liberalism*, Oxford University Press, Melbourne, pp. 294–305.

Chaney, F. (1986), 'National issues', in Y. Thompson, G. Brandis and T. Harley (eds), *Australian Liberalism: The Continuing Vision*, Liberal Forum, Melbourne, pp. 209–212.

Cook, I. (1992), *Fightback! as Political Theory*, Paper presented to the 1992 Australasian Political Studies Association Conference, Canberra, Australian National University.

Cook, I. (1993), 'Backflip to the future', *Australian Left Review* (148), pp. 14–16.

Ellicott, R. (1986), 'Liberals Forget that Policies are made for People', in Y. Thompson, G. Brandis and T. Harley (eds), *Australian Liberalism: The Continuing Vision*, Liberal Forum, Melbourne, pp. 188–190.

Elliott, G. and Graycar, A. (1979), 'Social welfare', in A. Patience and B. Head (eds), *From Whitlam to Fraser; Reform and Reaction in Australian Politics*, Oxford University Press, Melbourne, pp. 87–107.

Federal Parliamentary Labor Party (ed.) (1978), *The National Implications of Unemployment*; Proceedings of a Seminar Held at University of New South Wales, 21 May 1978, National Secretariat of ALP, Canberra.

Fraser, M. (1979), *The Liberal Party of Australia: Ready for the New Decade*, Melbourne, Address to the Victorian State Council of the Liberal Party of Australia, 17 November.

Fraser, M. (1993), 'Liberals need the "Forgotten People"', *Australian Financial Review*, 22 March, p. 15.

Gibson, D. (1990), 'Social Policy', in C. Jennett and R. Stewart (eds), *Hawke and Australian Public Policy: Consensus and Restructuring*, Macmillan, Melbourne, pp. 180–203.

Goot, M. (1979), 'Monitoring the public, marketing the parties', in H. Penniman (ed.), *The Australian National Elections of 1977*, American Enterprise Institute for Public Policy Research, Washington, pp. 185–230

Goot, M. (1983), 'The media and the campaign', in H. Penniman (ed.), *Australia at the Polls: The National Elections of 1980 and 1983*, Allen and Unwin, Sydney, pp. 140–215.

Greiner, N. (1986), 'Dry and warm', in Y. Thompson, G. Brandis and T. Harley (eds), *Australian Liberalism: The Continuing Vision*, Liberal Forum, Melbourne, pp. 199–200.

Harley, T. (1993), 'Search for a Broader Party', *Australian Financial Review*, 22 March, p. 15.

Hewson, J. and Fischer, T. (1991), *Fightback! It's Your Australia: The Way to Rebuild and Reward Australia*, Online Offset Printers, Canberra.

Hirschman, A. (1991), *The Rhetoric of Reaction; Perversity, Futility, Jeopardy*, Belknap, Cambridge (Mass.).

Hooper, N. (1993), 'Subdued Business Primed for Change', *Business Review Weekly*, 5 March, pp. 22–24.

House of Representatives (various dates), *Parliamentary Debates (Hansard)*, AGPS, Canberra.

Jaensch, D. (1989), *The Hawke-Keating Hijack*; The ALP in Transition, Allen and Unwin, Sydney.

Johnson, C. (1989), *The Labor Legacy; Curtin, Chifley, Whitlam, Hawke*, Allen and Unwin, Sydney.

Jones, B. (1993), 'Keating's Clan', *Sun-Herald*, 21 March.

Kelly, P. (1984), *The Hawke Ascendancy* Angus and Robertson, Sydney.

Kelly, P. (1992), *The End of Certainty; The Story of the 1980s*, Allen and Unwin, Sydney.

Liberal Party Committee of Review (1983), *Facing the Facts*, T. Eggleton, Canberra.

Liberal Party of Australia and National Party of Australia (1988), *Future Directions; It's Time For Plain Thinking*, Liberal Party of Australia and National Party of Australia, Barton, Canberra.

McAllister, I., and Moore, R. (eds), (1991), *Party Strategy and Change; Australian Political Leaders' Policy Speeches Since 1946*, Longman Cheshire, Melbourne

McEachern, D. (1991), *Business Mates: The Power and the Politics of the Hawke Era*, Prentice Hall, Sydney.

McMahon, W. (1972), *Federal Election 1972: Policy Speech*, Federal Secretariat, Liberal Party of Australia, Canberra.

Maddox, G. (1989), *The Hawke Government and Labor Tradition*, Penguin, Ringwood.

Manning, H. (1992), 'The ALP and the Union Movement: 'catch-all' Party or maintaining tradition?', *Australian Journal of Political Science*, 27(1), pp. 12–30.

Metherell, T. (1986), 'New Liberalism: its principles and its directions', in Y. Thompson, G. Brandis and T. Harley (eds), *Australian Liberalism: The Continuing Vision*, Liberal Forum, Melbourne, pp. 226–9.

Mills, S. (1986), *The New Machine Men: Polls and Persuasion in Australian Politics*, Penguin, Ringwood.

Missen, A. (1986), 'The relevance of Liberalism today', in Y. Thompson, G. Brandis and T. Harley (eds), *Australian Liberalism: The Continuing Vision*, Liberal Forum, Melbourne, pp. 182-4.

Oakes, L., and Solomon, D. (1974), *Grab for Power: Election '74*, Cheshire. Melbourne.

O'Brien, P. (1985), *The Liberals: Factions, Feuds and Fancies* , Viking, Ringwood.

O'Reilly, D. (1993), 'GST Was Hewson's Ball and Chain', *Bulletin*, 23 March.

Peacock, A. (1986), 'The Liberal approach to change', in Y. Thompson, G. Brandis and T. Harley (eds.), *Australian Liberalism: The Continuing Vision*, Liberal Forum, Melbourne, pp. 174–180.

Penniman, H. (ed.) 1979, *The Australian National Elections of 1977*, American Enterprise Institute for Public Policy Research, Washington,

Rawlinson, M. (1983), 'The Liberal Party', in Penniman (ed.), *Australia at the Polls: The National Elections of 1980 and 1983*, George Allen and Unwin, Sydney, pp. 35–54

Sawer, M. (1990), 'The battle for the family: family policy in Australian electoral politics in the 1980s', *Politics*, 25(1), pp. 48–61.

Scott, A. (1991), *Fading Loyalties; The Australian Labor Party and the Working Class*, Pluto Press, Sydney.

Sexton, M. (1979), *Illusions of Power; The Fate of a Reform Government*, Allen and Unwin, Sydney.

Simms, M. (1982), *A Liberal Nation: The Liberal Party and Australian Politics*, Hale and Iremonger, Sydney.

Singleton, G. (1990), *The Accord and the Australian Labour Movement*, Melbourne University Press, Melbourne.

Stutchbury, M. (1992), *Gain From the Pain: Australia Recovers from its Economic Boom-Bust*, The Financial Review Library, Sydney.

Watts, R. (1987), *The Foundations of the National Welfare State*, Allen and Unwin, Sydney,

Watts, R. (1989), ' "In Fractured Times": the Accord and social policy under Hawke', in R. Kennedy (ed.), *Australian Welfare: Historical Sociology*, Melbourne, Macmillan, pp. 104–131.

Whitlam, G. (1985), *The Whitlam Government 1972–1975* ,Viking, Ringwood.

Windschuttle, K. (1980), *Unemployment*, revised edn, Penguin, Ringwood.

CHAPTER FIVE

SOCIAL JUSTICE
New route to Utopia?

DAMIAN GRACE

INTRODUCTION

Shaping society to eliminate disadvantage and provide something like equal opportunities for all of its members is a very modern possibility. This possibility gives rise to a host of questions about fairness and equity grouped under the heading of social justice. For centuries, discussions of justice took place without the qualification 'social'. These discussions were, in the main, concerned with questions of legal and personal justice, with the rights and obligations of persons and groups under existing rules. However, the possibilities for a broader concept of justice, which has opened up in the modern era, have led to questions of distribution and equity which would have been inconceivable before. The term 'social justice' is a product of market societies (Miller, 1976) and thus has a remedial or 'prosthetic' (Raphael, 1964) quality about it. It is about changing social institutions and even attitudes to achieve a fairer society, and so embraces questions not only of philosophy, but of politics, economics, religion, education and even geography.

The pattern was set almost five hundred years ago, when Thomas More constructed the first recognisably modern design for a just society in his *Utopia*. This work is modern not only in the sense that it treats social institutions as raw material for planning, but in prefacing its plan with a structural attack on the shortcomings of contemporary Europe. In particular, More identifies the avarice of rulers and the unjust distribution of wealth they support as the causes of social corruption:

> *A king has no dignity when he exercises authority over beggars, only when he rules over prosperous and happy subjects…A solitary ruler who enjoys a life of*

pleasure and self-indulgence while all about him are grieving and groaning is acting like a jailer, not a king.

(More, 1516/1989:34)

Here More was making three important and connected points. First, there is something wrong at a personal level with living well in the midst of deprivation. Even if one's comforts were not the cause of another's hardship, an indifference to suffering reveals a character lacking the virtues of generosity, justice and nobility. More's second point is that institutional justice is wanting if those charged with protecting the collective welfare, in this case a king, pursue self-interest instead. Justice in rulers requires fairness in distribution as well as the virtue of generosity or charity. Thirdly and most audaciously, the assumption underlying More's work is that society is plastic, its advantages and disadvantages can be shaped by human agency, nature and fortune notwithstanding. All these points have a strong echo in current arguments about social justice (Boulding, 1988). Much else, however, has changed.

When More wrote his classic, he brought ancient principles of justice to the modern task of designing a society. Cicero had written in *De officiis*:

*The first office of justice is to keep one man from doing harm to another ...
and the next is to lead men to use common possessions for the common
interests, private property for their own.*

(1913: I.20)

For Cicero, as for More, society was sustained by the 'common bonds' of justice and its close relation, charity. Today, many believe that only the first office of justice is defensible, and that the chief function of the state is the defence of individual interests. Social needs should no longer be a state responsibility but become a matter for individuals. In reaction to this view, there has recently been a re-emphasis on the social dimension of justice. Hence, the notion of social justice, affirmed in Australian Government policy in 1988, indicates an obligation to distribute resources in the interests of the whole society.

The concept of socially held and distributed property is harder to grasp today than it used to be because we are used to private distributions through the market. In a liberal society, the prosperity of the individual is conceivable without reference to the prosperity of the whole. Ironically, in times of accepted inequality, this was an object of moral concern, whereas in an age of professed egalitarianism it is possible to make a plausible argument that social justice is a violation of individual rights and freedoms and an affront to good sense.

Since More's time, the growth of liberal individualism in Western industrial so-cieties has cast doubt on two interrelated assumptions: the first is the existence of a real entity called society which can be said to distribute resources and opportunities throughout its membership. The second is whether there is anything that can be said to belong to a society for it to distribute. Like More we usually understand society to be something more than simply the site of individual interactions. There is a general impression that society is a corporate entity with powers of possession and agency. In More's time common grazing areas were taken as a collective right and their alienation was a perennial political issue. Now, the commons, like the kind of community which supported them, are all but gone, and some seem to believe that the bulk of social property should go the same way. Even the use of a remedial term like 'social justice' connotes individualism in concentrating on the entitlements of beneficiaries and evading the problem of distributing social burdens (see for example,. Australian Catholic Social Justice Council, 1990; Miller, 1976:22; cf. the cautions of Jackson, 1986:16 and Lucas, 1980:163).[1]

Libertarians and radical liberals insist, however, that the concept of justice ap-plies only to individuals and not at all to the nominal collectivities we call societies. As there is nothing to distribute and no agency of distribution, there is no entity and no action to which the term injustice could apply. Social justice in this view has as much reality as Utopia.

Is there a social agent?

Plato believed that virtue could be expressed in persons or societies. He thought the best way for individuals to understand justice was to examine it writ large in a just society. But this assumes that societies can possess the virtues of individuals. Liberalism, especially in its most individualistic forms, challenges this assumption.

Foremost amongst liberal sceptics are F. A. Hayek and Robert Nozick. Hayek argued that society could not be unjust. If some people are poor or the victims of misfortune, society cannot be blamed for this. Society is a complex of interactions some of which have unintended and unforeseen if regrettable consequences for some people. But this does not entitle us to infer that society owes those who do not gain from its normal processes a special share of its benefits (Hayek, 1976:64–5).

Perhaps Hayek's point could be illustrated in this way: a person takes out superannuation and lives in comfortable retirement. Another person chooses not to take superannuation and lives with difficulty on a pension. Why is anything owed to the person who chose not to take an option to improve his life in advancing age? Say a person was not in a position to contribute to superannuation.

Why is anything owed to this person? Why is anything owed to those who have not achieved as much in life as others? Obviously many people would willingly contribute towards the welfare of the destitute and disadvantaged, but the crucial word here is willingly. Charities work on this principle. People contribute to causes which they judge to be worthy. But this is not what happens with redistribution conducted by the state in the name of social justice. Far from being about justice, this process is about power and coercion, for the labour and assets of some are forcibly acquired by the state for the benefit of others.

Underlying Hayek's rejection of social justice is a belief in the operations of the market and other voluntary social processes protected by law. Uncoerced agreements between parties give rise to questions of justice, not the unintended social misadventures which befall some people. Interventions by government agencies will, according to Hayek, always be subjective and, in consequence, ineffective (Gray, 1984:71–5).

The crucial point for Hayek is that injustice must be the product of intentional action. Unfortunate third parties whose condition results from the unintended side-effects of a just contract between two others have no claim upon them. If one has no opportunity to contribute to superannuation, this is a misfortune but hardly an injustice. Presumably, well-off people have a better chance of winning a lottery than the less well-off because they can afford to buy more tickets. Are we then to say that it is unjust for the poor not to win more lotteries and for the well-off to become even richer by a win? It may be unfortunate that lottery wins do not favour the poor, but who could seriously claim that it is unjust? Hayek's point is that misfortune is not to be confused with injustice.

But take the example of a developer who secures government approval to develop part of the Daintree rainforest in Queensland. There is no intention here to harm the interests of third parties. But to claim that this obviates injustice because there was no intention to harm is to make inadvertence, neglect, oversight, and indifference non-culpable. Of course, Hayek would respond that these faults are indeed culpable with respect to voluntary relationships entered into by responsible parties. What he would deny is that they are socially culpable; that societies or social groups should bear any responsibility or share a stake in matters which lie outside their explicit commitments.

Hayek's brand of liberalism takes society to be a collection of individuals, distinguished from associations and organisations by its very diversity. For whereas the latter have collective purposes, to which each of their members in some way subscribes, society has no such purpose or structure. Along with many other economic thinkers of this century, Hayek rejects the notion that a modern (liberal) society has an end. Instead, its members have purposes, often conflicting ones, which make any notion of a common good not only implausible but authoritarian. Freedom relies on people being able to pursue their own purposes and interests without the imposition of some state-endorsed good. This is the condition of civil rights in a liberal secular state and underwrites not only market freedoms but political and religious ones as well. The notion of a pattern to which a society should conform — even for the sake of the disadvantaged — is anathema to Hayek. It is important for the freedom and self-respect of every citizen that conformity not be imposed in the name of socially approved ends. Society is not about bringing into being some supposed pattern of good, but is a cooperative arrangement governed by impartial procedures and laws which allow people to live with a minimum of interference. It must be said, however, that Hayek's views suggest that social policy is too difficult even to attempt. Finding that the best is unattainable, he makes it the enemy of the good. Ironically, Hayek's use of blueprint principles makes him as utopian as his social justice adversaries.

The view that society is not an actor as individuals are actors means that societies cannot be the bearers of virtues as individuals are. Antony Flew makes this point well. He warns against the temptation common among social scientists to attribute intention and organisation to outcomes which are neither intended nor foreseen:

> Among those studying or discussing who ends up holding what capitals and enjoying what incomes, it is the almost universal practice to speak of showing how Society distributes its wealth and its income. But in most of the countries to which such studies and discussions refer there is in fact no such centralised, active and controlled distribution. No super-person and no committee decides what everyone is to have and to hold.
>
> (Flew, 1991: 69)

Robert Nozick argues exactly the same point in his seminal defence of individual rights, Anarchy, State and Utopia:

> We are not in the position of children who have been given portions of pie by someone who now makes last-minute adjustments to rectify careless cutting. There is no central distribution, no person or group entitled to control all the resources, jointly deciding how they are to be doled out.
>
> (Nozick, 1974: 149)

To summarise, there is no structural injustice possible in the distribution of benefits in society as Flew, Hayek and Nozick describe it. But more than this, there is no pattern of society from which its failures, its injustices, might be measured. For while such patterns are common in Utopian literature, they are not the stuff of liberal democratic societies which reject centralised control and respect individual rights and autonomy. The hard truth for idealists is that if a pattern is to be imposed on society so that certain outcomes will be produced, such as equality of wealth, then a centralised agency must be instituted and individual and group autonomy reduced. Equality of this kind entails abridgments of freedom.

Secondly, there is, on this view of society, no common property to distribute. What is held for the society in public ownership should only be what is necessary for the continued operation of the state. A state which assumes more than minimal functions courts injustice, because it necessarily abridges property and other rights of its citizens.

There are, of course, liberal thinkers who do not agree with these arguments. The best known is John Rawls whose pivotal work, *A Theory of Justice* (1972) has inspired many attempts to reconcile the liberal emphasis on personal freedom with a requirement for fair distributions of wealth (e.g. Reiman, 1990). In a famous thought experiment he asks us to imagine rational, mutually disinterested people who have come together to agree on the principles of justice in advance of forming a society. Rawls calls this the 'original position'. In this condition, people do not know their class or social status, abilities, attainments or intelligence. They have no concept of their own good, nor a personal identity. This Rawls calls a 'veil of ignorance'. It is supposed to remove bias and personal interest from rational deliberation on the principles of justice (1972:11–12). Hence, the initial conditions for the decision are fair and the criteria produced are styled 'justice as fairness'. Rawls believes that people in the original position would be cautious and choose principles which would ensure their wellbeing in case it turned out that they were amongst the worst-off in society.

What principles of justice would be chosen in the original position? Rawls holds that the following principles would emerge in strict 'lexical' priority. First, that every person be equally free; secondly, that offices and positions be accessible to all but that if there are to be social and economic inequalities, they must be to the advantage of everybody and not merely for the good of the majority (1972:60). This qualification to the second principle Rawls calls 'the difference principle', and it guarantees that the least advantaged always get some benefit from inequality. Rawls assumes that initially all would favour equal distributions of what he calls the primary goods at the disposal of society, namely, 'rights and liberties, powers and opportunities, and income and wealth' (1972: 62). These goods are primary in the sense that every rational person requires them, but at their centre is self-respect, without which personal goods are hard to pursue and life loses its worth. While inequalities of wealth might eventually be found to benefit everyone, even the least advantaged, equal liberty could only be denied if it was necessary for a 'level of civilisation' enabling equal freedom (1972:152).

Under this principle of equality, no-one's interests are expendable: even the happiness of the majority must not be purchased with the misery or disadvantage of the few. This is the protection of justice. Thus Rawls builds his theory upon the values of equality, liberty and notional consent which together rule out a utilitarian basis for distribution.

By opting for what he calls a 'thin' theory of the good, Rawls has preserved a strongly liberal character to his theory of social justice, and avoided imposing upon society a plan which might conflict with the particular forms of good life chosen by individuals. Procedure replaces pattern as the criterion of justice, and *right* takes precedence over notions of *good* (1972:396). Because Rawls founds his theory on a pre-social condition which would be agreed upon by all contracting parties as fair, the redistributive aspects of decisions arising from it do not trespass upon individual rights. Transfers of wealth are what rational people would agree to in the original position, so welfare rights are part of a package deal on justice which precludes the separation of private property from public policy, at least on the ground of rights. No-one is entitled, then, to claim that welfare, public education and health are violations of property rights just because they do not happen to favour spending on these items.

Rawls builds into his theory a kind of permanent reminder of the under-class in society. This is not the Marxian argument that the better-off benefit at the expense of the poor, but an acknowledgment that people are equal in the face of life's vicissitudes and that today's tycoon might be tomorrow's pauper. Hence, totally disinterested parties to an agreement about fair rules for society would always provide for the unwelcome eventuality that might see them disadvantaged.

Rawls seems to have reconciled a strong theory of individual freedom with a compelling argument for welfare. At the same time, in refusing to specify all but a few goods as primary, he has kept his liberal credentials intact: people can choose their own goods, and only the rules, not the ends of justice need be specified. Rawls believed he had found a common basis for justice in a world of pluralistic desires by addressing standards of right conduct and refusing to impose his own version of good on society.

Rawls' success, however, is achieved by resting his case on certain unacknowledged culturally derived assumptions. Among these are the views that rationality is necessarily disinterested, that it precludes risk-taking and enjoins the safety net of the difference principle, and that it dictates a narrow materialistic conception of self-interest. In proposing a thin theory of the good as necessary to secure agreement on the principles of justice, he rules out a host of goods which might be regarded as equally fundamental. Why are the goods Rawls nominates preferable to others? Why is politics among the goods excluded when it is the means to resolve issues about what is good and what is not? Rawls' bewitchment with finding the right formula leads him from genuine politics and the participation of real citizens to a hypothetical type of administration whose connection with the world is tangential (Jackson, 1986:21, 161–4). In other words, Rawls' conception of society is still emaciated and shadowy in the manner characteristic of liberal theories. It resembles a political science seminar rather more than any society familiar to most of his readers.

Is there anything social to distribute?

While much discussion has focussed on the criteria which should apply to distributions, there is a more fundamental question of whether redistribution is justified in the first place. Who gets what and whether this is more or less equitable is rightly of concern to advocates of social justice. But there is a prior question in the debate on equality. Robert Nozick raised it in a particularly dramatic way in the 70s in *Anarchy, State and Utopia*. This prior question is whether there is anything socially owned to distribute.

Distributive justice assumes that there is something held in common which may properly be distributed or redistributed in society. Why is this a problem? The problem arises because in market economies, private property holds a special place and the right to private property governs much else. In such societies, individuals have to supply from their labour or assets the wealth which is redistributed to others. What then becomes of private property? What of the implication that taxes for redistribution are, in effect, a form of forced labour?

Social justice assumes something communal to distribute, but according to Nozick there is no common property because property comes attached to individuals. As there is no common pool to distribute, there can only be distributions from party to party, and these are vitiated only by coercion and fraud. In other words, there is room only for procedural not social justice. As long as coercion and fraud are avoided, there can be no injustice no matter how disparate living standards, wealth and opportunity become in a society. As social justice assumes that there is common or socially owned property, it must be shown how bad luck, disadvantage, or marginality can be the basis of claims for distributions and how these can be converted into claims against those deemed to have a surplus of wealth or property.

Ken Minogue has argued that 'an eleventh commandment has been insinuated into the consciences of the West: *'Thou shalt not be in more fortunate circumstances than another'* (1989:n3). The guilt associated with the failure to keep this commandment assumes not only that inequalities per se are unjust, but that sufficient knowledge and power are available to ensure that such failures could be rectified and in future prevented. It is the implausibility of such planning goals and their authoritarian implications which worry liberal writers (Friedman, 1980, ch.5).

The most common justification for redistribution is the principle of equality. In the name of equality it is often argued and more often assumed that the state should reshape social advantages to remove inequalities. This is reckoned to be just. But, as Michael Jackson points out, justice is not a matter of comparisons, or more correctly, *merely* a matter of comparisons (1986:49). Income disparity statistics and wealth distribution figures can alert one to areas of disadvantage. Such statistics, however are also much relied upon as proof of unfairness and inequality, as though justice were a matter of ensuring that everyone had equal quantities of wealth. This might be a feasible arrangement in Utopia, but not in the real world. The various statistics compiled by critics of inequality, seldom reveal how people came by their wealth, opportunities or income. Simply to point to differences is not to show unfairness. To give everyone equal shares regardless of merit or exertion is to reward mediocrity and laziness and discount exertion, talent, and excellence. The simplistic use of statistics on income and wealth differences can suggest quite gratuitously that there is something morally or legally dubious about a society which does not fit a desired pattern of justice. This is the force of liberal criticisms (Minogue, 1989).

Rawls' achievement was to focus attention on the requirements of justice for those who are least well-off in liberal societies. His rejection of utilitarianism and adoption of the difference principle — ruling out extra social burdens for those already in distress — give his theory a commonsense appeal in liberal welfare states. But Nozick's *Anarchy, State and Utopia* opened up the seam between individual rights and social welfare which Rawls tried to close. Nozick begins, like Rawls, with the bold declaration that 'Individuals have rights, and there are things that no person or group may do to them'. This immediately raises the issue of whether the state can have authority over individuals at all without their consent. If individual rights are inviolable, then taxation, conscription, social welfare and many other functions commonly adopted by modern states seem to be unjust. For Nozick, the state is a kind of legitimate protection racket whose authority comes from usage rather than design. Its just functions are limited to policing and defence. It has no business providing services in health, education and welfare because these services must be paid for by taxing the just earnings of citizens. Not even a good cause can justify violating property rights, for ultimately the compulsory transfers of taxation involve a violation of rights to one's own body and its labour. A state is necessary, but only to secure its citizens from fraud, coercion and invasion, not to impose some kind of moral or social goal on them. This minimal state, as Nozick terms it, is the most extensive form of state that can be justified.

Individualism has encouraged both its advocates and critics to focus on the plurality of goods rather than the plurality of choosers. Liberal theory suggests that each of us has our own preferences which we identify as subjective goods. The implication is that if freedom and responsibility are to be respected, then others are not entitled to prescribe goods for one. Hence, justice becomes pre-eminently a matter of procedure as Hayek, Rawls and Nozick argue. This conception of justice serves as a protection against the elision of choice through the prescription of substantive goods. This fear of authoritarianism on the liberal side is matched by something akin to despair on the part of its critics, who are equally emphatic about the absence of shared conceptions of the good in modern secular societies (e.g. MacIntyre, 1981; Hauerwas, 1991). Both sides exaggerate the diversity of goods preferred and the political consequences of individual choice.

Yet, if one thing characterises the modern market society it is the survival of choices through group demand. The choices and goods available in our society are not merely matters of whim, but, as in the case of the environment or Aboriginal land rights, are negotiated socially, often through the political process. Liberalism has not destroyed the social fabric or replaced common identities with anomie. The basic goods and the preferences of people can be identified more clearly today by social scientists, marketers, and politicians than ever before. But the plurality of choosers, both in the market and in politics has been translated by liberals and critics of liberalism into an ethic of difference.

One of the most cogent reassertions of a basic goods as a foundation for justice has been the recent work of John Finnis, *Natural Rights and Natural Law* (1980). Finnis takes as his starting point the intelligibility of goods, that is, he makes them matters of reason and not just taste or preference. If reason is able to deliberate about goods, then there is the possibility of genuine argument, rational agreement and disagreement about what is good: good is not simply subjective. And if this is so, there is the possibility of arriving (not easily) at a reasonable conception of the common good (Finnis, 1980: ch.2 esp 33–4; 1983: chs. 1 and 2).

Finnis uses Aristotle's notion of basic goods to identify categories of goods which are ends in themselves rather than merely means to further ends. These basic goods can be manifested in many ways, indefinitely, across a variety of different cultures. Finnis ensures this by the generality of his list which he insists is not exhaustive. It comprises life, knowledge, play, aesthetic experience, friendship, practical reasonableness and freedom, and religion, a term he uses in a very wide sense. These goods are basic in the sense that they are expressed irreducibly in human actions. As such they represent possibilities for human participation and growth, for human 'flourishing'. Every person should respect these goods and their realisation in the lives of others, even if they have no personal interest in pursuing any of them. To deprive others of participation in these goods deliberately is unjust: they have not only a fundamental status in Finnis' philosophy, but an absolute one as well. Fostering participation in and respect for these goods is the mark of a virtuous person and a good society. Given the variety of forms the basic goods can take, there is no reason to assume that their adoption has illiberal implications. Quite the contrary. In multicultural societies like Australia, an important component of the identity of the whole is the acknowledgment of the goods of the component cultures.

Hence, it would not be enough for a good society simply to refrain from interfering in the endeavours of others, for that might bring about decline and hardship rather than flourishing. This, however, would be the effect of a liberal emphasis on individual freedom such as Nozick's. Cicero writes that justice 'is the most comprehensive bond that unites together men as men and all to all', and confers the 'common right to all things that Nature has produced for the common use'. He cites the following maxims to illustrate this right:

> *Deny no one the water that flows by; Let anyone who will take fire from your fire; Honest counsel give to one who is in doubt; for such acts are useful to the recipient and cause the giver no loss.*
>
> (De offic. I.50)

It is commonplace for modern states to assign public property to private tenants for the public good. For example, mining companies are given leases, broadcasters are licensed to use the electromagnetic spectrum, airspace is allotted to aircraft operators, and doctors have visiting rights in public hospitals. There is no perceived loss here to the public interest, and it is now a commonplace that private capital must be attracted for public projects like highways in times of fiscal restraint. But the redistribution of property through taxation to provide for health, education and income support, elicits more hostility. This is understandable. It is one thing for recognisably common property to be distributed by the state, and quite another for ostensibly private property to be designated public to enable redistribution. The former involves no breach of individual rights; the latter is seen by libertarians to involve just such a violation.

How can the common good require as a matter of right, not of charity, the redistribution of property or equitable access to common enterprises as conditions of human flourishing? The justification for some distributions, like the assigning of mineral leases or radio frequencies, is public benefit. But this justification is harder to sustain for welfare services. If we remember More's point quoted at the beginning of this chapter, we can see the separateness and interrelatedness of private and public goods. To allow some to live in poverty or deprivation which can be remedied through income transfers is unjust. Private property is not an unqualified right. In time of war it may be expropriated and applied to the common defence. This kind of argument has a clarity which is not affected by talk of rights, probably because it embraces the self-interest of parties affected by the expropriation. But to defend the flourishing of those harmed by poverty, lack of opportunity or some social, physical or mental disability is seen as a violation of the rights of those who are taxed. This attitude is understandable in a mentality where every transfer of property is held to require consent. But such a place is a market, not a society. The ties of society will, under certain circumstances, transcend consent. Justice is more than the keeping promises and commitments voluntarily entered into. Defence of those least advantaged is a form of social defence as real as raising an army.

Hence, there is something exaggerated in the appeal to natural rights against state-imposed taxes for the needy. If one is to redistribute wealth a justification is needed. But this will not be a justification of the deliberate harming of citizens judged to be well-off, or of the imposition of reduced circumstances on some because others deserve a turn at winning in the lottery of life. It will be a justification which appeals to the same criteria as the believer in the absolute right to property. For that right is founded on the inviolability of the human person. Where personal survival is at stake, property is an inviolable right. Where the survival of others is threatened, property is a qualified right. This is recognised by Locke and other writers in the liberal tradition. By extension, the flourishing of one person may not arbitrarily be sacrificed to enable others to flourish, but nor can some be allowed to perish because others claim not only the right to flourish, but the unrestricted enjoyment of property. In other words, it is not morally justified simply to claim that one's wealth is not the cause of another's misery, and that nothing is owed to the disadvantaged by the well-endowed. To do nothing about preventable impediments to the flourishing of others is morally culpable.

This is not to say that placing moral requirements in a liberal society upon the relatively well-off to care for those less fortunate is trouble free. It might seem to extreme liberals at best to be a form of utilitarianism wrapped in a new guise, and at worst a justification for the excesses of communism. Finnis is as aware as Rawls and Nozick of the authoritarian potential of policy framed for the common good, and is as resistant to utilitarian arguments as they are. As he puts it:

Common enterprises and the exploitation and creation of a common stock of assets are alike for the common good because they are for the benefit of the individual members of the community...(but) no common enterprise can itself bring about the all-round flourishing of any individual. An attempt, for the sake of the common good, to absorb the individual altogether into common enterprises would thus be disastrous for the common good ...

(Finnis, 1980:168)

Already it will be clear that Finnis departs from the liberal assumptions of Rawls and Nozick. He affirms what they deny, namely the rationality of human goods, the worth of society in itself and not merely for the realisation of individual projects, and the reality of a common good (1980:165). That is, he offers positive answers to the two questions of distributive justice: there is common stock for distribution, and there is an agency for distributing it. Of course, Finnis then goes on to offer criteria for just distributions, but, unlike Rawls' basic principles of justice, these emerge from his concepts of society and the common good, not from some notional view of fairness imputed to unreal people.

Adopting the notion of a certain minimum necessary for flourishing, Finnis gives priority in his list of criteria for distributive justice to *need*. Then comes *function*, that is, the social role of the person in the society, as in a doctor having first claim on use of a car in case of an accident. Next, *capacity*: clearly it is wasteful of both a resource and a human talent to give the best instrument to the least capable player, ignoring the claims of the best player. Finnis' fourth criterion is *deserts and contributions*, and his fifth is a slightly difficult one to express but is nonetheless familiar: the acceptance of *foreseen and avoidable risks* (1980:174–5).

Finnis does not, like Rawls, give lexical priority to these criteria, nor does he claim that they will give one no trouble in application (1980:76). This is not a matrix of principles imposed on the world but the kind of considerations a reasonable person will take into account depending on their situation and the kind of distributive problem they are faced with.

CONCLUSION

In the end, social justice is not a complete solution to the problems of refashioning social advantage. A regime of moral rights and legal instruments might be necessary, but will not be sufficient to bring about the just society: a concern for others is also required. A society operating only on the basis of rights claims, and which is distrustful of institutional and personal channels of charity and concern is hardly a society at all. Ironically, both extreme liberals and some welfare advocates conceive of social relations in just such impoverished terms. To place property rights on the same plane as the human rights to which they owe their force is muddled (Griffin, 1986: ch.13, especially 307 ff). No less so are attempts by welfare advocates to remove the stigma attending disadvantage and its relief by placing social justice at the centre of social relations. This gets rid of the old Charity Society Organisation distinction between deserving and undeserving poor, but also implicitly denies the very human qualities that welfare wishes to affirm and promote. Social justice can only ever be part of the answer to deprivation. Unless people care about each other, as Titmuss argued in *The Gift Relationship* (1970), then social relations will become contractual, and suspicion, envy, and even animosity will assume more importance than friendship. Two thousand years ago, Cicero saw this very clearly: 'of all the bonds of fellowship, there is none more noble, none more powerful than . . . friendship'. And of all the virtues which make us love our friends, 'justice and generosity do so most of all' (1913:I.55–6).

Contemporary society takes for granted the benefits of planning in contexts such as technology, economics, education and health. This sense of control gives rise to questions of justice in a peculiarly modern way. If social systems can be designed like a car or plane, then they ought to be relatively fault-free, like the machines which travel in the sky and highway. Dysfunctional social systems are those which violate assumed operating principles like equality, but instead of being called faulty like the Pinto or the Comet, they are said to be unjust. Thus, questions of social justice can seem to be questions about better design or getting the right formulae. In accepting this equivalence we are, like Marx, children of the Enlightenment, of science and social science, of industrial rationality. As such we expect that if justice is possible it will be a matter of rationally arriving at the correct formula for distributions. Once that is obtained, our society can act collectively through its governments to implement that formula. The merit of Hayek and Nozick is to disturb such assumptions and the use made of them by writers like Rawls. The merit of Rawls is to reconcile liberal values with concern for the least advantaged. But, as Michael Jackson (1986: chs.3, 5) points out, neither side adequately realises the role society plays in making us not just fungible rational agents, but the very people we are, persons with commitments and attachments arising from our social identities.

These comments bear on the question of justice, for the sense of justice we possess will come from recognising what is due to people with whom we can identify, whose narratives are morally intelligible to us, rather than from pondering the outcomes of clever thought experiments. The only way in which individuals can have the kind of identity that elicits a sense of moral concern is as part of a shared system of social values. A sense of justice obviously must extend beyond those known to us personally to those who are known to us because of their social identity. Social justice is the translation of that sense of justice, as well as an informed view about equity, into social policy.

Social justice conceived as an abstract plan of reform for society has already set off for Utopia. The possibilities offered for change in the world of fiction will always be more promising than the world of real people and the societies in which they have their being. Those who make social justice the whole of justice, morality or religion, destroy their own case and must resort to coercive means which are sure to make radical liberalism more attractive. If social justice becomes the imposition of policy at the behest of interested groups it will, like More's original, be nothing more than a rhetorical route to Utopia.

---

[1] Of course in emphasising the distribution of benefits, contemporary discussions of social justice are also talking about the distribution of burdens, even if indirectly or unconsciously.

REFERENCES

Australian Catholic Social Justice Council (1990), *Social Justice in Everyday Life*, Collins Dove, Melbourne.

Boulding, K. (1988), 'Social justice as a Holy Grail: the endless quest', *Social Justice Research*, 2(1), pp. 49–60.

Brown, Alan (1986), *Modern Political Philosophy*, Penguin, Harmondsworth.

Cicero, *De Officiis*, trans. W. Miller, (1913), Loeb Classical Library, Cambridge Mass. and London.

Finnis, J. (1980), *Natural Law and Natural Rights*, Clarendon Press, Oxford.

Finnis, J. (1983), *Fundamentals of Ethics*, Clarendon Press, Oxford.

Flew, A. (1991), *Thinking About Social Thinking*, 2nd edn, Fontana, London.

Friedman, M. and R. (1980), *Free to Choose*, Macmillan, Melbourne.

Gray, J. (1984), *Hayek on Liberty*, 2nd edn, Blackwell, Oxford.

Griffin, J. (1986), *Well-Being*, Clarendon Press, Oxford.

Hauerwas, S. (1991), *After Christendom?* Abingdon Press, Nashville.

Hayek, F. A. (1976), *Law, Legislation and Liberty, Vol. 2, The Mirage of Social Justice*, Routledge and Kegan Paul, London.

Jackson, M. W. (1986), *Matters of Justice*, Croom Helm, London.

Lucas, J. (1980), *On Justice*, Clarendon Press, Oxford.

MacIntyre, A. (1981), *After Virtue*, University of Notre Dame Press, Notre Dame, Indiana.

Miller, D. (1976), *Social Justice*, Clarendon Press, Oxford.

Minogue, K. (1989), *The Egalitarian Conceit*, The Centre For Independent Studies, St. Leonards NSW.

More, T. (1989), *Utopia*, ed. G. M. Logan and R. M. Adams, Cambridge University Press, Cambridge.

Nozick, R. (1974), *Anarchy, State, and Utopia*, Blackwell, Oxford

Raphael, D. D. (1964), 'Conservative and Prosthetic Justice', *Political Studies* (12) pp. 149–162.

Rawls, J. (1972), *A Theory of Justice*, Clarendon Press, Oxford.

Reiman, J. (1990), *Justice and Modern Moral Philosophy*, Yale University Press, New Haven.

Titmuss, R. (1970), *The Gift Relationship*, Penguin, Harmondsworth.

PART TWO

Distribution and redistribution

CHAPTER SIX

SOCIAL CLASS AND COMMUNITY SERVICES
The paths to privilege

ADAM JAMROZIK

INTRODUCTION

The key element in contemporary industrialised societies is the role performed by governments under the concept and principles of 'the welfare state'. In broad terms, this role entails allocation of resources to economic production and to the consumption of goods and services so as to enable the economy to function and to ensure the wellbeing of the population. In discharging this role the welfare state is responsible for a range of functions, which may be divided broadly into two distinct, though not always mutually exclusive categories:

1. Facilitating functions: enabling the market economy to function and enabling people to function in the system by developing and enhancing their capacities for production and consumption;
2. Maintaining functions: keeping the system under control and providing means for physical survival of those individuals and groups who do not obtain these means (or do not obtain sufficient means) from the market.

It needs to be noted that the state performs these functions within the system of so-called 'free market' capitalism, the characteristic feature of which is inequality in access to resources and corresponding social divisions, exemplified empirically as socioeconomic stratification and referred to conceptually as class structure. The contemporary welfare state thus functions in an 'uneasy alliance' with the capitalist system, commonly called 'mixed economy', but perhaps more appropriately defined as 'welfare capitalism' (Esping-Andersen, 1990).

In the conventional perceptions of the welfare state it is seen as an ameliorative institution, whose important function is to alleviate, if not exactly counteract, the inequalities generated in the market. This function is expected to be carried out by two kinds of provisions: income support for those who need it in the form of pensions and other cash transfers, that is, the 'maintaining' provisions; and community services such as health, education and a diversity of personal services aimed to assist people in their social functioning in the market, that is, the 'enabling' provisions. This diversity of functions and provisions gives the welfare state a 'problematic' character, for while some provisions may indeed alleviate marginally and temporarily some of the extreme inequalities of the market economy, other provisions may indeed maintain those inequalities or even reinforce them. Additionally, through various mechanisms which regulate, facilitate or restrict access and use, some important 'enabling' provisions may become a source of new inequalities and new 'paths to privilege' in society. It is this issue that is the subject of this chapter.

Contrary to the social reality of the wide range of functions performed by the welfare state in contemporary industrialised society within the system of welfare capitalism, conventional perceptions of welfare services and their recipients present an interesting dichotomy. 'Welfare' means pensions, benefits, emergency financial relief, food vouchers, rent assistance, other cash payments, and personal services such as child protection, control of young offenders, and intervention in family crises. Recipients of these services are identified as the unemployed, single parents, pensioners, immigrants and 'the poor'; in sum, the people who are often seen to be a 'burden' on society and on its 'taxpayers'. In some perceptions projected by the mass media and by some social analysts and commentators the recipients of these services are now frequently referred to as the 'new underclass': an aggregate of individuals and families with inferred or even overly ascribed common characteristics of 'inadequate personalities', mentally or emotionally 'maladjusted', 'chronically lazy', relying on public 'handouts', and often 'morally suspect', not adverse to occasional cheating and 'abusing the system'.

By contrast, subsidised private schools, tertiary institutions, subsidised child care, occupational 'fringe' benefits are not seen as welfare services; recipients of these services are not seen to be 'welfare recipients' and neither do they see themselves as such. Yet it is access to these important and relatively costly services paid for by the whole community that leads to good professional jobs, often in the public sector, good income, security of employment and progress on the career ladder, followed by a reasonable retirement income via generous superannuation. In sum, access to these services means access to privilege and membership of the affluent 'new' middle class, with corresponding social status and respect in the community.

The dichotomy of conventional perceptions on welfare and on the recipients of welfare services is fully reflected in the literature on the subject and in numerous research monographs. Studies of poverty and unemployment abound: researchers are using a variety of ostensibly 'scientific' or 'objective' methods of analysis and manipulation of empirical and simulation data, attempting to reify and measure such abstract and arbitrary concepts as the 'poverty line', or even reviving the once-discarded concept of the 'culture of poverty'. Related to these perceptions and methods of analysis are policies and methods of intervention into the lives of individuals and families by state authorities and their diverse 'helping professions'. Social and welfare workers, teachers, ministers of religion, psychologists and psychiatrists, teachers, youth workers, counsellors of all kinds and for all occasions, even police, work with 'the poor' and 'the disadvantaged'. The interventions are carried out with manifest aims of support, assistance, or child protection, but common elements and effects are surveillance, social control and maintenance of the existing social order.

These dichotomous perceptions serve to maintain a number of myths of considerable political and social significance. The first myth is based on the belief that the welfare system alleviates those inequalities that are unavoidable in the market economy and prevents individuals and families from sinking into poverty. By focusing on 'disadvantage' a myth is created of a 'caring society', of a 'caring government', or 'caring helping professions'. Undoubtedly, this belief is genuinely and sincerely held by many people, including the people who provide welfare services and some who receive them. It is also true that such unemployment benefits (now called 'job search allowance'), age pension, sole parent pension, or sickness benefit assist people at times in coping with difficult circumstances. The value of such measures has to be acknowledged. However, alleviating poverty does not reduce inequality if the social order which regulates and controls access to society's resources remains undisturbed.

The image of a caring society created by public expressions of concern about 'the poor' and 'the disadvantaged' and reinforced by research and interventions directed at the same population serves to maintain another myth, namely, that Australia still is, or at least still aims to be, a fairly egalitarian society, ensuring a fair and equitable access to resources to all its citizens. However, this belief serves to legitimise social and economic inequalities by a diversity of explanations such as: difficult, though believed to be short-term, economic conditions; the need to restructure industry; or the recessionary state of the world economy, aggravated by selfish policies of some other countries who either do not want to buy Australian products or undersell them on the world market by unfair subsidies to their own producers. Underneath such explanations there always remain traditionally entrenched beliefs that 'the poor' are perhaps 'different' in their personal characteristics from the rest of the population. The image of an 'underclass', separated from the rest of society by the reified 'poverty line' sustains the legitimacy of such beliefs. The legitimacy is reinforced by the contrived logic of some economic arguments which lead to an increasingly accepted belief that in order to develop and maintain efficiency of industry and competitiveness in the world market, some people, rather unfortunately, have to be left outside the mainstream of social and economic life. Assistance rendered to them through income support and a variety of counselling methods serves to demonstrate to them society's concern and to adjust to their status of marginalised citizens. Such measures also serve to ease the conscience of the affluent middle classes.

The focus of attention in welfare literature and research, directed solely at the marginalised population strata, presents the welfare state and welfare services in a 'truncated perspective', through which these population strata are perceived outside the societal context. Such perspective also excludes from public view and scrutiny some of the important and valuable welfare services and benefits provided by the state, as well as the recipients of these services and benefits. As a result, inequalities in access to the resources provided by the welfare state, which bestow 'advantage' on certain population strata are thus effectively concealed.

This chapter examines the reasons for this dichotomy in the perceptions of welfare and points to the negative outcomes of these perceptions, not only for the people who 'miss out' but also for the society as a whole. From the outset it is emphasised that the issue of inequality in access to society's resources, has to be seen in terms of unequal 'command over resources through time' as argued by Titmuss (1963), which is the inherent feature of a capitalist market economy and welfare capitalism.

A few words of clarification of the terms used in this chapter will be pertinent at this point. First, the term 'resources' encompasses material resources and human resources. Material resources such as income from employment or business and material property, or capital, of all kinds are mainly provided by the market and include things that can be bought, such as food, clothing, housing, entertainment, motor vehicles and holidays. Human or personal resources such as education, specialised occupational skills, family and friends, social status in the community, and the like, which collectively may be called human capital, are different: their possession give a person an individual and group identity and they define the person's place in the socioeconomic stratification system and in the class structure. These include those provided by the state and the community: a wide range and diversity of infrastructure services such as health, education, child care, roads, power and water supply, libraries, art galleries, parks and gardens, police protection, and the legal system among others. These resources are, in effect, public property or 'commonly owned' by the whole community, but access to them is governed by various laws, administrative regulations and controls, social conventions and constraints, user-pays principles, and people's capacity and need to use them. It is the operation of these mechanisms that creates inequalities of access to these valuable resources, and inequalities tend to increase when some of these resources are taken out of public ownership by a device called 'privatisation'.

The extent to which a person has access to all these resources determines that person's position in the structure of society's socioeconomic stratification system and his or her social class. Class, as the term is used in this chapter, is thus not considered solely as an economic concept but one which includes also elements of power and influence. Access does not necessarily mean private ownership; the term 'command' rather than 'ownership' is therefore appropriate to use in this perspective as a person's accessibility to a resource may be just as valuable as private ownership. The value of such resources as health and education services lies in their accessibility to a person and the person's ability to use the service to his or her advantage.

It is common knowledge that access to, or command over, all kinds of society's resources is not equal. It is easy to observe in everyday life that causal links exist among the various kinds of resources, in that access to one kind of resource is usually associated with, or facilitates, access to another kind. For example, access to material resources such as income facilitates access to education, and access to education facilitates access to employment and income. This seemingly circular process of creating and maintaining advantage is a feature of societal arrangements which plays an important role in maintaining social and economic inequalities.

Command over resources 'over time' is a further important factor in maintaining the stability of the socioeconomic stratification system and class structure. It means that resources, once acquired, can be held over a period of time, even a lifetime, and can also be transferred from one person to another in the same generation or from one generation to another. Transfers may take place between individuals but an important instrument for effecting such transfers is the institution of the family. Material resources are transferred through transfer of the title of ownership but transfer of access to such resources as education is more complex because it entails access to material resources as well as the personal capacity to use education services. Later in this chapter, intergenerational transfer of access to such resources as education services is discussed. This tends to be largely influenced, if not entirely determined, by the position of the family in the class structure.

The resources provided by the state — health, education, and the like — are important community services because access to them facilitates access to material resources provided by the market. For example, good education is a prerequisite for obtaining good employment, or even obtaining employment at all, and good employment means a good income and consequently access to other goods and services the market has to offer. Considering that resource availability and allocation in the market is inherently unequal, it would then follow that the availability of access to resources provided by the state, which facilitate access to goods and services in the market is also unequal. This then becomes an important element in creating, maintaining and/or reinforcing inequality. The process through which this occurs is considered in this chapter, and the resources examined are education, employment, and child care services. As will be seen, these three kinds of resources are closely related, and access to one facilitates access to the other two, sometimes in a linear and at other times in a somewhat circular process.

Education

The system of arrangements through which education resources are created and provided to the community is one of the most significant part of community services. The significance of arrangements lies in the education system's societal function of developing human resources into productive social forces, in the reproduction of these forces, and in the maintenance and reproduction of society's identity and its culture. This function is performed through transfer of knowledge (a process of developing the minds), teaching certain skills (developing personal capabilities), and instilling or enforcing certain social norms of behaviour and social values (socialisation). In addition to performing these functions, the education system is an important 'sorting mechanism' which opens or closes the doors of opportunity for the recipients of its services (pupils, students). Education thus enables or prevents them taking up certain positions in the system of economic production and in the socioeconomic stratification and class structure.

The significance of education and its role in the development and assigning of human resources to certain stations in society has been examined and commented upon by many writers (e.g Bourdieu and Passeron, 1990). In Australia, prominent among these have been Anderson (1988), Connell et al. (1982), Encel et al. (1974) and Jones (1982).

The 'sorting out' function performed by the education system does not mean simply allocating people to certain individual positions in society but allocating them certain positions in the socioeconomic stratification system and in the class structure. The 'sorting out' processes consist of a range of diverse forms: a hierarchy of 'progressive' or 'selective' schools; systems of 'streaming' students within a school; divisions between 'academic' and 'practical' subjects; exit points which allow a process of 'weeding out' to take place at various stages of secondary education; and a host of assessment procedures through which children and young people are encouraged or effectively discouraged to proceed in certain directions by being convinced of the validity of the assessments. Aptitude tests, IQ tests, and a variety of counselling methods may have some rational bases but they are all value-laden, mediated, as it were, through the mirror of cultural, social, political and class perceptions.

In Australia, in addition to the mentioned mechanisms, the 'sorting out' process is entrenched, on a broad scale, in the dual system of education which has played an important role in the maintenance of social stratification of the population, typical of a class structure. According to Anderson (1988:215), 'Australia's dual public/private schooling systems have their roots in the beginning of European colonisation of the continent two hundred years ago'. It needs to be emphasised that this is not simply a dual system which indicates diversity, but a system which maintains and reproduces inequality and serves to maintain the stability of class structure in Australian society.

The inequality generated by this dual education system has not diminished since the Labor party came to power in 1983. If anything, the differences have increased since then, despite the government's claimed commitment to equality in education. Evidence provided by surveys conducted by the Australian Bureau of Statistics and by numerous research projects does not support such a claim.

Responsibility for primary and secondary education in Australia, however, rests with State governments, but the Federal government also supports directly both systems and its support clearly favours the private school system, thus contributing to its growth at the expense of the public system. Table 6.1, shows that over the ten years from 1982 to 1991 there has been a shift of student population from the public to the private system: while the total number of students in both systems increased over this period by 2.7 per cent, the numbers in the private system increased by 20.5 per cent, but those in the public system decreased by 2.9 per cent. The differences have been even greater in secondary schools where the number of students in the private system increased by 29.1 per cent and those in public schools increased only by 6.1 per cent. Over the same period, Federal government's allocation to the private school system has been maintained at a much higher rate than its support to the public school system. It can be ascertained from Table 6.1 that in 1992 the Federal government's allocations amounted to $1619 per student in private schools and only $526 per student in public schools, a ratio of over three to one in favour of the private school system. In addition to Federal government's support, all State governments also support private schools. With all governments' continued support, the capacity of the private school system has increased and the facilities for students in private schools have remained generally superior to those in the public school system. It is therefore not surprising that more middle-class parents have been sending their children to private schools, especially for secondary education. Furthermore, as observed by McIntyre (1985:115):

> The advantages of the private school lie not just in its superior material resources, its more spacious grounds, smaller class sizes and better libraries, but above all in its ability to reproduce ideological and cultural values.

The attraction of the advantage of private schools is reflected in their ability to retain students up to the final year of high-school education. Official statistics clearly show that, while retention rates to Year 12 over the past decade increased in both systems, those in the private system have continued to outstrip the rates in the public school system (in 1991 the rates were 71.3 per cent in all schools: 66.9 per cent in public schools; 71.9 per cent in Catholic schools; and 98.4 in other private schools — ABS 1992, Catalogue 4221.0). These data, like all indicators of group average, conceal the extremes in both parts of the education system. The retention rates, especially those in the public schools vary among the States, and then within each State. For example, as recently as 1989, some high schools in the outer suburbs of Sydney recorded retention rates under 20 per cent (Jamrozik, 1991:163).

The effect of the dual system of education is clearly evident in the entry of students into tertiary education. Students from private schools are more likely to enter into tertiary education than students from public schools. As shown in Table 6.2, 275.6 thousand students between 15 and 24 years of age left school in 1991: nearly three-quarters of these (73.6 per cent) were students from public schools and 23.5 per cent came from private schools. However, students from private schools accounted for 40.1 per cent of entrants to higher

TABLE 6.1

Commonwealth Government expenditure on schools, student attendance and teaching staff, Australia, 1982 and 1991.

Expenditure/ Student enrolment	1982		1991		Change 1982–91+	
	N	%	N	%	N	%
Government expenditure (M$) (1)	1175.8	100.0	2623.4	100.0	1447.6	123.1
• Public schools	527.3	44.8	1165.1	44.4	637.8	121.0
• Private schools	604.8	51.4	1388.9	52.9	784.1	129.6
• Joint programs	43.8	3.7	69.4	2.6	25.6	58.4
Student enrolments ('000) (2)						
All schools	2994.6	100.0	3075.1	100.0	80.5	2.7
• Primary schools	1849.0	61.7	1786.5	58.1	−62.5	−3.4
• Secondary schools	1145.7	38.3	1288.6	41.9	142.9	12.5
• Public schools	2283.0	76.2	2217.2	72.1	−65.8	−2.9
• Private schools	711.7	23.8	857.9	27.9	146.2	20.5
Primary schools	1849.0	100.0	1786.5	100.0	−62.5	−3.4
• Public schools	1454.9	78.7	1338.6	74.9	−116.3	−8.0
• Private schools	394.1	21.3	447.9	25.1	103.8	26.3
Secondary schools	1145.7	100.0	1288.6	100.0	142.9	12.5
• Public schools	828.1	72.3	878.6	68.2	50.5	6.1
• Private schools	317.6	27.7	410.0	31.8	92.4	29.1
Teaching Staff ('000)						
All schools	196.7	100.0	199.5	100.0	2.8	1.4
• Public schools	148.3	75.4	145.9	73.1	−2.4	−1.6
• Private schools	48.4	24.6	53.6	26.9	5.2	10.7

+ Change means increase except where a minus sign is shown
(1) Budget expenditure for 1982–83 and 1991–92, current prices
(2) Student enrolment and teaching staff (equivalent full-time staff) for 1982 and 1991

Source: Commonwealth Government: Budget Paper No. 1 1983–84 and 1992–93
          Department of Education, Employment and Training (1987) Schooling in Australia, Statistical Profile No.1
          Australian Bureau of Statistics (1992) Schools Australia 1991, Cat. No. 4221.0

education in the subsequent year (1992). Indeed, close to one-half (46.3 per cent) of students from private schools went into tertiary education, while only 21.1 per cent of those from public schools did so. Thus a student attending a private school is more than twice as likely to proceed to tertiary education than a student attending a public school.

TABLE 6.2

Persons 15-24 years who attended school in 1991 but were not attending in May 1992, Australia (N='OOO)

Activity in May 1992	Type of school attended in 1991								
	(1)+ All schools		(2) Public schools			(3) Private schools		
	N	%	N	%	% of (1)	N	%	% of (1)
All who attended school in 1991	275.6	100.0	202.8	100.0	73.6	65.5	100.0	23.8
Attending further education	151.2	54.9	99.8	49.2	66.0	47.8	73.0	31.6
* Higher education	75.6	27.4	42.8	21.1	56.6	30.3	46.3	40.1
* TAFE	64.3	23.3	49.1	24.2	76.4	14.3	21.8	22.2
* Other	11.3	4.2	7.9	3.9	69.9	3.2	4.9	28.3
Not attending	124.4	45.1	103.0	50.8	82.8	17.7	27.0	14.2

+ Includes 7300 persons who were not asked the type of school attended

Source: Australian Bureau of Statistics (1992) Transition from Education to Work, Australia, May 1992. Cat. No. 6227.0

The effect of the dual system of education is thus indisputably evident in tertiary education, where class divisions in student population have remained prominent. For example, relying on evidence from the results of a number of studies, Anderson concludes (1988:225) that 'the overwhelming impression from these results is one of little change in the socioeconomic profile of students commencing higher education over the past decade'. He further adds that the expansion of tertiary education has not changed this socioeconomic profile. He observes:

> *Apparently, even when the system expands substantially …*
> *a disproportionate number of families which are well-placed in the social order*
> *are able to use their advantage (private schools, good home environment for*
> *studying, and so on) to secure additional places for their children.*
>
> (1988:227)

Anderson, who has studied the Australian education system for many years, is certainly not the only person who has considered the issue of inequality in the system. Some years ago Encel et al. observed (1974:196) that social class was a significant factor in access to higher education, and higher education was 'a powerful agent of class stability for this reason, despite the mythology which treats it as a force for social mobility'.

Employment

The labour market in the industrialised societies has always been a source of inequality, as organisation of production has always been hierarchical in related terms of skill, responsibility and reward. A person's position in the hierarchy of the labour market, identified by occupation, industry and level of organisational responsibility, has been, and continues to be, regarded as the main indicator of that person's social class. The hierarchical structure of the labour market is thus reflected in the social structure, with corresponding hierarchy of prestige, social status and access to society's resources.

Another reason for inequality in the labour market has been the scarcity of work: full employment in the industrialised countries has been experienced only for relatively short periods of time, the most recent such period, and perhaps the longest, occurred from the 1940s to the early 1970s. Since then, unemployment has been on the rise in most industrialised countries and now it has reached an endemic condition, with no sign that the situation might improve in the foreseeable future. However, unemployment has not affected all occupational groups of the labour force equally; while it has been experienced to varied degrees in most occupations, it has also become increasingly entrenched as a long-term or permanent state in the lower occupational strata of manual labour, creating a growing social stratum of marginalised population, excluded from the mainstream of economic and social life.

One of the main causes of the growing inequality in access to employment has been the profound change in the technology of economic production. It has been a feature of industrialised societies that progressively fewer people are employed in the production of material goods and more people are employed in the distribution of goods, in the provision of services, in the management of economic and social production and in the regulation and control of economic and social life (Jamrozik, 1991). This change has not only brought on the emergence and growth of new industries and decline or demise of others, but has also created a wide and diverse range of new occupations, has reduced demand for other occupations and has made some occupations entirely redundant. Most negatively affected have been manual trades and unskilled labour previously engaged in the production of material goods. At the same time new opportunities have arisen for professional, para-professional and related non-manual occupations in industries engaged in the management of finance and property, in public administration and in the broad field of community services such as health, education and welfare.

These three sectors of industry share a number of common characteristics. First, as all three are engaged in the management and control of material and human resources, they may appropriately be referred to as 'management industries'. Second, they are labour-intensive, and, as a group, the three sectors have recorded the fastest growth of employment since the mid 1960s, with the rate of increase over three times the rate of increase in total employment. Third, these industries now constitute the main field of employment for women: while accounting (in 1992) for 36 per cent of all employed persons, they account for nearly one-half (47.7 per cent) of all employed women (Table 6.4). Fourth, these sectors also account for the large majority of employed professional and para-professional persons, of both sexes, most of whom hold high educational qualifications obtained through studies at tertiary institutions.

Changes in the structure of industries and corresponding changes in the structure of occupations have made education, more than ever before, an increasingly important prerequisite for securing employment and even more so for securing quality employment. People with post-school qualifications, especially those with tertiary degrees, have a distinct advantage in the labour market over persons without such qualifications: they record higher participation rates, higher rates of full-time employment, and very much lower rates of unemployment (see Table 6.3). In addition, persons with professional qualifications are more likely to enter and hold employment which offers an above-average salary, career structure, relative security of employment, varied degrees of autonomy, occupational 'fringe' benefits, and usually good retirement benefits (Jamrozik, 1991).

TABLE 6.3

Educational attainment and labour force status, persons 15-69 years, Australia, February 1992 (N='OOO)

Labour force status			All persons	With post-school qualifications				Without
				All with qualifi- cations (1)	Degree	Trade Diploma Other	Certificate	qualifi- cations
All persons			12155.2	5076.5	1139.5	1620.2	2272.8	6485.2
In labour force	N		8557.2	4174.8	1010.0	1359.4	1772.1	4196.0
	%	(2)	70.4	82.2	88.6	83.9	78.0	64.7
Employed	N		7571.1	3830.2	950.5	1240.8	1610.2	3599.5
	%	(3)	88.5	91.7	94.1	91.3	90.9	84.8
Employed full-time	N		5873.7	3160.5	813.5	1140.8	1183.6	2711.5
		(4)	77.6	82.5	85.6	91.9	73.5	76.2
Employed part-time	N		1697.4	669.6	137.0	100.0	426.6	887.9
	%	(4)	22.4	17.5	14.4	8.1	26.5	24.9
Unemployed	N		986.1	344.6	59.4	118.6	161.9	596.6
	%	(3)	11.5	8.3	5.9	8.7	9.1	14.2
Not in labour force	N		3598.0	901.8	129.5	260.8	500.7	2289.2
	%	(2)	29.6	17.8	11.4	16.1	22.0	35.3

(1) Includes persons with other (not stated here) qualifications
(2) Per cent of population 15–69 years
(3) Per cent of population in labour force
(4) Per cent of employed population

Source: Australian Bureau of Statistics (1992) Labour Force Status and Educational Attainment, Australia, February 1992, Cat. No. 6235.0

Education being the key to gaining advantage in the labour market, the path to that advantage is thus laid down in the education system. As discussed earlier in this chapter, the Australian education system has an in-built inequality which tends to ensure that young people from more affluent middle-class families have an advantage in access to tertiary education and obtaining the credentials which are now so important in gaining advantage in the labour market. Inequality of opportunity to gain that advantage in the labour market is thus a reflection of the inequality generated by the education system.

The growth of employment in professional and para-professional occupations has been due mainly to the growth of employment in community services. In terms of persons employed, this is the largest of the three sectors in the 'management industries'. Also, the rapid growth and emergence of this sector has been a direct outcome of policies and services provided by the welfare state. In the mid 1960s employment in community services accounted for 10 per cent of total employment in Australia, and the three sectors of 'management industries' together accounted for slightly less than one-fifth (19.6 per cent) of total employment (ABS 1987, Cat. No. 6204.0). In 1992, as shown in Table 6.4, community services alone accounted for close to one-fifth (19.4 per cent) of total employment, and employment in the 'management industries' rose to 35.6 per cent of the total employment in all industries. More significant is the occupational structure of these industries; while a wide range of occupations find a place in that sector, the most prominent are professional and para-professional occupations. Of all employed persons in these occupations, three-quarters are found in the 'management industries': two-thirds of all employed men in these occupations and close to nine out of ten women (87.6 per cent) employed in these occupations are found in these three sectors of industry. Community services account for over one-half (55.1 per cent) of all employed persons in professional and para-professionals occupations: 39.3 per cent of all employed men and 75.4 per cent of all employed women in these occupations. Community services is thus a sector of industry of considerable economic significance in the magnitude of employment it offers, particularly in the quality of human resources that it musters.

Community services is also the sector of industry of considerable social and political significance. Except for some activities in community services which provide tangible services such as refuse collection and maintenance of parks and gardens, or services of direct social control such as police or prisons, the services this sector of industry mainly provides are the knowledge and skills of professional and related personnel.

TABLE 6.4

Employed persons, Australia, August 1992: all industries, management industries and community services (N='OOO)

Employed persons/ Occupational group N %	(1) All industries		(2)++ Management industries			(3) Community Services		
	N	%	N	%	% of (1)	N	%	% of (1)
All employed persons	7679.3	100.0	2735.5	100.0	35.6	1490.5	100.0	19.4
• Men	4433.4	57.7	1186.1	43.4	26.8	509.5	34.2	11.5
• Women	3245.8	42.3	1549.3	56.6	47.7	981.0	65.8	30.2
Group 1+	869.5	11.3	139.2	5.1	16.0	37.5	2.5	4.3
• Men	651.2	74.9	105.1	75.5	16.1	21.8	58.1	3.3
• Women	218.3	25.1	33.9	24.5	15.5	15.6	41.6	7.1
Group 2+	1529.2	19.9	1155.1	42.2	75.5	842.3	56.5	55.1
• Men	860.7	56.3	569.8	49.3	66.2	338.2	40.2	39.3
• Women	668.5	43.7	585.5	50.7	87.6	504.1	59.8	75.4
Group 3+	2453.0	31.9	983.9	36.0	40.1	361.0	24.2	14.7
• Men	692.4	28.2	242.8	24.7	35.1	35.1	9.7	5.1
• Women	1760.5	71.8	741.2	75.3	42.1	325.8	90.3	18.5
Group 4+	1696.8	22.1	137.8	5.0	8.1	70.2	4.7	4.1
• Men	1500.8	88.4	116.4	84.5	7.8	53.2	75.8	3.5
• Women	196.0	11.6	21.4	15.5	10.9	17.0	24.2	8.7
Group 5+	1130.9	14.7	319.5	11.7	28.3	179.6	12.0	15.9
• Men	728.2	64.4	152.1	47.6	20.9	61.1	34.0	8.4
• Women	402.6	35.6	167.4	52.4	41.6	118.5	66.0	29.4

Group 1: managers and administrators
"   2: professionals, para-professionals
"   3: clerks, salespersons, personal service workers
"   4: tradespersons, plant operators, drivers
"   5: labourers and related occupations
+   Percentages of all persons employed in a group are those of all persons employed listed in the column; percentages for men and women are those for each group
++ Management industries as defined in text (finance, property and business services; public administration; community services)

Source: Australian Bureau of Statistics (1992) The Labour Force, Australia, August 1992, Cat. No. 6203.0

The professional service providers in community services operate on people rather than things: they manage, organise, teach, control behaviour, cure, counsel, adjudicate, examine, research, advise on policy, formulate and implement policies, and engage in a host of related activities. Depending on the nature of these activities, community services facilitate some people's social functioning or inhibit other people's social functioning. In effect, community services control and regulate access to society's resources and in doing so they are also instrumental in maintaining the inequalities of the social order in the market economy.

In discharging these functions, community services play an important role in relation to social and economic organisation by maintaining the supply of labour for the market and by taking care of the human residue of the market economy: the unemployed, the disabled, the sick and the retired.

It is this dual nature of community services that receives little attention in discourse on the welfare state and welfare services. Neither is much attention given to the significance of the opportunities provided, through the growth of community services, for tertiary-educated professional persons of both sexes. The growth and concurrent professionalisation of employment in community services and opportunities created in this process for both sexes have been important factors in the growth of two-income, high-income families — the relatively affluent families of the new middle class in Australian society.

Child care

Child care is another community service which is not regarded in common perceptions or in the literature and research as 'welfare', and users of child care services are not seen, and do not see themselves, as 'welfare recipients'. Yet, child care, provided by various organisations and with financial, administrative and professional support by the state, is a form of 'substitute care'. In essence, it is not different from substitute care which has been provided to this day and continues to be provided by welfare agencies under state authority and state laws. In each case, substitute care is provided when the family cannot fulfil this function, for whatever reason. The difference is not in the need for substitute care but in the perceptions of the need for such care: one form is seen as 'welfare', with certain negative connotation about the family; the other is 'care', perceived as an important service assisting the family in its social functioning.

Why are there differences in perceptions and interpretations? Viewed in a longer-term perspective, child care services have been a subject of changing public attitudes, government policies, and class interests. It is appropriate to note at this point that child care was originally introduced in Australia in the early 1900s under the name of creches or kindergartens as a charitable service for poor children; the aim of service providers was to ensure that these children grew up into 'useful citizens'. Later, as the value of these services became apparent, they were 'appropriated' by middle-class families, and children of working-class families were excluded. With State governments' support, kindergartens grew in numbers and were used mainly by children of middle-class families. When working-class families needed child care they had to use commercially run 'child minding' services (Sweeney and Jamrozik, 1982). The Commonwealth government, rather reluctantly, began to provide support for child care services in the mid 1960s, when middle-class professional women began to enter the workforce in large numbers and their organisations began to lobby for such services. The Child Care Act was passed in 1972 by the then Coalition government; it authorised the Commonwealth government to provide support for child care services, subject to certain priorities of need, but without legal obligation to do so.

During the Labor government of 1972–75, early childhood services were to become a universal service, still aimed primarily to be a service for children rather than families, and emphasis was to be on both care and educational-developmental aspects of young children. The Coalition government of 1975–83 aimed to convert the services into a residual 'welfare' service for 'families in need', but it did not succeed in achieving this. By that time the value of child care services was fully recognised by the increasingly well-organised, articulate, and politically influential middle-class women's lobby who, claiming to act in the interest of all women, demanded child care services 'as a right'. The incoming Labor government in 1983 again promised universality of these services for all children under 15 years of age, but it soon converted child care into an arm of economic policy and, also mindful of the middle-class vote, has in effect made the priority of access to the service by the middle class a reality. State-supported child care services have now become a form of occupational welfare, used predominantly by relatively affluent two-income middle-class families of professional people (Sweeney and Jamrozik, 1982, 1984; Jamrozik, 1991).

Despite claims to the contrary by the child-care lobby, repeated surveys conducted by the Australian Bureau of Statistics have shown consistently higher rates of usage of child care services by higher-income families. Some results of the last such survey, conducted in November 1990, are shown in Table 6.5.

TABLE 6.5

Families with children under 12 years of age: income and use of formal child care, Australia, November 1990 (N='OOO

Parents' combined income p.w.($)	(1) * All families		(2) Families using formal care			(3) ** Working families using formal care		
	N	%	N	%	% of (1)	N	%	% of (1)
All families *	1829.4	100.0	466.5	100.0	25.5	266.5	100.0	14.6
0–159	53.5	2.9	10.4	2.2	19.4	3.7	1.4	6.9
160–319	264.0	14.4	54.9	11.8	20.8	15.7	5.9	5.9
320–479	310.5	17.0	78.2	16.8	25.2	32.5	12.2	10.5
480–639	325.9	17.8	76.3	16.4	23.4	34.9	13.1	10.7
640–799	260.5	14.2	62.5	13.4	24.0	38.8	14.6	14.9
800 & over	496.7	27.2	158.9	34.1	32.0	124.0	46.5	25.0
Don't know	118.3	6.5	25.7	5.5	21.7	16.8	6.3	14.2

* Includes one-parent and two-parent families
** Working families means two-parent families in which both parents are employed and one-parent families in which the sole parent is employed

Source: Australian Bureau of Statistics (1992) Child Care, Australia, November 1990, Cat. No.4402.0

At the time of the survey there were 1829.4 thousand families with children under 12 years of age in Australia. Of these, 466.5 thousand families (25.5 per cent) used some type of formal child care and over one-half of the users (57.1 per cent) were 'working families', that is, two-parent families in which both parents were in employment, or the employed parent in one-parent families. Over one-third of all families (34.1 per cent) using formal child care were recorded by the survey to be in the highest income range ($800 per week and over), a rate of usage over three-times greater than that for families in the $160-319 per week income range (11.8 per cent). The distribution of usage in 'working families' was shown to favour even more extensively the families in the highest income range: close to one-half (46.5 per cent) of families in this group using formal child care services were families in the highest income range, recording nearly eight times the rate of usage by the families in the $160–319 income range (46.5/5.9 = 7.88).

Commonwealth government expenditure on child care services now exceeds half a million dollars ($536.7 million in Budget Estimates for 1992–93 — Budget Paper No.1, 1992–93), and all State governments also expend considerable public funds on these services. It is a very important and valuable service and is universally needed by most families with young children. The problem lies in the access to the service, which continues to favour the affluent new middle class of high-income, two-income families. The low-income families, if they need to use child care services are forced to use 'informal' care, either commercially operated or provided by friends or neighbours. The problem is aggravated by the frequent denials of the inequality in access to this community service, emanating from the active middle-class 'child-care lobby'. A previous Minister for Social Security acknowledged this problem by stating:

> It worries me a lot that some of the people who are activists in the child-care movement seem to be more concerned about looking after the interests of people at the higher end of the income scale than the people at the lower end.
> (Grimes, reported by Wyndham, 1985)

The inequality of access to child care services is an outstanding example of a 'shift of perception' which occurs where a service, originally introduced as a 'welfare' service aimed at socialisation and social control of children from poor working-class families, later becomes recognised as a service of universal value. The service then tends to become the property of a class-based interest group which is politically influential and has the capacity to protect and enhance its class interest, especially when the service remains scarce. It is also an example of a social welfare service which has been, in effect, subjugated to the demands of the market economy. As the employment opportunities in that economy favour the educationally qualified professional people of both sexes, child care services have become, for the middle-class two-income family, a valuable form of occupational welfare.

Community services or paths to privilege?

The three kinds of community services discussed in this chapter are closely interrelated, and all three constitute significant resources provided directly or indirectly by the state. It is true that the bulk of employment in the industrialised 'mixed economies' is provided by the private sectors of these economies but the governments in the welfare states are ultimately responsible for maintaining employment and are judged accordingly. In Australia, the public sector accounts for approximately 30 per cent of total employment (ABS 1992, Cat. No. 6248.0) and through governments' expenditure on various goods, services and income support, many more jobs are created and maintained in the private sector of the labour market. In community services, many people, such as medical practitioners and lawyers, see themselves to be in the private sector, either as employees or employers or self-employed persons, but most of their incomes comes from government expenditure.

Community services are important social provisions and, although they are rarely perceived as such, they may be appropriately regarded as 'primary welfare services'. As argued by Marshall:

> *Welfare fulfils itself above all in those services which are its own in every sense — health, education and 'personal social services' and, with increasing emphasis, community services for the preservation and development of the physical, social and cultural environment. It is by strengthening these that the civilising powers of welfare can be most effectively increased.*
>
> (1981: 135)

The name 'community services' implies that these services are established to serve the entire community. However, as demonstrated in this chapter, access to these services is certainly not equal to all who need them. For those who secure access, the advantages tend to be cumulative, as access to one service, such as higher education, provides the paths to other resources such as employment and good income, social status and prestige of membership of influential and affluent social class.

The first and most significant beneficiaries of access to community services are, of course, the service providers themselves, as they derive income from them as well as positions of advantage in the access to society's other resources. It is also an established fact, which logically follows from the nature of community services, that service providers in community services are also among the main consumers of the services, such as education and child care.

It needs to be recognised that the welfare state in the system of welfare capitalism has not eliminated or even reduced inequalities generated in the market. Moreover, by establishing and providing some services which are not equally accessible to all who need them, the welfare state has created new inequalities, new forms of socioeconomic stratification and a new class structure.

CONCLUSION

The argument presented in this chapter is not, and it must not be seen as, an argument against community services as such On the contrary, it is an argument for the necessity to recognise the importance of these services as 'primary welfare' and to ensure equal access to them, as a right, to all people who need them. This is certainly not the case now, and for this reason community services have become paths of advantage for the middle classes, especially for the new middle class whose members have a dual access to these services, as providers of services and as consumers.

The advantage in access to community services as an advantage of a relatively privileged social class has been, rather unwittingly perhaps, concealed by the 'truncated perceptions' of the welfare state, traditionally maintained by the population and reinforced by much of the literature on social policy and welfare services. The welfare state in these perceptions is seen as an 'ameliorative state' or as a 'remedial state' rather as a 'facilitative' or 'enabling' state, which it is, but now only for some. If community services are to serve the whole community with equality of access, the first step in that direction needs to be taken by widening the perceptions of the nature of welfare state and its potential as a facilitative and enabling state.

REFERENCES

Anderson, D.S. (1988), 'Education and the social order', in J.M. Najman and J. Western (eds), *A Sociology of Australian Society*, Macmillan, Melbourne, pp. 214–38.

Australian Bureau of Statistics (1987), *Labour Force, Australia: Historical Summary, 1966–1984*, Catalogue No. 6204.0.

Australian Bureau of Statistics (1992), *Schools, Australia*, Catalogue No. 4221.0.

Australian Bureau of Statistics (1992), *Labour Force and Educational Attainment, Australia, February 1992*, Catalogue No. 6235.0.

Australian Bureau of Statistics (1992), *Transition from Education to Work, Australia*, May 1992, Catalogue No. 6227.0.

Australian Bureau of Statistics (1992), *Child Care, Australia*, November 1990, Catalogue No. 4402.0.

Australian Bureau of Statistics (1992), *Labour Force, Australia*, August 1992, Catalogue No. 6203.

Bourdieu, P. and Passeron, J-C. (1990), *Reproduction in Education, Society and Culture*, (translated by R. Nice), Sage, London.

Connell, R. W., Ashenden, D. J., Kessler, S., and Dowsett, G. D. (1982), *Making the Difference: Schools, Families and Social Division*, Allen and Unwin, Sydney.

Commonwealth Government Budget Papers, (1983, 1992), Budget Paper No.1, Australian Government Publishing Service, Canberra.

Department of Education, Employment and Training (1987), *Schooling in Australia, Statistical Profile No. 1*, Australian Government Publishing Service, Canberra.

Encel, S., Mackenzie, N. and Tebbutt, M (1974), *Women and Society: An Australian Study*, Cheshire, Melbourne.

Esping-Andersen, G. (1990), *The Three Worlds of Welfare Capitalism*, Polity Press, Cambridge.

Jamrozik, A. (1991), *Class, Inequality and the State: Social Change, Social Policy and the New Middle Class*, Macmillan, Melbourne.

Jones, B. (1982), *Sleepers, Wake! Technology and the Future of Work*, Oxford University Press, Melbourne.

McIntyre, S. (1985), *Winners and Losers: The Pursuit of Social Justice in Australian History*, Allen and Unwin, Sydney.

Marshall, T. H. (1981), *The Rght to Welfare and Other Essays*, Heinemann, London.

Sweeney, T. and Jamrozik, A. (1982), *Services for Young Children: Welfare service or Social Parenthood?*, Social Welfare Research Centre Reports and Proceedings No. 19, SWRC, University of New South Wales, Kensington.

Sweeney, T. and Jamrozik, A. (1984), *Perspectives in Child Care: Experiences of Parents and Service Providers*, Social Welfare Research Centre Reports and Proceedings No.44, SWRC, University of New South Wales, Kensington.

Titmuss, R. M. (1963), *Essays on the 'Welfare State'*, Unwin University Press, London.

Wyndham, S. (1985), 'Child Care or Volvos? The Middle Class Choice', *Good Weekend*, (The Sydney Morning Herald Magazine), 15 June.

CHAPTER SEVEN

PUBLIC OPINION, REDISTRIBUTION AND THE WELFARE STATE

ELIM PAPADAKIS

INTRODUCTION

A common assumption about the welfare state is that it serves, or should serve, the purpose of redistributing from the better off in society to the less well off. Donald (1986) has referred to the two major objectives of social security policy in Australia as poverty alleviation (in other words, 'ensuring at least a minimum acceptable income') and income maintenance (namely, 'encouraging and facilitating people's efforts to maintain and restore their income'). The third objective is referred to as income redistribution, namely:

> ... ensuring that, in combination, social security, taxation and other programs contribute to a more equal distribution of resources and life chances, both across the population at any point of time and from the relatively affluent to lower income phases of people's lives.
>
> (Donald, 1986:2)

Social democratic supporters of the welfare state have been highly critical of the failure by the Australian welfare state to serve this and other related purposes. Pusey (1991), in a well-publicised critique of the Australian state and of the senior executives who run it, has argued that the social democratic welfare state is 'not in very good shape'. Furthermore, the economic rationalists in Canberra have apparently rejected the values that underpin a redistributive social democratic welfare state: 'they are bolting the door against the sort of value commitments — to social justice and to participatory democracy — that underpin the welfare state and pluralist-progressive, social-democratic politics' (1991:125).

Pusey sees the welfare state as 'expiring' and is concerned about the decline both in resources and in commitment to certain values. With respect to resources, he is influenced by writers like Castles (1985, 1987) who, in comparing Australia to countries like Sweden, have argued that the welfare state here is both very poorly developed and highly vulnerable (Pusey, 1991:223). On the issue of moral commitment, the concerns by Pusey are shared by writers like Beilharz, Considine and Watts who argue that economic liberalism has 'regained control of the popular imagination and of the public agenda' (1992:51). Beilharz et. al. are deeply concerned that the ideas of social justice and citizenship, which are often tied in with notions of redistribution, and which have been influential at different stages in the history of the Australian welfare state, have diminished in significance over the past two decades in our 'sadly unequal society' (1992:3). For these writers, the purpose of the welfare state is much more than redistribution from the better off to the poor or the goal of efficiency ('cheap services'). Rather, it involves educating people 'for a democracy — for citizenship, self-development and active participation' (1992:151).

In a realistic account of the development of the welfare state over several centuries and in various countries, de Swann (1988) has demonstrated that the purpose of redistribution has often been not so much to achieve the goals espoused by social democratic reformers but by those who wish to maintain their power and influence over the economy. As he puts it:

> *The problem of the poor is to stay alive: the problem of poverty is a problem for the rich — the problem of distributing part of the surplus without altering the rules of its accumulation and conservation. In this perspective the solution is to distribute enough of the surplus to guarantee the long-term working capacity and reproduction of the working force, to pacify and terrify those who might attempt to change the rules of accumulation, and to prevent the ills from poverty — whether through crowding, contagion or discontent — from affecting the ranks of the well-to-do.*

(de Swann, 1988:14)

Approaches to dealing with the fundamental problem of the poor have changed over time and have ranged from the provision of private charity to massive intervention by the state. Many contemporary writers regard the recent emphasis on market forces as a return to feudal ideas about noblesse oblige and private charity (Beilharz et. al., 1992:14). The contrast is drawn between two quite different purposes of the welfare state: the first, to offer minimal provision for subsistence, the second, 'to enable human and social development', to provide welfare for citizenship as a fundamental right. In reality, these traditions are less clear-cut. The provision of a minimal level of subsistence, for instance, can be justified either in terms of a fundamental right to a basic level of provision or as an obligation to be met by charitable citizens.

In contrast to writers who have attempted to explain the development of the welfare state in forms of principled and altruistic behaviour, Dryzek and Goodin (1986) have presented a variant on arguments about self-interest. Unlike de Swann, who has focused on power relations between the rich and the poor, Dryzek and Goodin, in examining the shaping of the welfare state after the Second World War, found that risk-sharing and uncertainty have provided the main impetus. The experience of the Great Depression and of the war contributed to a much greater willingness on the part of the people to adopt a risk-sharing strategy rather than an individualist approach.

Politics involves compromises between a variety of traditions. Moreover, the development of the welfare state will, at different times and in different contexts, be influenced by historical legacies, institutional factors and particular events. Though they emphasise the contrast between economic liberal and social democratic traditions, Beilharz et al., for example, recognise that in recent times the Australian Labor Party (ALP) political regime 'attempted to develop a new compromise between economic liberal strategies of deficit reduction and an activist policy orientation that was more consistent with its traditional concern for the disadvantaged' (1992:123). The theme of compromise and the fusion of different traditions of welfare provision has also been addressed by Hindess (1987) and by Papadakis and Taylor-Gooby (1987).

The analysis of empirical data presented in this chapter demonstrates support, in different ways and in different contexts, for both state and private provision of services. There is a strong consensus about the need for statutory intervention in many spheres as well as an awareness of the advantages to certain groups in society of private provision of services (see Papadakis, 1990a).

The question as to who benefits from the welfare state is a controversial one. Different writers have referred to a wide variety of services and defined the welfare state in ways that have led to apparently conflicting conclusions. In Britain, for instance, there was a significant difference between the conclusions arrived at by Le Grand (1982) who argued that the middle classes made the greatest gains, and by O'Higgins (1985) who identified the impact of the welfare state in redistributing resources from the better off to the less well off. Similar issues have been addressed in Australia by writers like Harding (1984) and Gruen (1989).

Gruen has presented some useful arguments which throw new light on the common assumption that Australia has one of the least generous welfare states compared to other OECD (Organisation for Economic Cooperation and Development) countries. He has found that the Australian model, which focuses heavily on poverty alleviation, has become influential in other OECD countries:

Concentrating on poverty alleviation and leaving the provision of income maintenance to the private sector used to be a sure sign of a laggard Welfare State. We now find our poverty-alleviating policies gradually adopted elsewhere; coupled with suggestions from organisations such as OECD that this is the way social policy ought to be remade.

(Gruen, 1989:29)

Gruen tends to overestimate the shift away from statutory intervention, even with respect to income maintenance. Australia has been a wage-earners' welfare state, in other words, the state has played a crucial role in ensuring that wages are maintained at a certain level (see Castles, 1985). It is not simply a question of the private sector being solely responsible for income maintenance. Nevertheless, Gruen is correct in identifying (a) the shift in many countries towards poverty alleviation strategies and (b) the complexity of calculating how incomes are distributed.

The extent and causes of income and wealth inequality have been addressed in numerous ways. Meagher and Dixon (1986) have provided a useful analysis of methodological issues and the extent of income inequality in Australia (see also Browne, 1987; Piggott, 1987 and Whiteford, 1988). Yet, despite the gloomy prospects for income distribution, it is worth emphasising that welfare provision does alleviate some of the worst effect of primary income distribution both in Australia (see Moore and Whiteford, 1986) and elsewhere (see O'Higgins, 1985). Similarly, the taxation system can ensure that people are not made poorer (see Brown and Jackson, 1987).

Rather than identifying how the welfare state redistributes between different groups, this chapter focuses on how people perceive the process of redistribution between high-, middle- and low-income families; on whether or not there are similarities in perceptions among different social groups; and on explanations for these patterns.

Perceptions are important insofar as they legitimate the role of government in redistributing resources through mechanisms like social security and welfare provision. Governments usually attempt to redistribute resources through cash benefit transfers and through services in kind. The cash benefit transfers and services in kind can either be universal: available to all citizens; or categorical: directed towards particular sections of the population. Le Grand (1982) and Goodin and Le Grand (1987a) have argued that universal schemes lead to a serious compromise of the redistributive efforts of the welfare state since the middle class benefit substantially from them. Their education, their resources and their cultural background ensure that the middle classes are well positioned to exploit opportunities for welfare provision and even to derive benefits from programs that were originally designed for assisting the poorer sections of the community (see Goodin and Le Grand, 1987b). Governments, including social democratic ones, are especially keen to avoid an electoral backlash from the middle classes that stand to gain from the universal provision of services like health, education and old age pensions.

The provision of universal health care and education in Australia represents services in kind. The issue of providing universal health care has divided the major political parties in Australia in recent times and changes in government have led to major restructuring of health care arrangements. Over the past decade, Australia has had a universal health care system, created by a Federal Labor government. The controversy generated by conflicting ideas about arrangements for health care makes this a particularly interesting area for the study of popular perceptions of who gets best value for money.

The structure of public and private education has also aroused great controversy, especially with respect to the funding of government, Catholic and private schools and the efficiency of expenditures. The power of private schools to mobilise support and influence government decisions on educational policy has been a striking feature of Australian politics over the past few decades. In the 1950s and 1960s Catholic schools placed State Labor governments under intense pressure to provide them with financial aid. The formation of the Democratic Labor Party (DLP) (which represented a division within the ALP) was partly linked to this issue.

The politics of education is also reflected in the landmark decision by the Liberal government under Menzies to fund science laboratories in secondary schools, a decision which represented an attempt 'to make sure of DLP support and at the same time to exploit divisions over state aid within the Labor Party' (Macintyre, 1985:106). The capacity of affluent groups to organise, to lobby effectively and to voice their concerns can easily be demonstrated in the sphere of Australian educational policy (see Hogan, 1984). Perceptions of redistribution in this sphere are especially interesting because of the concerns expressed by both parents and politicians regarding the most appropriate ways of funding the educational system.

The survey

The remainder of this chapter analyses data from a national survey of attitudes to state and private welfare in Australia, conducted in 1988. The survey examined problems that have arisen from popular experiences of welfare provision as well as political arguments about the development of the welfare state. The survey differentiated between various aspects of statutory and private welfare. Data was also gathered on the personal characteristics and socioeconomic background of respondents. The original sample for the survey was 3507. The response rate (after removing 'non contacts') was 62 per cent (see Papadakis, 1990b, for a detailed report on the survey).

The following analysis focuses on perceptions of both statutory and private welfare, devoting particular attention to:

  a.   Views about the redistributive effects of the welfare state in the spheres of health and education;
  b.   The patterns of these views among people of different social background, economic power and status;
  c.   The relationship between perceptions of redistribution and views about taxation;
  d.   The level of support for state and private provision (both in Australia and in the United Kingdom);
  e.   The connection between perceptions of redistribution and support for state and private provision.

Perceptions of redistribution

As indicated above, welfare provision involves redistribution through taxation and subsidies. The question used to assess perceptions of redistribution is similar to one used in a national survey of attitudes to the welfare state in Britain (see Taylor-Gooby and Papadakis, 1985). The question, which asks about who gets best value for money from their taxes from various services, addresses the issue of redistribution between the better off and the poor. However, it avoids the hazards associated with trying to quantify welfare benefits, opting instead for subjective perceptions of what constitutes value for money, in general, for different groups (see also Taylor-Gooby, 1985).

With respect to the government health and education services, the most likely response is that low-income families get the best value for money (47 per cent and 40 per cent, respectively; see Table 7.1). Interestingly enough, only

7 per cent feel that middle income families get best value for money from government health services and 19 per cent from government education services. Yet, most survey respondents have ranked themselves as belonging to middle income households (refer to Table 7.2.).

TABLE 7.1

Perceptions of redistribution to different types of families [a]
(per cent)
(N=1807)
Value for money from ...

	Government health service	Government schools	Catholic schools
High-income families	20	14	29
Middle-income families	7	19	25
Low-income families	47	40	10
Don't know	24	22	28
No reply	2	6	8

[a] 'On the whole, which of these three types of family gets best value for money from their taxes from the government health service/government schools service/Catholic schools service?'

Source: E. Papadakis. *Attitudes to State and Private Welfare in Australia,* 1988 [computer file]. Social Science Data Archives, The Australian National University, Canberra, Study No. 595.

The overall patterns are remarkably similar to those identified by the UK survey (see Taylor-Gooby, 1985). The Australian survey also included a question about Catholic schools since they play an important role in the education system and rely heavily on government subsidies. Here, the pattern of perceptions is rather different, with most respondents identifying high- and middle-income families as the prime beneficiaries. As in the other questions, about a quarter of the sample indicated that they did not know who got the best value for money. This is a higher figure than in the UK Survey (about twice as high), and may reflect the methods used to elicit responses — in other words, a mail survey as opposed to face-to-face interviews — and/or the different historical legacies of private and public provision in both countries.

The next stage of the analysis sets out to compare the responses to the question about redistribution and value for money to the social characteristics of respondents — namely, to subjective as well as objective measures of class and income. The results are unsurprising, especially in the light of previous

TABLE 7.2

Perceptions of redistribution by income and class (per cent)

value for money for families on...

	GOVERNMENT HEALTH SERVICE					GOVERNMENT SCHOOLS SERVICE					CATHOLIC SCHOOLS SERVICE				
	High Income	Middle Income	Low Income	Don't know	(N=)	High Income	Middle Income	Low Income	Don't know	(N=)	High Income	Middle Income	Low Income	Don't know	(N=)
INCOME (OBJECTIVE)[a]															
High 1	8	9	73	10	(66)	6	28	59	7	(66)	18	41	21	19	(66)
2	15	3	66	15	(230)	10	18	54	18	(232)	25	36	14	26	(229)
3	20	6	58	17	(262)	12	19	48	21	(256)	35	28	9	28	(257)
Low 4	24	7	41	28	(222)	16	18	38	28	(210)	35	18	10	38	(205)
INCOME (SUBJECTIVE)[b]															
High	7	9	68	16	(86)	5	26	59	10	(85)	21	38	19	23	(83)
Middle	15	7	58	20	(921)	10	22	46	22	(906)	29	31	11	29	(895)
Low	30	7	34	29	(630)	21	17	36	27	(602)	39	20	9	33	(588)
CLASS (OBJECTIVE)[c]															
High 1	11	5	65	20	(287)	12	22	54	12	(288)	22	37	18	23	(280)
2	14	8	57	22	(301)	12	20	49	19	(293)	25	34	13	28	(288)
3	21	9	52	19	(265)	10	21	46	19	(293)	33	30	9	28	(251)
4	22	7	46	26	(327)	13	22	36	30	(318)	35	23	9	33	(317)
Low 5	28	7	42	23	(290)	19	17	36	28	(284)	44	19	5	32	(278)
CLASS (SUBJECTIVE)[d]															
Middle	11	8	63	17	(655)	10	23	51	17	(647)	25	32	14	28	(639)
Working	25	7	44	24	(716)	15	20	40	25	(694)	37	26	7	29	(682)
Lower	39	5	22	35	(144)	27	13	22	37	(134)	49	13	7	31	(134)

a 1 = over $65,000; 2 = $40,001 to $65,000; 3 = $25,001 to $40,000; and 4 = $10,000 to $25,000.
b 'Would you say that your household income is high, middle or low?'
c The scale for 'objective class' is derived from the Australian Standard Classification of Occupations Jones (1989) has used this to calculate occupational prestige rankings. Using these rankings, the sample was divided into five quintiles with similar numbers in each group. The groups were derived as follows: group 1, 56.6 to 100 points on the Jones scale; group 2, 36.0 to 56.5 points; group 3, 27.6 to 35.9 points; group 4, 17.0 to 27.5 points; and group 5, 0 to 16.99 points.
d 'If you were asked to use one of four names for your social class, which would you say you belong in; the lower class, the working class, the middle class or the upper class?'

Source: see Table 7.1

analyses carried out in the United Kingdom. People on high incomes are far more likely than those on low incomes to feel that families on low incomes get better value for money from government health and schools services (Table 7.2). The same pattern applies to subjective perceptions of income as well as to subjective and objective class location. People who perceive themselves as belonging to high-income households are four times less likely than those who perceive themselves as belonging to low-income households to feel that high-income families get best value for money from government health services (7 per cent and 30 per cent, respectively). A similar pattern applies to the views about education services (5 per cent and 21 per cent respectively). The overriding impression is that the better off feel that the poorer sections of society do best out of the system of health and education services, and vice-versa. In other words, most people think that socioeconomic groups other

TABLE 7.3

Perceptions of redistribution and of taxing the rich [a]
(per cent)
Government health services
value for money for families on ...

TAX THE RICH	High income	Middle income	Low income
Strongly agree/agree	73	54	43
Not sure	13	18	15
Strongly disagree/disagree	14	27	41
(N=)	(350)	(123)	(827)

GOVERNMENT SCHOOLS SERVICE

TAX THE RICH	High income	Middle income	Low income
Strongly agree/agree	72	57	45
Not sure	12	14	15
Strongly disagree/disagree	16	29	41
(N=)	(237)	(337)	(698)

[a] 'Would you agree or disagree that rich people should be taxed more heavily than they are now?'
Source: see Table 7.1.

TABLE 7.4

Support for government and private provision [a]
per cent
part A (Australia)

	Government Health	Private Health	Government Schools	Catholic Schools	Private Schools	Old Age Pensions	Superannuation
Very important	50	61	59	32	37	57	52
Fairly important	29	26	25	36	37	29	35
Not very important	11	7	6	15	13	7	6
Not at all important	7	3	4	9	7	4	4
Don't know	3	3	7	9	6	4	5

PART B (UNITED KINGDOM)
(N=1362)

	Government Health	Private Health	Government Schools	Private Schools	Old Age Pensions	Private Pensions
Very important	93	33	92	33	91	57
Fairly important	6	41	7	42	7	32
Not very important	1	18	1	17	1	7
Not at all important	0	7	0	6	1	2
Don't know	0	1	0	2	1	2

[a] 'How important is it to people in this country that government/private health care (etc...) continue to be available?'

Sources: Part A, see Table 7.1; Part B, Taylor-Gooby (1985).

than their own are getting the best value from the welfare state. That appears to reflect their experiences. The impression that perceptions are heavily influenced by self-interest is reinforced by the following finding: people who felt that better-off families got the best value for money from government health services were more likely than those who felt that poorer families got value for money to favour heavier taxes on the rich (73 per cent and 43 per cent, respectively — Table 7.3). Views about value for money from the government schools service and about taxing the rich were distributed in a very similar manner.

The wording of questions about welfare services can easily be used to create the impression that support for them is either low or high (see Smith, 1987; Papadakis, 1992). In the UK survey, an attempt was made to formulate questions which 'removed responses from the arena of self-interest as far as possible by focussing on the collective interests of the population' (Taylor-Gooby, 1985: 404). An identical question was used in the Australian survey (see Table 7. 4). The data show that in both countries there was strong support for both state and private welfare. The overwhelming majority of respondents felt that both government and private health and education as well as old age pensions and superannuation (private pensions) were either very important or fairly important. However, historically, the intensity of support for state services has been greater in the United Kingdom than in Australia. Conversely, support for private provision has been greater in Australia than in the United Kingdom. For instance, in Australia, 61 per cent of respondents felt that private health care was very important compared to 33 per cent of respondents in the United Kingdom. The data clearly reflect the different paths in the development of the welfare state in these two countries. In Australia, the wage earners' welfare state was not based on universal provision of services funded by compulsory social security contributions by those in paid employment, but on state intervention to ensure that all workers received a 'fair and reasonable wage' that would enable them to purchase health services and private housing (see Castles, 1985).

The introduction of a Medicare levy in Australia represents a step in the direction of a contributory system similar to the ones used in universal welfare states. By contrast, in the more universal welfare states like Britain there have been attempts to encourage more people to purchase services from the private sector (see Papadakis and Taylor-Gooby, 1987).

TABLE 7. 5

Perceptions of redistribution by support for government
and private provision
(per cent)

HEALTH

	Government			Private		
	Value for money for families on ...					
GOVERNMENT/PRIVATE PROVISION	High income	Middle income	Low income	High income	Middle income	Low income
Very important	61	52	44	62	53	66
Fairly important	25	41	31	26	32	26
Not very important	9	7	15	9	13	6
Not at all important	5	1	11	3	2	2
(N=)	(353)	(123)	(841)	(355)	(123)	(845)

EDUCATION

Very important	70	69	62	41	32	44
Fairly important	20	27	28	36	44	38
Not very important	7	3	7	15	19	12
Not at all important	3	2	3	8	5	6
(N=)	(242)	(339)	(708)	(236)	(333)	(708)

Source: see Table 7.1.

The difference in organisation of welfare provision in both countries is reflected by the following findings: whereas in the United Kingdom there was no connection between perceptions of redistribution to families on different incomes and support for the welfare state (see Taylor-Gooby, 1985), in Australia there was a modest association between these two variables (see Table 7.5). For instance, respondents who felt that low-income families got the best value for money from government health services were less likely than those felt that high-income families got best value for money to rate government provision as very important (44 per cent and 61 per cent, respectively). With respect to the private sector, the UK study revealed the following type of variation in views: respondents who felt that government services gave best value for money to low-income families were more likely to support private provision and vice versa (Taylor-Gooby, 1985:404). This pattern, however, is only partially replicated in Australia (Table 7.5). Those who regard low- or high-income families as the primary beneficiaries of government provision are more likely than those who regard middle-income families as the primary beneficiaries strongly to support the private sector.

CONCLUSION

Although much of the data presented so far suggests that one's experiences and self interest play an important part in shaping opinions about redistributions, some of the evidence suggests that there is strong support for both state and private provision across all sectors. Furthermore, experiences and self-interest can be construed in a variety of ways. For instance, self-interest can operate at the level of benefits derived from an individualistic reliance on market mechanisms, or, as Dryzek and Goodin (1986) have suggested, in terms of risk-sharing and uncertainty. It is also worth noting the findings of other analyses of the same data which draw attention to the recognition by most people of the importance of statutory intervention and of government spending on most areas of welfare including those that are associated with both universal as well as residual welfare states (see Papadakis, 1990a; 1992). These studies support the arguments presented by some writers that ethical considerations are important and that there is often only a weak connection between the specific interests or experiences of an individual (defined in terms of behaviour directed towards income maximisation) and their opinions or actions.

Finally, the analysis of perceptions of redistribution suggests that ideas about charity, noblesse oblige, market forces, social solidarity and altruism may all play a part in the development of the welfare state. It is therefore questionable to assume either that the primary purpose of the welfare state is a redistributive one or that economic liberalism has inevitably triumphed over notions of social justice and citizenship, or that there is a necessary and fundamental conflict between different traditions. Politics entails the art of compromise between various traditions. This is well illustrated by the development of the modern welfare state and is reflected by opinions about it.

REFERENCES

Beilharz, P. Considine, M. and Watts, R. (1992), *Arguing about the WelfareState*, Allen and Unwin, Sydney.

Brown, C.L. and Jackson, P.M. (1986), *Public Sector Economics*, Blackwell, Oxford.

Browne, P. (1987), '1981–1986: Poverty on the rise', *Australian Society*, April, pp. 34–5.

Castles, F.G. (1985), *The Working Class and Welfare*, Allen and Unwin, Sydney.

Castles, F.G. (1987), 'Australia and Sweden: the politics of economic vulnerability', *Thesis Eleven*, (16), pp. 112–21.

de Swann, A. (1988), *In Care of the State: Health Care, Education and Welfare in Europe and the USA in the Modern Era*, Polity Press, Cambridge.

Donald, O. (1986), *Social Security Reform*, Background Discussion Paper No. 2, Social Security Review, Department of Social Security, Canberra.

Dryzek, J. and Goodin, R. 1986. 'Risk-sharing and social justice: the motivational foundations of the post-war welfare state', *British Journal of Political Science*,16(1), pp. 1–34.

Goodin, R. and Le Grand, J. (1987a), *Not Only the Poor: The Middle Classes and the Welfare State*, Allen and Unwin, London.

Goodin, R. and Le Grand, J. (1987b),'Creeping universalism in the Australian welfare state' in R. Goodin and J. Le Grand (eds), *Not only the Poor:The Middle Classes and the Welfare State*, Allen and Unwin, London, pp. 108–126,

Gruen, F. (1989), *Australia's Welfare State: Rearguard or Avant Garde?* Discussion Paper no. 12, Centre for Economic Policy Research, Australian National University, Canberra.

Harding, A. (1984), *Who Benefits? The Australian Welfare State and Redistribution*, SWRC Reports and Proceedings, No. 45, Social Welfare Research Centre, University of New South Wales, Kensington.

Hindess, B. (1987), *Freedom, Equality and the Market*, Tavistock, London.

Hogan, M. (1984), *Public versus Private Schools*, Penguin, Ringwood, Victoria.

Jones, F. (1989), 'Occupational prestige in Australia', *Australian and New Zealand Journal of Sociology*, 25(2), pp. 187–99.

Le Grand, J. (1982), *The Strategy of Equality*, Allen & Unwin, London.

Macintyre, S. (1985), *Winners and Losers*, Allen and Unwin, Sydney.

Meagher, D.A., and Dixon, P.B. (1986), 'Analysing income distribution in Australia', *Economic Record*, 62(179), pp. 427–441.

Moore, J., and Whiteford, P. (1986), *Trends in the Disposable Income of Australian families, 1964–65 to 1985–86'*, Background Discussion Paper No. 11, Social Security Review, Department of Social Security, Canberra.

O'Higgins, M. (1985), 'Welfare, redistribution and inequality' in P. Bean, J. Ferris and D. Whynes (eds), *In Defence of Welfare*, Tavistock, London, pp. 162–179.

Papadakis, E. (1990a), 'Conjectures about public opinion and the Australian welfare state', *Australian and New Zealand Journal of Sociology*, 26(2), pp. 209–34.

Papadakis, E. (1990b), *Attitudes to State and Private Welfare: An Analysis of Results from a National Survey*, SPRC Reports and Proceedings No. 88, Social Policy Research Centre, University of New South Wales, Kensington.

Papadakis, E. (1992), 'Public opinion, public policy and the welfare state', *Political Studies*, 40(1), pp. 21–37.

Papadakis, E. and Taylor-Gooby, P. (1987), *The Private Provision of Public Welfare*, Wheatsheaf, Brighton.

Piggott, J. (1987),'The nation's private wealth: some new calculations for Australia', *Economic Record*, 63 (190), 61–73.

Pusey, M. (1991) *Economic Rationalism in Canberra*, Cambridge University Press, Cambridge.

Smith, T. (1987), 'That which we call welfare by any other name would smell sweeter: an analysis of the impact of question wording on response patterns', *Public Opinion Quarterly*, (51), pp. 75–83.

Taylor-Gooby, P. (1985), 'Pleasing any of the people, some of the time: perceptions of redistribution and attitudes to welfare', *Government and Opposition*, 20(3), pp. 396–406.

Taylor-Gooby, P. and Papadakis, E. (1985), Attitudes to Welfare - Final Report to ESRC, mimeo, University of Kent, Canterbury.

Whiteford, P. (1988), 'Income inequality rises', *Australian Society*, January, p. 8.

CHAPTER EIGHT

INTERVENTION IN CHILD WELFARE

An inflicted evil or solicited response?

JAN BRECKENRIDGE

INTRODUCTION

Historically, child and family welfare in Australia has been (and constitutionally, still is) the responsibility of the different States and Territories (Jamrozik et al. 1986:3). This responsibility has taken the form of child protection, with intervention occurring when the family was absent, or when it was assessed as being unwilling or incapable of providing competent care for the child or children. In reality, state supervision over child-rearing practices has not been necessary for the majority of Australian families, but has drawn disproportionately from the most marginalised, impoverished sections of the population (Carrington, 1991:109). In contrast, the Commonwealth government has only become directly involved in the child welfare arena as late as the 1970s. This limited involvement was primarily in the field of early childhood services (such as pre-schools and child care in its various forms), and was seen as a philosophical shift away from protective intervention into the area of prevention or community care (Mowbray, 1983:2). The appeal of this shift was presented as widening the scope of existing protection services to the population at large thereby addressing all children's needs rather than simply assuring the rights of some children to protection from harm.

One critical consequence of the legislative and administrative division between the States and Territories and between States and the Commonwealth has been the continually emerging variety of different philosophies, definitions, policy responses and allocation of resources within

Australia. These differences directly affect child welfare practice and also confirm that conceptions of child welfare in general and child protection in particular are not self-evident, consensual or universally held. Sweeney (1986:15) argues that it is precisely because of these differences and the resultant 'lack of clarity' that the state has been able to use the notion of 'child protection' as a means of intervention or a tool of social control in the lives of certain groups of poor families. Jamrozik (1983:68) whilst clearly acknowledging the multiplicity of legislative and bureaucratic responses as important, sees them as less influential in their own right. He claims that such responses are simply incorporated into and accommodated by existing practices and administrative structures thereby continuing the state's dual roles in child welfare of child protection and maintenance of social order.

The themes of social control and class-based state intervention are in clear evidence throughout the relevant literature. Carter (1983:1) describes those families who came 'under the welfare' before the 1970s as being from a special class of family who reproduced themselves from generation to generation in a 'cycle of deprivation'. Jamrozik argues even more forcefully that statutory child welfare agencies and even non-government welfare organisations have acted as 'instruments of class power and class control' (1983:70). Such explanations, while still holding some sway, are limited in terms of the complexity of the role of the state. They strongly portray individuals (and certain groups such as the working class) as passive 'objects' of state intervention. Van Krieken (1991:5) alleges that this type of explanation characterises a narrowness of focus that is best described as a 'welfare-centredness'. This focus consequently lacks the contextual analysis of more recent accounts of aspects of child welfare (such as Gordon, 1989; Allen, 1990; van Krieken, 1991) which highlight the capacity of individuals and groups to engage with the state and resist its impact.

This chapter will examine a case study in the area of child welfare which exemplifies the notion of 'resistance' and explores the role of state intervention into family life. The term 'resistance' refers to the suggestion by Foucault that 'it would not be possible for power relations to exist without points of insubordination which, by definition, are means of escape' i.e. resistance (cited in Dreyfus and Rainbow, 1982:225). The case study will elaborate on the politicisation of childhood sexual assault by feminist groups and child advocates in the 1980s in New South Wales, though similar social action took place in other Australian states during this period. Intrinsic to the account will be a detailed discussion of the conspicuous absence of appropriate therapeutic and social policy responses to child sexual assault prior to this time. This absence will be compared and contrasted to the extensive changes in legislation, social policy and service provision which have emerged in response to the above-mentioned campaigns. By unravelling the complex and unique combination of factors that had facilitated the taboo on the public discussion of child sexual assault, this chapter will address how child sexual assault came to be recognised as a significant social problem.

From protection to community care

O'Donnell and Craney argue that current perceptions of child abuse are determined by our history and culture and that unless the problem is situated in its historical context, we fail to understand the confusion of professionals and the welfare state regarding how best to define, explain and deal with the issue (1982:176). This is particularly the case when considering the relatively unique beginnings of Australia as a penal colony and the consequent practice of the transportation of British children to colonial outposts.

Whilst developments in child welfare varied from colony to colony throughout Australia, the recurrent themes of the necessary protection of children by the state and the control of delinquent behaviour, are evidenced in many historical accounts (see Allen, 1990; O'Donnell and Craney, 1982). Van Krieken alleges that the ideologies and institutional forms which characterised early child welfare provision were transported along with the convicts, soldiers and settlers (1991:45). In New South Wales, the nineteenth century child welfare policies which embodied these themes were underpinned by two main philosophies. First, there was an acceptance of explanations regarding the social reproduction of abuse as a working class phenomena. Second, there was the propagation of a strong moral imperative that children could and should be saved by state intervention as a means of producing a better society.

These philosophies drew directly from the focus of British religious reformers, who, in the first instance, had identified transportation as a means of separating children of the lower classes from their environments, to more suitable locations (van Krieken, 1991:48). In New South Wales, the establishment of orphanages, orphan and industrial schools (and subsequently, in the early 1880s, a boarding out system) were the responses of social policy implemented to achieve the improvement of working-class behaviour and morality by changing the environment of children; they also ensured the production of future citizens and a useful source of cheap labour (O'Donnell and Craney, 1982:182). Yet, despite the guise of 'child-saving' van Krieken alleges that 'set as they were within the context of fear and loathing of the lower orders, the intentions and practices of the people running the colonial child welfare institutions produced a form of child welfare that was difficult to distinguish from punishment and imprisonment' (1991:56).

Gordon (1989), in her historical analysis of family violence in Boston, Massachusetts, and van Krieken, in his exploration of social control and Australian child welfare, both assert that the success of the campaigns of the nineteenth century child reformers was primarily in the acceptance of their goals by the very group who were the object of reform — the working class. Many working class people embraced cultural values such as familial morality and respectability and subsequently sought intervention by the state where such values were not in evidence. Gordon speaks of the poignant irony of the label 'the Cruelty' which was awarded to the child welfare service in the Boston area in the nineteenth century (1989:28). Her research uncovered evidence that working class people were often the source of notification to the statutory authorities despite the punitive perception of the service. Such evidence is testament to the complexity of the relationship between the state and civil society and clearly shows that individuals are not simply passive objects of unwanted state intervention.

The twentieth century brought with it a greater rationalisation, systemisation and expansion of child welfare services largely achieved by increased legislative regulations and resulting in increased numbers of children and families under state supervision (van Krieken, 1991:84). The introduction of the New South Wales Child Welfare Act of 1923 and the establishment of a Child Welfare Department and Children's Courts in New South Wales strengthened the state's response to delinquent behaviour and poor parenting. In both cases, children were still removed from their environments, either to an institution or to an extension of the boarding out system that better emulated family-like settings — foster care. The distinction between children who were in need of protection and those considered delinquent not only resulted in different responses from the state but also encouraged a differentiation between potentially worthwhile and difficult children which still exists today.

The increased use of legislative responses had a very particular impact on the regulation of Aboriginal children in New South Wales. The amendment of the NSW Aboriginal Protection Act of 1909 led to the establishment in 1915 of the Aboriginal Protection Board; this Board gained total control ('loco-parentis') over Aboriginal children in New South Wales and proceeded to remove them from their families under an apprenticeship scheme. The denial of an Aboriginal culture allowed the state to frame intervention into Aboriginal life as a necessary act of morality which entailed providing a different and more suitable environment. While the philosophy underpinning state intervention into the family in the nineteenth century had emphasised environmentalist explanations, a significant shift to essentialism occurred early in the twentieth century. The shift was apparent in the reports of the NSW Royal Commission into Neglected and Delinquent and Mentally Deficient Children in 1912 which indicated that even the smallest portion of Aboriginal heritage was in some way 'pathological' (Goodall, 1990:7). The policy of removing children was a very powerful way of attacking Aboriginal communities as was evident in the claim by the Aboriginal Progressive Association in the 1920s that the state's policies were an attempt 'to exterminate the noble and ancient race of Australia' (Maynard cited in Goodall, 1990:8).

Allen (1982:21) claims that this shift to essentialism was substantially the result of a more general rise of eugenics as an explanation for social problems. In its extreme form, proponents of eugenics believed that immoral behaviours and social conditions such as crime, poverty, drunkenness and prostitution, were products of mental defectiveness transmitted by heredity. The more general (and moderate) implementation of this view in practice included the increased use of social categories which encouraged medical and psychological interventions that could 'offset the environmental influences that allowed for the realisation of unfit potentialities' (Allen, 1982:21). The popularity of the eugenics school of thought can be partly attributed to the growth of liberalism and the ideology of privacy which also emerged at the beginning of the twentieth century. From the prior understanding of child protection as a response to an environmental and class-based social problem, the eugenic philosophy encouraged a new understanding of intervention as a response to individual family peculiarity (O'Donnell and Craney, 1982:183). Intervention became highly individualised and professional in orientation. Disciplines such as medicine, psychology and psychiatry claimed a certain legitimacy by asserting that their intervention into pathological families was evidence of a more scientific understanding of child welfare. This scientifically informed and controlled human warmth, genuineness and community can be seen as a replacement of the predominance of religion in the nineteenth century by 'science' in the twentieth (van Krieken, 1991:123).

The medicalisation of child abuse was a telling example of the twentieth century search for a scientific approach embodied in professionalised, humanitarian intervention. The pinnacle of this medicalised approach was the introduction of the concept of 'a battered child syndrome' by Kempe in America in 1962. The concept was taken up in Australia by both medical practitioners and the child protection lobby and, to a limited degree, child abuse was established as a public concern (O'Donnell and Craney, 1982:178).

This concern was not reflected in corresponding child welfare policy developments or service provision. From the 1970s Australia generally witnessed a decrease in the use of protective interventions (particularly substitute care), and an increase in the use of preventative interventions. As a result, government intervention into children's lives had become altogether less coercive and more persuasive, as well as less remedial and more developmental (Carter, 1983:53). This change of focus corresponded with the entry of the Commonwealth into the child welfare arena, but more importantly it corresponded with the increasing pressure at that time to minimise welfare-related expenditure (Mowbray, 1983:2).

The move to community care

The popularisation of longstanding criticisms of institutional care as not being in the best interests of the child brought with it the accompanying view that 'the family is the natural and fundamental group unit of society and the state' (Australian Human Rights Commission Act 1981 as cited in Mowbray, 1992:4). Under the heading of 'Duckshoving as State Strategy', Mowbray (1983: 2) argues that the criticisms of institutional care were little more than attempts to disguise as compassionate and progressive social policy, the major concern of cost saving with its emphasis on private organisations and family care. These new provisions were broadly classified as community care, but were more specifically known as prevention, restoration, or substitute family care of various descriptions.

Welfare cuts based on cost saving not only increased the domestic burden on women but also provided a strong signal that the family should be a self-sufficient unit requiring ever-decreasing support from the state. The move toward an emphasis on families can be seen as an attempt to endow the government's economic policies with a spurious 'commonsense' legitimacy (Barrett and McIntosh, 1982:12). Regardless of the motivation, this new emphasis was clear evidence that families were not necessarily supported in their own right as an institution but only when politically and economically convenient for the state (Lewis in Carter, 1983:54).

Child sexual assault: An issue made public

The immediate context that preceded the feminist social action campaigns of the 1980s was not necessarily conducive to calls for greater state intervention in child welfare matters. The move to community care (with the ensuing philosophical and policy changes) had limited the success of the establishment of child abuse as a major issue; it was simply the last in a long line of social policies that had failed to address issues of sexual violence for children in terms of appropriate legislative and administrative responses.

In discussing some of the major trends in the development of child welfare provision earlier in this chapter there was a conspicuous absence of any specific discussion of child sexual assault. The reason is simple: prior to the 1980s in Australia, incest and the broader area of child sexual assault was subject to both a discourse of omission and an omission of discourse. Together, these discourses explained child sexual assault either as rare sexual perversion/fantasy, or failed to distinguish between generic child abuse (and the generic child protection response), and the very specific gender experiences and differences inherent in child sexual assault. The discourses suffered from a difficulty which Dickey identifies as characteristic of many accounts of welfare history and policy response — the objects of policy or intervention are often hard to see or hear in their own right and for the most part they are mediated through the perceptions and the actions of the decision makers (1987:87).

The constructions inherent in these discourses are not necessarily the result of scarce or inadequate research but are actually misrepresentations and distortions of the evidence available at the time (Gordon, 1989:207–9). Allen's account of sexual crimes against women and female children in Australia indicate the existence of rape and child sexual assault since the early days of colonisation with female victims of child sexual assault often coming before the courts on status offences such as 'uncontrollable', or the non-specific 'in moral danger' (1990:144). Definitional differences can result in disclosures of single occurrence and 'minor' forms of child sexual assault simply not appearing in incidence studies. As the extent of sexual violence against children cannot be comprehensively known, child sexual assault is either subsumed and obscured by class-based explanations that characterise the more general classification of child abuse or considered not to exist (Kelly, 1988:69). However, it is more beneficial to note the obstacles to the public discussion of sexual violence than to speculate on the unrecorded incidence and prevalence (Allen, 1990:226).

A discourse of omission

From the early twentieth century the medical, legal and welfare professions had dominated and shaped the understanding of, and responses to, child protection as the general discourse of Australian child welfare. Their impact on child sexual assault cannot be underestimated. In a sense, professional accounts of child sexual assault embody the notion of a 'discourse of omission' in that these accounts question the existence, prevalence and significance of sexual violence for children. As professionals in Australia had engaged in little or no research in the area of child sexual assault before the 1980s much of the theorising and practice in the area reflected the experiences of Europe, the United Kingdom and America.

The legacy of the psychoanalytic tradition and the work of Freud at the turn of the twentieth century in Vienna had a profound effect on later understandings of child sexual assault. Initially Freud's work provided a challenge to the discourse that abuse of children was a class-based phenomena. In 1896, in his seminal paper 'The Aetiology of Hysteria' Freud presented findings from his clinical practice (which included women from a variety of class backgrounds) citing child sexual assault as a direct cause of adult female hysteria and neurosis. His concern about the significance of this problem would seem to be warranted given the available statistical information documenting the extent of known sexual offences in Europe at this time (Breckenridge, 1992:19–21). In 1905 Freud surprisingly retracted this theory of seduction which had engendered the hostility of his colleagues. Instead, he proposed that such accusations were based on infantile fantasies — they reflected what children wanted their fathers to do, not what had actually happened. It was as if Freud himself realised the gender implications of his earlier work. In a letter to his colleague, Fliess, he explains ' the surprise that in all cases, the father, not excluding my own, had to be accused of being perverse' and concludes that 'surely such widespread perversions against children are not very probable' (in Masson, 1984:108).

The widespread acceptance of Freud's proposition that incest rarely occurred but was rather an allegation based on children's fantasies meant that, in Australia prior to the 1980s, many disclosures/complaints of incest were not given credence in clinical settings. There was little reason to develop any specific responses in terms of policy or provision of services because incest was an allegation with no substance.

The prominence of systems theory in the 1940s and 1950s resulted in a shift from the traditional psychiatric focus on individual pathology to the application of systems analysis to the family. When related to incest as one form of child sexual assault this approach no longer sought to deny its existence; instead, incest was framed as only a symptom of a more problematic family dysfunction. The functionalist tendencies of systems theory and the requisite acceptance of the family unit as the focus of intervention rendered the victim and the perpetrator of incest invisible. Policy and service provision were oriented toward support of the family and resolution of the family's dysfunction. Incest as a symptom would decrease or cease only when the more significant family problem was addressed. In a sense, the principle of community care was similar to this approach because it proposed that if families were better resourced and supported within a preventative approach there should be a decreased need for protective interventions.

Theories of deviance were also in evidence in the psychological literature at that time. As opposed to psychiatric and family dysfunction theories, psychological explanations successfully side-stepped issues of prevalence and significance by turning their attention to the identified offender. Retreating to essentialist understandings of child sexual assault, these theorists described adults who commit sexual offences against children as 'psychopathic, feeble-minded, physical and moral degenerates' (Finkelhor, 1979:20). Later research contradicted this representation in finding that only a small proportion of offenders were psychotic, senile or intellectually disabled (Russell, 1984:204). The result of such misrepresentation was that it allowed theorists to define offenders and the experiences of children out of the realm of the ordinary. Child sexual assault consequently became 'an exotic virtually negligible phenomena taking place between retarded girls and sociopathic fathers' (Summitt and Kryso in O'Donnell and Craney, 1982:156).

In theorising about child sexual assault, the professions were operating within a patriarchal ideology (MacLeod and Sararga, 1988:31). Functionalist assumptions about the family and power relations at a micro (family) and macro (societal) level characterised the nature of professional explanations. In accepting predominantly essentialist explanations of child sexual assault the professions failed to analyse sexual violence within its political, social and cultural context. The ensuing discourses took the form of distortions and misinterpretations of the available evidence, minimising the occurrence and significance of child sexual assault; in this sense they are 'discourses of omission'. The subsequent lack of appropriate and responsive social policy development and service provision in Australia prior to the 1980s was not surprising. Waldby (1987:47) claims that the data from the NSW phone-in against incest repeatedly confirms the professional discounting of incest and the resultant ineffective 'treatment' as well as the inappropriateness and inability of existing services to respond to the needs of children and adult survivors of child sexual assault. Therapeutic, social policy and legislative responses were characterised by their inadequacies at best, their absence at worst.

An omission of discourse

The rise of critical theory in the 1960s and 1970s coincided, in New South Wales with the move to community care in child welfare and perhaps even facilitated this move by raising questions about the role of the state in civil society. Prior to this time, state intervention had been framed as a form of humanitarian progress but now it was being portrayed as thinly disguised social control of individuals and groups who deviated from the accepted social and political norms of society (van Krieken, 1991:16). In relation to child welfare this revisionist social theory had concentrated on the oppression of working class families by means of state intervention. Jamrozik (1983:70) succinctly exemplifies this view in his assertion that 'practice intervention by the state was for the sole purpose of controlling the behaviour of the lower classes'. The concept that has been lost in this account is that children actually are abused, not just in working class families but also in other socioeconomic groups. Sweeney goes further by suggesting that the identification of child abuse serves the political function of 'legitimating coercive state intervention, usually in poor families at a time when other reasons for intervention, such as destitution, have been declining' (1986:35). An understanding of state intervention that relies on social control as the total explanatory factor runs into a number of difficulties, not the least being the inability to conceptualise child abuse as a social problem. Just as the discourse of the critical theorists was unable to conceptualise actual abuse, child sexual assault was completely omitted from their consideration. This was not simply the result of some form of collusion with, or expansion of, the distortions and misrepresentations embodied in the professional discourses outlined earlier. Much of the criticism of critical theory was in fact aimed at professional self-interest. For example, Sweeney (1986:36) argues that at the administrative level, the identification of child abuse in New South Wales has provided professionals with the ammunition necessary to expand their area of expertise.

The failure of critical theory to incorporate any analysis of gender into their predominantly class-based critiques of child abuse in Australia is pertinent. By omitting any discussion of gender, critical accounts such as Jamrozik (1983), and Sweeney (1986) were unable to explain the gendered nature of sexual violence and the gender differences of victims and offenders. MacLeod and Saraga (1988:44) suggest that, in reality, traditional critical theorists in their male hegemony are no less threatened by a feminist critique than the more conservative theorists who openly support functionalist views of the family. The ensuing lack of explanatory power in relation to child sexual assault results in its omission from their discourse and places the emphasis on the inevitable generic notion of abuse.

The combined impact of 'the discourse of omission and the omission of discourse' on the development of appropriate and specific therapeutic, social policy and legislative responses to child sexual assault was profound. The refusal of the state, the professions and critical theorists to incorporate the structural and material context of gender oppression in their analyses resulted in an inability to explain the specific patriarchal power relations which engender sexual violence. Before the feminist social action campaigns of the 1980s in New South Wales, child sexual assault was conspicuous for its presumed absence.

Breaking the silence: The politicisation of child sexual assault

In the same way that the 1960s had witnessed the rise of critical social theory the corresponding emergence of civil rights movements in western cultures challenged the social control of individuals by the state. In exposing the structural inequalities which oppressed certain marginalised groups, civil rights movements demanded that such inequalities be addressed by policies which embraced notions of equality. The second wave of the women's liberation movement emerged during this period of social upheaval and, as a consequence, the 1970s and the early 1980s saw the issues of rape and domestic violence forced onto the political agenda throughout Australia and more specifically in New South Wales. The women's movement and feminists in key bureaucratic positions exerted intense pressure aimed at promoting research into these areas, instigating policy and legislative changes, and establishing appropriate services for victims of sexual violence.

An unforseen consequence of research into sexual violence and the accompanying developments in social policy and service provision in the area of adult sexual violence was the unearthing of a significant number of women who had been sexually assaulted as children by an adult family member (Waldby, 1987:10). When the NSW Department of Health established nine specialist adult sexual assault centres in hospitals in 1979, an increasing number of children were referred there for assessment and help. A similar experience was noted by the Sydney Rape Crisis Centre when, in July 1979, following their phone-in on child sexual assault, referrals in this area rose to one-third of all contacts (Calvert, 1991:106). This phenomenon was not limited to New South Wales but also occurred across Australia. Feminist agencies and sexual assault services organised phone-ins and surveys, results of which substantiated the finding that child sexual assault was a significant, if previously undisclosed social problem (Breckenridge, 1992:32). In New South Wales this information was complemented by an increasing number of women and children seeking assistance from women's health centres and adult sexual assault centres in order to deal with the consequences of childhood sexual violence.

The interest of the media was another telling factor in breaking the silence surrounding child sexual assault. Advocates for children were successful in highlighting issues of poor intervention and statutory neglect in cases of child abuse. The publicisation of such instances facilitated the beginnings of necessary enquiries into how child welfare departments did (or more accurately in some cases, did not) respond to child abuse (O'Donnell and Craney, 1982:180). Within this broader context of enquiry the media also began to pick up the specific issue of incest. In April 1981 'The Australian Women's Weekly', a normally conservative publication, invited its readership to write in and tell of any unwanted childhood sexual experiences. The magazine was overwhelmed by 30 000 responses from its female readers and concluded that three per cent of them had been sexually assaulted as children by a family member; however each year throughout Australia there were only about thirty prosecutions for incest (Scutt, 1983:67).

In 1983, in New South Wales, feminist social action campaigns became increasingly focused with the formation of the Women Against Incest collective. The collective aimed at formulating a feminist analysis of incestuous abuse as well as providing a way of coordinating responses to the emerging problem of child sexual assault. In February 1984 the collective held a well-publicised three-day incest phone-in and received 340 calls. Under the slogan 'Breaking the Silence', this campaign aimed (as had the previous surveys and phone-ins) to make the privatised experience of child sexual assault a public issue. In this sense it was not merely a neutral method of information gathering but a political act. Waldby contends that the survey 'acted not only as a point of data collection but also as a point of feminist mobilisation and community education' (1987:22). It was the very process of information gathering and documentation that distinguished the feminist campaigns from previous attempts to 'explain' child sexual assault. Women and children (particularly women survivors) were no longer simply the 'objects' of state concern and intervention; instead they were active participants in setting future agendas and resisting professional domination. It was the beginning of the elevation of the experience of women and children to the level of theory (Waldby, 1987:22).

The necessary engagement with the state

In exposing child sexual assault as a social problem feminists highlighted the extent to which it was not dealt with adequately or competently by existing welfare services and the criminal justice system. At this juncture feminists had to engage with the state because of the state's monopoly over the control of sexual violence amongst its citizens (Franzway et al., 1989:114). In New South Wales the social action campaigns had created a strategically useful context for such engagement to occur. Feminist claims were based on the growing body of knowledge that encompassed the personal accounts of women and children who had experienced sexual violence; these accounts succeeded in producing a compelling impetus for change. By concurrently providing a credible theory of child sexual assault that directly addressed the experiences and needs of victims, feminists had challenged the dominance of the assertion by the child protection lobby that child sexual assault was simply part of a generic problem of child abuse. Structural change was the next goal.

The strategy of engagement developed in most Australian states involved the establishment of child sexual assault task forces which sought to 'identify problems associated with the existing laws and current methods of service delivery and to recommend on ways of integrating and coordinating policies and services' (Franzway et al. 1989:119). In appealing to the state to act on their demands, feminists were expecting the state to regulate its own role in the perpetration and perpetuation of oppressive power relations — a seeming paradox. The New South Wales Child Sexual Assault Task Force was established in 1984 and reported back to the NSW Premier one year later after extensive community consultation. There were a number of key elements that facilitated the relationship between feminist claims and the state's response — in particular, Calvert identifies the networking between feminists in the bureaucracy and the non-government sector as a critical factor (1991:110). Combined with support from key people such as the Premier (then Mr Wran), the Director General of Youth and Community Services in New South Wales and the Director of the Women's Co-ordination Unit, the issue was able to be defined as 'attention worthy'. These factors matched the government's concern to present itself as a social reformist government and accordingly allow child sexual assault to be placed on the public policy agenda.

The meshing of feminism and liberal state ideology was clearly evidenced in the various Task Force Reports commissioned by almost all State governments across Australia at that time. The comment that ' what feminism demanded, the state responded to, in turn, by incorporating and containing those demands' (Game 1985:107) accurately describes the situation. However, the NSW Task Force did bring about reforms, the extent of which varied from the other states due to the divergent interests of the respective welfare and criminal justice departments. The sixty-five recommendations of the NSW Task Force covered the areas of community education, training, the law and service development. In 1985, Premier Wran announced the establishment of a four-year Child Sexual Assault Programme containing key aspects such as: the law reform package; the 1.87 million dollar special allocation for service development across government departments in the first year of the program; and the 6.4 million dollar allocation in the second year. Service development included the formation of the Child Protection Council as the central body to co-ordinate the Child Sexual Assault Programme. The additional mandate given to the Council involved the coordination, monitoring and evaluation of child protection programs in New South Wales (NSW Child Protection Council, 1986:5). This latter mandate amounted in part to an official recognition that, prior to this time, services had been organised on an ad hoc basis without adequately meeting the needs of clients especially those who had experienced childhood sexual assault. The emergence of child sexual assault as a serious social problem was a clear example of how the way in which policy defines a social problem can influence the public perception of the issue; definitions can create a demand for more (or less) public resources and directly influence development and provision of services.

Feminism, the state and child welfare: A fraught relationship?

While the state response did fall short of what feminists had demanded, the significance of the state's acceptance of child sexual assault, as a social problem aligned to the broader concept of sexual violence, cannot be underestimated. In not subsuming child sexual assault into the generic child abuse amalgam, the state had adopted the fundamental principle of feminist resistance — the gendered nature of child sexual assault. The importance of this alignment was the state's toleration of feminism's attempt to stop the collusion of past theory with sexual politics by making sexual violence against children visible and thereby constructing a different meaning for it (MacLeod and Saraga, 1988:43). Feminists invited the state to accept the possibility of a different response to the problem of child sexual assault. This shift in thinking marked a movement away from the traditional polarised views of child welfare intervention as either progressive or a means of social control to a more complex appreciation of the issues. Intervention into the family could no longer be dismissed as inherently damaging because women and children, by disclosing instances of child sexual assault, were now seen to publicly make use of both non-government and statutory agencies to redress some of the imbalance of power within the family. To appreciate the complexity of child welfare intervention necessarily involves an acceptance that 'the relationship between state agencies and family life is often characterised by osmosis and complex alliances and compromises' (van Krieken, 1991:7).

It is only by acknowledging the recursive nature of the workings of power in society that studies of resistance have any meaning. Without a concept of resistance, individuals and certain marginalised groups are reduced to becoming passive objects of state intervention, and the state is then in danger of being given independent existence as the source of all change and improvement (Dickey, 1987:94).

CONCLUSION

The case study presented in this chapter outlines the importance of developing analyses which do not reduce all policy needs and responses to unitary explanations, such as class. Equally important is the necessity of avoiding a forced choice of either protective intervention or prevention as the only response capable of ensuring the welfare of children. Since the introduction of the concept of community care in the 1970s, child welfare debates have been somewhat characterised by oppositional and mutually exclusive policy responses and service provision. More often than not, the conflicts of protection and prevention are specialised versions of the general policy problem of whether services should be residual or universally provided — addressing children's needs or rights (Carter, 1983:6). This predominance of oppositional concepts not only results in confusion amongst service providers but also underscores the many contradictory and inadequate policy responses in the child welfare arena. The feminist social action campaigns clearly aimed to ensure that policy responses both protected the victims of sexual violence and prevented future occurrences by politicising the issue.

The future challenge for social policy in this area is to go beyond the uniform and deterministic ideologies which underpin facile solutions.(Williams, 1992:7). A useful starting point is the suggestion that child welfare needs to be reconceptualised so that the issues will not be seen simply as the need for 'more welfare' (Jamrozik, 1983: 67). The next logical step is to access the experiences and meanings attributed to traditional concepts like child welfare by individuals and groups who are other than white, middle class, heterosexual and live in a nuclear family unit. By seeking out and consequently understanding differences in experience it is possible to conceptualise a social problem in alternative ways. There is the possibility of less prescriptive responses that address specific needs , such as those of differently abled people, or the Aboriginal community, or a combination of these and other constituents of identity.

A new conceptualisation of issues like child sexual assault will only be achieved by the continual examination of the impact of any changes that take place in policy development and service provision. This examination is a crucial element in exploring the ways in which the need for welfare provision may be reconciled with the need to meet diversity and difference in striving to distribute advantage to the child.

REFERENCES

Allen, J. (1982), 'The invention of the pathological family: a historical study of family violence in NSW', in C. O'Donnell and J. Craney (eds), *Family Violence in Australia*, Longman Cheshire, Melbourne, pp. 1–27.

Allen, J. (1990), *Sex and Secrets — Crimes Involving Australian Women Since 1880* , Oxford University Press, Melbourne.

Barrett, M., and McIntosh, M. (1982), *The Anti-social Family*, Verso, London.

Breckenridge, J. (1992) 'An Exotic phenomenon? Incest and child rape' in J. Breckenridge and M. Carmody (eds), *Crimes of Violence: Australian Responses to Rape and Child Sexual Assault* , Allen and Unwin, Sydney, pp. 18–37.

Calvert, G. (1991), 'Getting Child Abuse on the Political Agenda' in E. Baldry and T. Vinson (eds), *Actions Speak*, Longman Cheshire, Melbourne, pp. 105–118.

Carrington, K. (1991), 'Policing families and controlling the young' *Journal of Australian Studies*, (31), pp. 108–117.

Carter, J. (1983), *Protection to Prevention : Child Welfare Policies*, SWRC Reports and Proceedings, No. 29, Social Welfare Research Centre, University of NSW, Kensington.

Dickey, B. (1987), ' Problems in writing welfare history' in *Journal of Australian Studies*, (21), pp. 80–95.

Dreyfus, H & Rabinow, P. (1982), *Michel Foucault — Beyond Structuralism and Hermeneutics*, Harvester Press, Brighton (UK).

Finkelhor, D. (1979), *Sexually Victimised Children*, The Free Press, New York.

Franzway, S., Court, D., and Connell, R. W. (1989), *Staking a Claim: Feminism, Bureaucracy and the State*, Allen and Unwin, Sydney.

Game, A. (1985), 'Child sexual assault: the liberal state's response' in *Legal Services Bulletin*, 10 (4), pp. 107–110.

Goodall, H. (1990), 'Saving the children —gender and the colonisation of Aboriginal children in NSW 1788-1990', *Aboriginal Law Bulletin*, 2 (44), pp. 69.

Gordon, L. (1988), 'The politics of child sexual abuse: notes from American history' in *Feminist Review*, (28), pp. 56–64.

Gordon, L. (1989), *Heroes of their Own Lives : The Politics and History of Family Violence*, Virago Press, London.

Helfer, R. and Kempe, R. (1988), *The Battered Child*, 4th edn, University of Chicago Press, Chicago,

Jamrozik, A. (1983), *Changing Concepts and Practices in Child Welfare and Options for the Future*, SWRC Reports and Proceedings, Social Welfare Research Centre No. 34, University of NSW, Kensington.

Jamrozik, A., Drury, S., and Sweeny, T. (1986), *Innovation and Change in the Child Welfare System*, SWRC Reports and Proceedings No. 57, Social Welfare Research Centre, University of NSW, Kensington.

Kelly, L. (1988), 'What's in a name?: defining child sexual abuse', *Feminist Review*, (28), pp. 65-73.

MacLeod, M. and Saraga, E. (1988), 'Challenging the orthodoxy : towards a feminist theory and practice', *Feminist Review* (28), pp. 16–55.

Masson, J. M. (1984), *The Assault on Truth — Freud's Suppression of the Seduction Theory*, Penguin Books, New York.

Merquior, J.G. (1985), *Foucault*, Fontana, London.

Mowbray, M. (1983), 'Restructuring child welfare : deinstitutionalisation and austerity in the NSW Department of Youth and Community Services', *Australian Social Work*, 36(3), pp. 4–12.

Mowbray, M. (1992),'The political economy of substitute care: developments in child welfare in NSW', *Caring*,16(3), pp. 2–9.

O'Donnell, C., and Craney, J. (1982),'Incest and the reproduction of the patriarchal family' in C. O'Donnell and J. Craney (eds), *Family Violence in Australia*, Longman Cheshire, Melbourne, pp. 155–175.

Parton, N. (1985), *The Politics of Child Abuse*, Macmillan, London.

New South Wales Child Sexual Assault Task Force (1985), *Report of the NSW Child Sexual Assault Task Force*, NSW Govt Printer, Sydney.

Russell, D. (1984), *Sexual Exploitation: Rape, Child Sexual Abuse and Workplace Harassment*, Sage, California.

Scutt, J. (1983), *Even in the Best of Homes: Violence in the Family*, Penguin, Ringwood.

Sweeney, T. (1986), 'Worker's perceptions and definitions of child abuse: implications for policy', SWRC Paper given at the Sixth International Congress on Child Abuse and Neglect, 11–14 August, Sydney, Social Welfare Research Centre Publication, University of NSW, Kensington.

NSW Child Protection Council (1986), *Child Sexual Assault Training Manual* NSW Child Protection Council, Sydney.

van Krieken, R. (1991), *Children and the State: Social control and the formation of Australian child welfare*, Allen and Unwin, Sydney,

Waldby, C. (1987), 'Breaking the Silence: a report based on the findings of the Women Against Incest Phone-In Survey', Dympna House, Sydney.

Williams, F. (1992) ' Somewhere over the rainbow: universality and diversity in social policy' *Social Policy Review* (4), pp. 1–19.

CHAPTER NINE

SOCIAL JUSTICE AND THE AUSTRALIAN CITY
Developments in urban and housing policies

MARTIN MOWBRAY

INTRODUCTION

The next decade will continue to witness rapid urban sprawl, the polarization of Melbourne into housing rich and housing poor, and an increase in the ranks of private tenants and the inadequately housed.

(Burke and Hayward, 1990: 148)

The projection by Burke and Hayward has, as will be seen, a good deal of support, and is not out of place in relation to the other major cities of Australia. Little has happened since the prognosis to question its accuracy.

Effective and creative targeting of the welfare system has improved the position of the poorest Australians over the last few years. Nevertheless, the evidence is that overall income inequality in Australia has increased since 1980 (Harding and Landt, 1992; Raskall and Urquhart, 1993). This has been reflected in the growing distinction between the housing of the rich and housing of the poor. Key findings of the National Housing Strategy (NHS — a major Commonwealth review of housing, 1990–2) were that adequate housing became less affordable for a significant proportion of the Australian population, and that it may well remain so. During the 1980s, increases in house prices and interest rates decreased accessibility of home purchase, especially for low-income households. Between 1979 and 1990, accessibility to home purchase declined by a half for Australia as a whole. Within the same period, housing costs also increased faster than renters' incomes. Between 1982 and 1988, the position of low-income home renters deteriorated against those of high-income renters (NHS, IP2:x,13, 21). More recently, reduced housing prices and declining interest rates appear to have moderated the problem, particularly for those income units (individuals or groups living together and sharing expenditure) earning average incomes or above. Future housing markets are, however, uncertain. In a period of some growth in housing construction, since 1991, and during which a degree of pent-up demand was satisfied, both the Federal Treasury and the building industry forecasted a downturn in construction for 1993–94 (*Weekend Australian*, 8 May 1993:3; *Sydney Morning Herald*, 10 May 1993:3).

Currently, there is a great deal of up-to-date published information on Australian housing and urban planning infrastructure. Most of this is in report form and generated by various government organisations. The most important source has been the National Housing Strategy, which published seven issues papers (IP), fifteen background papers and three discussion papers. The Department of Prime Minister and Cabinet has published a series of reports through its Social Justice Research Program into Locational Disadvantage (e.g. Financing Urban Infrastructure, 1991); the Economic Planning and Advisory Council (EPAC) has published a number of papers on urban issues (e.g. Urban and Regional Trends and Issues, 1991) as have Standing Committees of the House of Representatives on Aboriginal and Torres Strait Islander Affairs ('Mainly Urban', 1992) and Long Term Strategies ('Patterns of Urban Settlement', 1992). Contributions have also been made for the Australian Bureau of Statistics (ABS) (e.g,. Housing Characteristics and Decisions, Edwards and Madden, 1992) and the CSIRO (e.g. Homelessness in Australia, Neil and Fopp, 1992). Numerous other Commonwealth, State and local government agencies have weighed in with reports and prescriptive documents on housing and urban issues. This chapter synthesises a cross-section of such material. It reviews data about the current and future housing condition, and overviews emerging urban and housing policies and programs. Developments are related to the broader Australian political economy.

THE GOOD NEWS

Overall, Australian housing presents a very mixed picture, though one somewhat blurred by the paucity of systematic data about the top end of the housing market. Information about the distribution of housing wealth and housing incomes, other than in Yates' (1991; 1992) work, and the actual value of government assistance to housing the wealthy, for example, is largely unavailable. Accounts of the extent of housing wealth tend to be on an individual basis. Nonetheless, such wealth can be impressive.

Warren Anderson is a prominent Australian businessman and a resident of Peppermint Grove, Perth. His home there, quaintly named Bungalow, is built on land acquired for over $10 million (*Business Review Weekly*, 17 May 1991:72). Mr Anderson listed two of his Sydney homes for sale in 1993. One was Boomerang, a 1926 Hollywood style mansion, set behind its high pink stucco garden walls on a one-acre waterfront block in the inner suburb of Elizabeth Bay. Anderson reportedly bought it for $5.1 million in 1985. The property features marble, silk, oak and mahogany internal linings, five bedrooms with their own dressing rooms, bathrooms and balconies, a 40-seat cinema, cellars, formal gardens with fountains and colonnades, a pool and a deep-water jetty, as well as an adjoining residence. Boomerang was described as 'Australia's finest' example of Spanish Mission style architecture — also known as 'Hollywood Fantasy' (*Australian Financial Review*, 28 April 1993:49).

Anderson's other residence on the market was a very private 10-bedroom, 1842 colonial mansion at Mulgoa, just west of Sydney. Fern Hill, labelled the 'State's finest Greek temple revival', occupies 730 hectares, and was bought for $2.8 million in 1980. Both homes have been expansively decorated by Anderson. One of Anderson's large Northern Territory properties, Tipperary, bought for $15.8 million around 1985 and which features a private zoo, was described as his 'personal Xanadu' (*Sydney Morning Herald*, 3 April 1993:81; *Business Review Weekly*, 17 May 1993:72).

Most Australians do not share Mr Anderson's housing wealth, but they live in dwellings which are of good quality, and comparatively new. Eighty per cent of their dwellings are, like Boomerang and Fern Hill, single, detached houses (NHS, IP1:ix–x). More than 90 per cent of homes owned or being purchased were single, detached dwellings, according to the 1988 National Housing Survey. To the Australian Bureau of Statistics, this figure is 'indicative of the continuing strength of the "great Australian dream" of owning a home on its own block of land' (ABS, 1992:314). About 70 per cent of households live in dwellings they own or partially own, a percentage that has been relatively constant since 1961. This figure is buttressed by the fact that the age group most likely to own its homes, the aged, is increasing relative to the rest of the population. The remainder of households rent privately (20 per cent), rent publicly (6 per cent) or live in boarding houses, caravans and so on, or are homeless (4 per cent) (NHS, IP1: 4). In 1988–89, less than ten per cent ($51m) of the estimated total value of owner- or purchaser-occupied housing

($537m) was mortgage debt (Yates, 1992: 116). Approximately 85 per cent of Australians buy a home at some stage in their lives (NHS, IP1:9).

Despite the fact that housing is the most significant single item of expenditure during the lifetime of Australians, on average only 12.6 to 14 per cent of household incomes are spent on housing (NHS IP1:3, 6; NHS, IP2:10). Australians, overall, spend about the same amount on accommodation, as residents of other OECD countries. This is despite having a higher rate of population growth and household formation (NHS IP1:18), as well as having around the highest rate of home ownership.

Housing is much more than an expenditure item. If the impact of imputed rent (market rental value) of dwellings on income distribution is taken into account, as recommended by the United Nations, a very different picture of overall incomes emerges. Yates' analysis shows that the average net imputed income for all Australian households was $46 per week in 1988–89. Benefits are, however, unevenly spread and depend greatly on type of tenure as well as income levels. The average net imputed income for those who own homes outright was $137 per week (Yates, 1991: 35). Such effective income is tax free, although it was not always so.

The 1988 Housing Survey estimated that of income units which owned or were purchasing their current dwelling, ten per cent either owned or were buying one or more additional properties (ABS, 1992:319). This statistic is consistent with the evidence that rental housing stock is widely spread — small landlords control more than half of all rented properties in the country (NHS, IP1:47). The amount of lightly used housing would also appear to be extensive. On Census night in 1986, over 500 000 private dwellings (of a total of just under six million dwellings) were unoccupied, and 26 per cent of these were holiday homes (ABS, 1992:321).

In general, investment in housing in Australia is a relatively attractive proposition. The Real Estate Institute, for example, has claimed that investments in residential property outperformed shares and fixed security investments over 10 years to 1982 — with average annual compound growth rates of 16.2 to 17.3 per cent in the capital cities (*Sun-Herald*, 25 April 1993:5). The highly tax-favoured treatment of negatively geared (where any losses incurred on an investment are deductible from taxable income) rental investments underpins the strength of such investment (Pender and Ross, 1993:11).

Indicators of housing conditions are frequently positive. The 1988 Household Survey confirmed a trend towards a greater amount of domestic space available to Australians. Whilst between 1976 and 1986 the size of dwellings increased, household sizes decreased from 3.1 to 2.9 persons per household (ABS, 1992: 318). The size of new dwellings increased over the 1970s and 1980s, despite the tighter economic environment. The average new home grew from 130 square metres in the early 1970s to 180 square metres, at about 1990. Repeat buyers, who accounted for 60 per cent of new homes built for owner occupation, may have been the prime beneficiaries (NHS, IP1: 38).

The amount of housing space per occupant also appears to have increased. On average, there were less residents than there were bedrooms for most types of dwellings (detached and semi-detached houses, and medium density and hig-rise flats). Only for the category of low-rise flats and units were there no more bedrooms (average 1.8 per dwelling) than people (also, average 1.8) (ABS, 1992: 318). Along with the move towards larger dwellings, there has been a movement from use of wood and fibro cement to brick veneer, concrete and stone walls (NHS, IP1:38). There has also been a steady increase in alterations and additions as a proportion of building activity (NHS, IP1: 39).

As another indicator of relative well-being, the 1990 ABS Survey of Income and Housing Costs and Amenities found that Australian homes averaged 1.3 bathtubs and could park 1.4 cars under cover. The 1985–86 National Energy Survey found that nearly all dwellings had a refrigerator, 95 per cent had a phone and 93 per cent had a washing machine, half had clothes dryers and freezers, a third had air conditioners and microwave ovens, and a fifth had a dishwasher. Detached dwellings were more likely to have such features (ABS, 1992: 320–1).

In 1988, there were over 5.8 million dwellings in Australia, representing an increase of 69 per cent over 20 years. This increase was all in the form of private dwellings. Non-private dwellings, such as boarding houses and migrant hostels, decreased (ABS, 1992:313). The latter development was despite an extensive national deinstitutionalisation program over the same period, which has put some pressure on alternative, community-based accommodation such as boarding houses.

Assistance for home ownership

The extent of Australian home ownership reflects government encouragement through a range of direct forms of assistance in the way of cash and, less visible, tax expenditures. Between 1964 and 1990 the Federal government provided cash subsidies for first home buyers; between 1974–78 and 1982–83 the Commonwealth also allowed first home buyers tax deductions on their mortgage interest payments; first home buyers have been given preferential treatment on payment of State taxes and charges, such as stamp duty; since

1945, state governments have also provided home loans at subsidised interest rates, or on low-cost repayment schedules; and under the Commonwealth States Housing Agreement (CSHA) the States have also facilitated short-term mortgage relief (NHS, IPs1:14; 2:78–92).

Governments have also provided a range of more important, but less obvious types of assistance to home owners. The bulk of this indirect encouragement is through the tax system and is, therefore, less readily understood as part of the overall provisions of the welfare state. Fiscal welfare (Titmuss, 1974) assistance is automatically allowed to home owners through exemption of returns on investment in their dwellings. The imputed rent (market rental value) of dwellings that are not commercially rented is not taxable. Indeed, unlike in many other countries, Australia does not include imputed income for housing in its income distribution statistics. Capital embodied in homes and home improvement is an effective tax haven, rendering housing a form of investment, as well as a source of shelter and, possibly, enjoyment. This facility of tax exemption on imputed rent extends to additional dwellings such as holiday homes. Paradoxically, an approximation of imputed rental income is shown in National Accounts (at five per cent of estimated property values). Capital gains that may accrue on primary place of residence are also treated in a concessionary way. Such income for home owners and purchasers, which is often very considerable, is tax exempt, as was capital gains on second homes until 1987.

Another form of fiscal welfare for home owners is administered at the local government level. Pensioner home owners are allowed discounts on local rates. No equivalent assistance is accorded to pensioners who are tenants, despite the fact that they are likely to be in greater need of assistance and pay rates through their rent. Pensioner home owners, and eventually the beneficiaries of their estates, also benefit from exemption of dwellings from the pension assets test, introduced in 1985.

Governments have also advantaged home purchasers through intervention in interest rates. Before 1986, the Commonwealth regulated savings bank mortgage interest rates, ensuring a degree of access to home purchase finance to the lower-income earner. Banks cross-subsidised home owners by being obliged to set home loan rates below those for personal loans. Home owners have been aided through the subsidised provision of infrastructure (such as roads, water, seweraage and electricity, and services, like transport, retail centres, health and recreational facilities) for new housing developments. This help has come from general government revenue, but has been reduced over recent years through greater use of levies on developers. However, the cost of these levies is likely to be passed on to buyers (Mowbray, 1991).

The drying up of some forms of direct government assistance for home ownership is contributing to a degree of inter-generational inequity, on top of any other population-category-related biases, such as gender. The aging 'baby boom' generation, which left parental homes in the 1960s and 70s, has been favoured by policies that are not available to the current generation of young adults. These advantages have gone well beyond housing (see Thompson and Tapper, 1993).

The historical and central role of local government in protecting, if not maximising, property values, through amenity provision, building regulation and land use control is another means by which home owners have been assisted by the state. Contrary to popular belief, local government has not been simply financed by property owner ratepayers, but by tenants (who pay rates in their rents) as well as through fees, charges and general State and Federal government revenue (Mowbray, 1984).

THE BAD NEWS

Australians benefit from housing policy and resources unevenly. Despite the high national rate, home ownership varies sharply with type of household. Married couples with dependent children, for example, are more likely to own a home outright, than male sole parents. The latter are, in turn, more likely to own a home outright than female sole parents (at 36.8 per cent, 34.8 per cent, and 28.3 per cent, respectively). Of married couples without dependent children, who are more likely to be older, 55.3 per cent were outright owners (Cass, 1991:11,14). One Federal government estimate is that some 200 000 households are unlikely to ever satisfy their housing needs through home ownership (NHS, IP6:77).

While average weekly earnings in real terms have declined over recent years (NHS, IP1:32) Gross Domestic Product has grown, as has average household disposable income. The latter increase was influenced earlier by real wage increases, and later by increased paid labour force participation of women (NHS, IP1:30). Nevertheless, there is general agreement that there has been a long-term decline in housing affordability, with those on low and moderate incomes worst affected (NHS, IP1:48). As Kendig has commented, the rise of two-income families may be seen as both a cause and a response to rising house prices (NHS, IP1:49).

The ABS reports that over the 1980s, housing costs increased more rapidly than overall cost of living. In the five years leading up to 1990–91, total housing costs increased by 43 per cent. This compared to an increase of 31 per cent in the cost of living and a 28 per cent growth in average weekly earnings. Regional variations were very considerable (ABS, 1992:323).

In Sydney and Melbourne each year from 1960 to 1989, median house prices increased in real terms by 3.5 per cent and 3.3 per cent, respectively. Increases were not uniform for all homeowners. Capital gains greatly depended on the years of purchase and sale. Rates of price change also varied greatly between cities, within cities, and between price categories. Increases were highest in the higher price locations (NHS, IP1: 43–4).

The 1988 National Housing Survey indicated that nearly 60 per cent of single-parent income units rented because they could not afford their own homes. One-parent income units renting private detached dwellings spent, on average, 37 per cent of their incomes on rent (ABS, 1992: 317, 324). With such data in mind, it is not surprising that single parents renting privately have been most likely to evince the highest incidence of real poverty (Yates and Vipond, 1991: 241). This is despite the fact that approximately 665 000 people receive private rental assistance, through either the Department of Social Security or Department of Veteran's Affairs (NHS, IP2: 87). The position of young purchasers, especially those in lower income categories, has been grim. In 1988, those in the second income quintile and under 34 years paid on average 36 per cent of their incomes on housing (NHS IP2:18).

The public housing waiting list in 1988-89 was over 197 000 and growing (NHS, IP2: 6). Although the Federal government's National Housing Strategy offered assurance that there is not yet any overall 'housing crisis' (NHS, IP1: xiv, 94), and there certainly is not for upper classes, it also reported that accessibility to home purchase declined by 50 per cent between 1979 and 1990. However, the rate of owner occupancy remained steady, at around 70 per cent of all households. This is because of the increased propensity to ownership through an ageing population. The home purchase rate of 25–34 year olds declined (NHS, IP2:13).

Of the various approaches to the measurement of accessibility of home ownership that are available, the deposit gap method is prominent. The deposit gap is the ratio of the amount that may be borrowed by an income unit relative to the purchase price of a home. An increased ratio means that a larger deposit is required and, hence, there is decreased affordability. In 1985, the deposit required to buy a median-priced house for someone on average weekly earnings was one and a half times their annual income. By 1991 the deposit required had increased to one and three-quarter times their annual income. Regional and population category variations are, again, very considerable (ABS, 1992:325–6).

Another measure of accessibility, the Housing Affordability Index of the Commonwealth Bank and the Housing Industry Association, has been used to suggest a marked improvement in home purchase affordability between 1989 and 1993 (ABS, 1993:220). The measure employed is, however, problematic. Amongst other difficulties, it uses estimates of average incomes, and house prices inappropriate to first home buyers (NHS, IP2:58). It appears correct, though, that reduced housing prices and declining interest rates have moderated the affordability problem, particularly for those income units with above-average incomes. As noted before, however, some authorities predict another downturn in construction for 1993–94, and commensurate increases in house prices (*Sun-Herald*, 23 May 1993:47).

With a view to developing targeted housing assistance measures, the National Housing Strategy sought to quantify the degree of (financial) 'housing stress'. This term was conservatively defined as denoting income units in the lowest 40 per cent of the income distribution range spending 30 per cent or more of their incomes on housing (NHS, IP2:7). The NHS found that 21 per cent of (the 2.3 million) low-income units (the lowest two-income quintiles) fell under the housing stress threshold. However, 34 per cent in this income category spent 25 per cent or more of their incomes on housing, and eight per cent laid out 50 per cent or more of their incomes on housing (NHS, IP2: 26–8). Proportional to their numbers in the total population, private renters, social security recipients, single-income units and women were much more likely to be in housing stress (NHS, IP2:28; Cass, 1991:18).

While, overall, income units spent an average of 12.6 per cent of their incomes on housing (NHS, IP2: 10) in 1988, sole parents spent 36.1 per cent of theirs and, single people, aged people 65 and over, spent 38.9 per cent. Low-income, private renters in general paid out more than 40 per cent of their incomes on accommodation (NHS, IP2: 21).

CSIRO-based research, itself a degree less optimistic in its projections on housing affordability than the NHS, stressed the likelihood of increased risk of homelessness — 'via a trickle down effect' (Neil and Fopp, 1992:191). There is, however, no accurate current data on the number of homeless people in Australia. The census data collection techniques are inadequate to reach many of the homeless population, and other efforts to establish indicative data have been too restricted. No concerted and adequately resourced attempt has been made to establish overall numbers of people without homes (Neil and Fopp, 1992:29–33). Informed sources suggest a trend towards increased youth homelessness (National Inquiry into Homeless Children, 1989:115).

PROJECTIONS

With the assistance of the National Institute of Economic and Industry Research, the NHS identified a range of economic and demographic trends which were seen as likely to help change the pattern of demand for housing over the next twenty years. These included an aging population increasingly likely to live independently, and a growing proportion of childless income units. The NHS projection was that until at least the year 2006 the proportion of owner/purchaser occupation of households will remain around 70 per cent. However, the NHS expected that a much higher proportion of such households will be made up of one or two persons 60 years and older.

A significantly lower proportion of owner/purchasers would be younger couples 25 to 34 years, 'unless house prices remain sluggish and there is a significant turnaround in the state of the economy by the mid 1990s' (NHS, IPI:83). The latter age cohort has been seen as increasingly likely to look to the rental housing market, which will have a decreased vacancy rate and be relatively less affordable than at the present. The NHS went on to note the possibility of greater forced dependence of younger people on shared dwellings, institutions and caravans (NHS, IP1:83).

The Indicative Planning Council has projected an underlying demand for 146 000 new dwellings per annum through the 1990s (NHS, IP4: 11). In Sydney, 80 per cent of additions to the housing stock in the 1980s have been on the metropolitan fringe. If Australian cities are to continue this pattern, another 1.25 million, mostly detached, dwellings will have to be built on semi-rural 'greenfields' locations on the fringes of Adelaide, Brisbane, Melbourne, Perth and Sydney by 2011. This is a quantity of dwellings roughly equal to the total number in Sydney in 1991 (NHS, IP4: 18). Continuing research confirms the likelihood that sprawling low-density dwellings serviced by car transport will continue to characterise growth in the Australian capitals (Weekend Australian, 8 May 1993:37).

The cost of new, serviced, subdivisions is considerable. The NHS gives the indicative average development costs on fringe land for the five largest cities as $50 800 per allotment , and up to $71 000 in Sydney. On average, 41 per cent of the costs were recovered and the balance paid for through the public sector (NHS, IP4:66).

One area for development in Sydney is South Creek, ten kilometres beyond the existing western metropolis. The Department of Planning sees the area as accommodating about 60 000 households, at $50 000 per block, including necessary infrastructure. Another area slated for urban expansion is Macarthur South, south of Campbelltown, which would provide more than 60 000 building lots at an average cost of significantly more than $50 000 (Birrell, 1991:208–213). For a 24 000 lot development at Rouse Hill EPAC gives the average cost of physical services as $36 130, and social services as $15 310, in 1988 prices (EPAC 1991:40).

Finding additional housing: A dry agenda

Governments are confronted with projections on underlying demand for housing and related urban infrastructure. As articulated by the National Housing Strategy, the Federal government's responsibility is seen as one of ensuring the availability of 'more affordable and appropriate housing choices' in order to meet future needs (NHS, IP7: 118).

Despite a limited number of modest and highly selective increases in public expenditure, current economic orthodoxy remains overwhelmingly against any significant move towards concerted growth in public resource commitment to housing and related problems. There is little disagreement that governments, with bipartisan agreement, will remain committed to minimising intervention and expenditure on social objectives. Investors guided by high profile and self-appointed custodians of economic rectitude, such as US credit rating agencies Moody's and Standard and Poor's, do much to strengthen government's resolve on monetary and fiscal policy settings.

The NHS affirmed the stance that 'governments will be unable to increase resources available for housing assistance' and will have to try new approaches. These will entail effective focusing 'towards those in greatest need'. 'At a time of fiscal restraint', the NHS said, governments must determine 'how to assist lower income renters and home purchasers in cost effective ways' (NHS, IP1:xiii, xv).

In this view, essentially what is required is (micro) economic reform. In summarising its view of future policy challenges, the NHS argued that governments, in association with industry and unions, must 'take advantage of opportunities that world economic growth presents'. Increased productivity should be sought, the NHS suggests, through investments in education and training and infrastructure, award restructuring, encouragement of exports, minimisation of 'burdens on industry' and effective financial sector management (NHS, IP1:xiii, 87).

> If Australia succeeds in catching up with 'world best' practice in terms of productivity, there should be no 'housing crisis' (in terms of significantly worsened housing affordability) between now and the year 2006.
>
> (NHS, IP1:xiii)

Burke and Hayward have suggested that expenditure on housing may be reduced in favour of a commitment to investment in industry which would produce exports or import replacements, and thereby reduce the current account deficit:

> ... with the increasing need to concentrate resources in the trade exposed sectors of the economy, governments may well seek to find ways to redirect resources away from housing. As has already been the case in the 1980s, attempts may be made to both lower housing expectations and housing standards.
>
> (Burke and Hayward, 1990: 126)

The NHS has helped substantiate this speculation with formulations such as that housing 'is arguably an area from which investment capital may need to be redirected if high current account deficits are to be reduced' (NHS, IP1: 17; see also xiii, 87). On a related tack, the NHS suggested that its own proposals for housing reform may significantly contribute to 'the micro-economic reform agenda and to building a stronger, more competitive Australian economy' (NHS, IP7:11).

Part of the overall discussion about housing policy and economic growth is the argument that because of tax advantages, there is over-investment in housing in Australia. Pender and Ross, for example, suggest in an EPAC publication that the concessional treatment of housing in the tax system distorts investment decisions. They reason that while taxation of imputed rent 'would be a political and administrative nightmare' other measures to redress the problem may be warranted. They list as alternatives: 'requiring better returns from water and sewage authorities, broadening land taxes, introduction of capital gains taxation on principal residence and introduction of betterment taxes' (Pender and Ross, 1993:13, 27).

It is important to recognise that the implication behind much of such discussion is that the domestic, dwelling-based, environment is essentially one of consumption. Whilst the NHS allows that housing is an investment good, as well as a consumption good, it does so in rather limited terms. These appear to be confined to points about untaxed imputed rental income and capital gains (NHS, IP1:17). Otherwise, investment in housing seems to be projected as a drain on the real economy and as an alternative to investment in economically productive activity. In this, there is a perception that investment in housing crowds out investment in production. Amongst other things, this understanding tends to ignore the value of domestic, predominantly female, labour (see Watts, 1993). The home is itself a site of production (and re-production of the labour force). The amount of wealth generated in the home may well be sensitive to the physical nature of the dwelling itself. Little interest in this issue is evident in the current discourse.

It should be noted that in the recent housing and urban policy discourse, it has become commonplace to also explain excessive investment in housing, by referring to the historically prevailing, below-cost, publicly subsidised, prices for new housing developments (NHS, IP1:17). The currency of such formulations has provided a normative context for specific governments' urban and housing policies.

POLICY DIRECTIONS

At this point, it is important to review the range and directions of programs concerning housing and the shape of Australian cities. In drawing these together, special attention will be paid to courses of action canvassed in the National Housing Strategy's Agenda for Action (NHS, IP7). This is not simply because Agenda for Action is the major official document reviewing directions and possibilities for Federal, State and local governments, but because it is tempered by an understanding of what is currently acceptable to governments at each level in Australia. In many respects the document synthesises established policy trends. At the same time, it represents an attempt, in Orchard's words...

> ... to carve out a progressive urban strategy in the context of the general move to the right in Australian politics and the policy dominance of economic rationalism.
>
> (Orchard, 1992:19)

The starting point for this review of policy and program trends is that there is an established need to increase the supply of affordable and accessible dwellings in Australia. It is also agreed that there is an associated need to increase the supply and appropriateness of urban infrastructure and services, such as public transport, most notably rail. These need to be strategically integrated with existing and emerging employment opportunities. Many facets of the approach to reform are built into the Building Better Cities program announced in the 1991–92 Federal budget. In this exemplar, the Commonwealth is meant to provide $816 million to the states over five years to help finance specific urban renewal style projects to model improved coordination and land-use strategies, linkage of housing with infrastructure, services, employment, training and environmental enhancement.

Urban consolidation and housing supply

At the core of policy reform is the concept of urban consolidation, referring to measures intended to increase residential density, by increasing the density of dwellings or of the population, or both. Governments, at least at the Federal and State levels, are in agreement that housing densities need to be raised. This is meant to diminish the overall costs of the land component of housing and of infrastructure provision. Increased densities are also seen as a necessary condition for increased efficiency in access to infrastructure and services and reduction of the consequential negative environmental impacts of sprawl. Medium, high, and mixed-housing densities should be encouraged, and detached dwellings should be made more compact (on smaller lots), to conserve space. This approach should be adopted for both development at the urban fringe, as well as in established urban areas.

Advocates of urban consolidation claim the following benefits:

1. *greater economic efficiency through higher utilization levels of new and existing infrastructure and consequent reduced demand for new infrastructure;*

2. *environmental benefits through greater use of public transport;*

3. *social equity through greater proximity to existing facilities.*

(Australia, Parliament, 1992:84).

Population decline in older suburbs should be reversed or arrested, through urban infill techniques such as encouragement of dual occupancy of existing detached dwelling sites (e.g. 'granny flats') and redevelopment of redundant industrial land. Residential use of inner cities should be encouraged, through recycling commercial buildings and new high-density residential construction. Encouragement may be given through offering incentives by relaxing rules to allow, for example, more floor area than otherwise permissable.

Urban design preferences have to be altered so that cities become more rational in their use of scarce resources, such as land, energy and clean air. Broader ecological, and national or societal, impacts of urban development need to be considered.

As a measure of this trend in urban planning, state governments now have target densities of 14–15 dwellings per hectare on the metropolitan fringe, rather than 8–10 dwellings per hectare (Australia, Parliament, 1992:84). They have also granted automatic dual occupancy entitlements to residents in established suburbs, and the States are trying to eradicate obstacles to increased medium density, townhouse style, developments in both new and established suburbs.

A study for Federal and NSW government agencies concluded that for every 1000 dwelling units built for urban consolidation in Sydney, rather than fringe development, the overall cost saving would be between 17 and 31 million dollars. Public sector budget savings were put at between 8 and 14 million dollars. The differences in projected savings largely reflected sensitivity to lot sizes on the urban fringe and density targets for the consolidated areas — generally costs were found to reduce with density up to 50 dwellings per hectare, and then increase slightly, up to 150 per hectare (Hughes Trueman Ludlow, 1991:iv).

One existing scheme with consolidation objectives is the Greenstreet program (first known as the Joint Venture for More Affordable Housing). Greenstreet is a joint Commonwealth–State enterprise which originated in the early 1980s. It is a limited scale trial and demonstration program officially aimed at making homes more affordable. Features are: use of smaller allotments; zero lot lining; reduced front, rear and side set-backs; house siting and orientation to optimise light, privacy and visual amenity; elimination of street footpaths; narrower streets without through traffic; overground stormwater run off and common trenching for utilities.

Local governments have often resisted Greenstreet innovations and a number of criticisms of Greenstreet approaches have been raised. For example, there is evidence that savings from Greenstreet type approaches, especially as used by the private sector, have not been passed on to consumers; projects tend to be shaped for the middle- and higher-income groups, rather than for those most in need; and reduced engineering requirements, as in thinner road paving, may result in higher maintenance costs.

There have also been very strident criticisms of the efficacy of urban consolidation strategies as a whole (see review in Australia, Parliament, 1992:85ff). Some of these criticisms question the assumptions upon which the cost-saving potential of urban consolidation programs are based. Others take up equity considerations, especially in respect to the questions of who benefits and who pays?

The House of Representatives Standing Committee for Long Term Strategies reviewed reasons such as the following as to why the capacity of urban consolidation policies to save space, and produce economic, environmental and social benefits, is limited. Explanations included: first, that perhaps only two per cent of a city's housing stock may be added each year, so that opportunity for transformation is very gradual; second, reducing average household sizes counteracts increased dwelling densities; third, non-residential land uses, which make up large parts of cities, are not so amenable to compression as residential uses; fourth, more compact urban form is partly reliant on better public transport replacing car use, an unlikely prospect for the immediate future at least. Lastly, the effectiveness of opposition to consolidation measures in many suburban locations restricts the total capacity of a city to incorporate higher density living. In any case, even by the most favourable scenario, two-thirds of urban growth can still be expected to take place at the suburban fringe (Australia, Parliament, 1992:xii–xiii).

The Standing Committee made the critical observation that over the past ten years the market's response to Commonwealth policy initiatives has had more impact on urban form and use of infrastructure than the explicit planning initiatives of the State governments. Relevant Commonwealth policies included general economic policies and taxation, finance for transport infrastructure, especially roads, immigration policy, industry restructuring and sectoral reform (Australia, Parliament, 1992:xv).

There is a commonplace commitment to making housing production more efficient and diverse. This, it is felt, can be achieved through reducing barriers to supply, by such means as minimising regulations and streamlining building and development approval processes, revising construction techniques and industrial practices, using newer building materials, and offering greater choice in land titling arrangements. The latter includes, for example, provision in New South Wales for a form of collective title for what are now being termed Manufactured Home Estates. From 1993, relocatable or mobile dwelling parks may be established with common title for communal facilities and individual titles for home sites. The latter may be as small as 130 square metres — a long way from the proverbial quarter acre (1000m^2) block.

Housing choices are seen as needing to be expanded, through such means as providing dwellings of a size and design appropriate to decreasing household size and changing household composition; more flexible home loan 'products'; and increasing the relative benefits of rental accommodation in respect of security of tenure and control. The legalisation in New South Wales of long-term caravan living and, its derivation, manufactured home estates also illustrates this development. Factory-built homes can be assembled (even disassembled) in various, flexible, configurations. Since 1992, their sites may be leased for up to 20 years, and with individual lot title possible, home loans will become feasible.

Financing and pricing

Another feature of the discourse on urban and housing policy reform is the search for and development of alternative methods of housing finance. These, it is generally agreed at least in the official discourse, should not rely on substantial increases in public expenditure. Acceptable ideas include, for example, facilitation of access to an individual's superannuation savings to finance home deposits. This was a feature of both Labor and Coalition election platforms in 1993. Other housing finance proposals within the realm of current acceptability to governments include: tax advantaged housing bonds (to raise investment capital); reverse equity loan schemes (in which equity in a home can be converted to income); mortgage insurance arrangements (to reduce vendor risk and allow lower interest charges); and encouragement of increased use of shared home purchase schemes (which facilitate fractional owner equity in a dwelling and payment of rent on the balance).

Also a trend with strong support is the call for revised residential land development pricing regimes. New serviced allotments should be priced so that they encourage more efficient use of resources. Claims on public expenditure, it is argued, can be contained by pricing services in new development areas so as to better reflect their real costs. This can be achieved through greater recovery of real costs of installation of roads, open space and services by public providers. Up-front levies by local governments on developers, who may then pass on costs to consumers, constitutes one popular device. Another is the levying of special rates directly on consumers. Alternatively, local governments may require developers to install amenities, such as recreation centres, as a condition of development approval.

This trend has international standing. The OECD gives the challenge to its member countries of 'finding ways of financing the continued provision and maintenance of urban infrastructure in the face of constrained budgets, restrictions on borrowing and inadequate revenues' as one of the two outstanding tasks facing those responsible for urban infrastructure. The other task is improving efficiency. The OECD also notes that in Australia 'an increasing proportion of funds will have to be devoted to the management and maintenance of existing infrastructure networks in the larger cities' (OECD, 1990:22, 29).

Social housing

Despite a strong commitment to supply side responses to housing provision, the NHS and others have not seen increased supply of public housing as a practical answer to housing deficiencies. However, a modestly expanded social housing sector has been considered vital by the NHS (NHS, IPs 6: xii; 7: 35). Social housing denotes dwellings managed for social purposes, rather than for profit. It includes public housing and community housing. The latter entails delivery of housing by private not-for-profit organisations, such as cooperatives. Presently, there are about 12 000 dwellings managed by community groups, compared to 360 000 in the public sector and about one million private rental dwellings (NHS, IP6:86). The NHS proposed 445 000 public sector dwellings and 25 000 community sector dwellings by the year 2000 or 6.5 per cent of total housing stock (NHS, IP7:49). This would represent an increase of about half a per cent for the social housing sector as a whole.

While it is commonly felt that public housing provision should not, or cannot, be expanded, a strong place is seen for public supply of land for residential and related purposes. This does not include advocating serious involvement of government in land acquisition and release so as to affect overall prices. It does include, however, the release of existing holdings considered surplus. Defence land, railway yards and former state institutions, for example, are being sold off around the country, often at bargain prices. Some such disposals are being incorporated into Building Better Cities projects, as is the disused waterfront and railway land on Newcastle Harbour (Honeysuckle) and at Pyrmont and Eveleigh in Sydney ('City West'). There is the hope that such developments will encourage large-scale investment by big capital.

Greater equity in access to housing needs satisfaction, at minimal levels anyhow, is to be sought. This should be primarily through more effective targeting by government, also a common element of government housing policies in Europe (Harloe, 1993:4). The NHS advocates better focussing of direct government assistance through the use of a 'housing affordability benchmark'. This is a measure of affordability, or stress, to be fully implemented for low-income renters by the year 2000.

The NHS saw an appropriate 'housing affordability benchmark' as a ratio of housing costs to income. This, it suggested, should be 30 per cent, or lower and 25 per cent of incomes of long-term private renters. Adoption of a 'benchmark response' to housing affordability problems would 'facilitate the targeting of assistance to those in greatest need'. The necessary funds would come from reallocation of existing unevenly distributed housing subsidies or through provision of additional funds (NHS, IP2:41, 50). Special assistance schemes are recommended for people with distinctive needs, such as women with children, people with disabilities and Aboriginal people. Emphasis is on achieving 'minimum acceptable standards' (NHS, IP7:37), rather than comprehensive redistribution of support for housing.

Education and information

Another policy direction concerns (re)education. The staid expectations or felt needs of consumers, planners, builders and developers, are seen to be in need of modification (away from what is seen as an over reliance on single dwellings on large blocks of land). To this end, the NHS proposed implementation of a National Housing Information Strategy and heavy use of demonstration projects. Also based on the recognition, at least implicit, that the market is a social construction, modification of consumer expectations is also an objective.

Finally, there is a recurrent call for better overall monitoring, evaluation, research and training mechanisms for shaping housing and urban policy on a national basis. Intergovernmental cooperation and planning are seen as in need of improvement, with the Commonwealth playing a leadership role. The newly established Australian Housing and Urban Research Institute may be seen as part of such a strategy.

Notable for their omissions are increased government expenditures, major tax reforms, significant market intervention or monetary policy to control affordability, decentralisation, or significant efforts to redistribute housing wealth.

CONCLUSION

A number of problems in relation to the supply of housing have emerged or become much more apparent over the last decade or so. These include access and affordability (at least for lower-income groups), future supply, distribution, appropriateness for a changing population profile, the cost of supporting infrastructure, environmental and aesthetic problems. Other issues, such as the degree of overall inequity in the distribution of housing wealth have received less attention. Whilst government has a clear interest in addressing most of these problems, current political exigencies restrict its capacity or preparedness to either increase its own level of expenditure, or to make any fundamental changes to the tax system which unevenly supports private home ownership.

In the context of a broader ideological commitment to structural reform, the state is also under continuing pressure to make conditions more conducive to housing and construction industry investment and profitability. This is reflected in the efforts it is making to facilitate supply of new housing through producing a less encumbered planning and building environment. There is also increasing recognition of problematic externalities, such as environmental damage, and their costs. The Economic Planning and Advisory Council (EPAC) has estimated partial economic costs of pollution and congestion, for example, at 4 billion dollars per annum (EPAC, 1991:31–2).

Across each level of government, the state is likely to continue its high levels of off-budget, fiscal Keynesian (Smith 1991:7) support for owner occupied housing. Taxing profits on the sale of owner-occupied housing, for example, would carry extreme political risks that are unlikely to be countenanced. It would also probably entail radical political and ideological reform. While continuing indirect support for home ownership, it seems clear that governments will seek to minimise their overall level of on-budget expenditure on housing. As a consequence, those directly and indirectly assisted through such aid, but excluded from owner occupation, will be relatively disadvantaged. The state will continue to try to find innovative mechanisms of intervention through such devices as user pays pricing systems for infrastructure finance, and rationalised planning and building standards, construction methods and approvals processes. These devices will be supported through means like new regulations, model programs, improved research and re-education.

The mechanisms for achieving this are likely to be through reduced effective commitment to public housing; reduced direct provision of urban infrastructure and greater reliance on user pays arrangements; encouragement of reduced use of land for housing, smaller and more economical housing, and more economical use of urban infrastructure. In doing so, it runs considerable risk of diminishing the social wage and residential living conditions particularly of lower-income recipients.

REFERENCES

Australian Bureau of Statistics, (1992), *Social Indicators, Number 5*, ABS, Canberra.

Australian Bureau of Statistics, (1993), *Women in Australia*, ABS, Canberra.

Australia, Parliament, (1992), *Patterns of Urban Settlement: Consolidating the Future*, Report of the House of Representatives Standing Committee for Long Term Strategies, AGPS, Canberra.

Birrell, R. (1991), 'Infrastructure costs on the urban fringe', Working Paper No.8, in Economic Planning Advisory Council, *Background Papers on Urban and Regional Trends and Issues*, Background Paper 46, AGPS, Canberra, pp. 203–32.

Burke, T., and Hayward, D. (1990), 'Housing Melbournians for the next twenty years: problems, prospects and possibilities', *Urban Policy and Research*, 8(3), pp. 122–51.

Cass, B.(1991), *The Housing Needs of Women and Children*, National Housing Strategy, Discussion Paper, AGPS, Canberra.

Economic Planning Advisory Council (EPAC). (1991), *Urban and Regional Trends and Issues*, Council Paper 46, AGPS, Canberra.

Edwards, M., and Madden, R (1992), *Housing Characteristics and Decisions: A comparative study of Sydney, Melbourne, Adelaide and Canberra, 1991*, ABS, Canberra

Harding, A., and Landt, J. (1992), 'Policy and poverty: trends in disposable incomes, March 1983 to September 1991', *Australian Quarterly* 64(1), pp. 19–48.

Harloe, M. (1993), *The Social Construction of Social Housing*, Working Paper 24, Urban Research Program, Research School of Social Sciences, Australian National University, Canberra.

Hughes Trueman Ludlow, (1991), *Public Sector Cost Savings of Urban Consolidation*, Final Report for the NSW Department of Planning, the Sydney Water Board and the Department of Industry, Technology and Commerce, Sydney.

Mowbray, M., (1984), 'Fiscal welfare and local government: distributive and ideological effects of the rating system', in J. Halligan and C. Paris (eds), *Australian Urban Politics*, Longman Chesire, Melbourne, pp. 73–87.

Mowbray, M., (1991), 'Political dimensions of local social planning in NSW', *Urban Policy and Research*, 9(3), pp. 133–40.

National Housing Strategy, (1991), *Australian Housing: The Demographic, Economic and Social Environment*, Issues Paper 1, AGPS, Canberra.

National Housing Strategy, (1991), *The Affordability of Australian Housing*, Issues Paper 2, AGPS, Canberra.

National Housing Strategy, (1991), *The Efficient Supply of Affordable Land and Housing*: The Urban Challenge, Issues Paper 4, AGPS, Canberra.

National Housing Strategy, (1992), *Housing Choice: Reducing the Barriers*, Issues Paper 6, AGPS, Canberra.

National Housing Strategy, (1992), *National Housing Strategy: Agenda for Action*, Issues Paper 7, AGPS, Canberra.

National Inquiry into Homeless Children (1989), *Our Homeless Children*, (Burdekin) Report, AGPS, Canberra.

Neil, C., and Fopp, R. (1992), *Homelessness in Australia: Causes and Consequences*, CSIRO, Melbourne.

OECD, Group on Urban Affairs, Project Group on Urban Infrastructure Policies, (1990) *Financing and Managing Urban Infrastructure*, Draft Final Report, May, OECD, Paris.

Orchard, L, (1992), *A Blinkered Vision? The Emerging National Agenda for Australian Cities and Housing or Where's the Social Democratic Middle?*, Working Paper No.1, Planning Education Foundation of South Australia, University of South Australia, Adelaide.

Pender, H., and Ross, S. (1993), *Income Tax and Asset Choice in Australia*, Economic Planning and Advisory Council (EPAC), Research paper No.3, Canberra.

Raskall, P. and Urquhart, R. 'Inequality, Living Standards and the Social Wage during the 1980s', paper presented to the 4th Australisn Family Research confernce, Australian Institute of family studies, 19 Februarry 1993.

Smith, M.P. (1991), *City, State, and Market: The Political Economy of Urban Society*, Blackwell, Oxford.

Thompson, D and Tapper, A (1993), 'Meet the Luckies — and the Unluckies', *The Independent*, April, pp. 20-3.

Titmuss, R. (1974), 'The social division of welfare: some reflections on the search for equity', in R. Titmuss (ed), *Essays on The Welfare State*, Allen and Unwin, London, pp. 34–55.

Watts, R. (1993), 'Australian living standards: some gender considerations', *Australian Journal of Social Issues*, 28(1), pp. 1–19.

Yates, J., and Vipond, J.(1991), 'Housing and urban inequalities', in J. O'Leary, and R. Sharp (eds), *Inequality in Australia: Slicing the cake*, Heinemann, Melbourne, pp. 234–57.

Yates, J., (1991), *Australia's Owner-Occupied Housing Wealth and its Impact on Income Distribution*, SPRC Reports and Proceedings No.92, Social Policy Research Centre, University of NSW, Kensington.

Yates, J., (1992), 'Imputed Income and Income Distribution', in Phil Raskall and Peter Saunders (eds), *Economic Inequality in Australia*, Volume 2, Social Policy Research Centre, University of NSW, Kensington, pp. 111–31.

CHAPTER TEN

DIS/CLAIMING CITIZENSHIP?

Social rights, social justice and welfare in the 1990s

MICHAEL WEARING

INTRODUCTION

The concept of a citizen is that of a person who can hold his head up high and participate fully and with dignity in the life of his or her society.

(King and Walden, 1988:443)

Part of the intellectual history of social policy analysis is the use of normative principles and ideas to generate debate on the development of welfare states. One such principle is the ideal of social citizenship or the maximisation of social rights to protect and promote the welfare of disadvantaged and marginal groups. This chapter uses the ideal of social citizenship within broad debates about citizenship theory to discuss strategic and material shifts in current welfare arrangements in Australia. The specific argument is that a transition has occurred in the liberal ideal of citizenship in the Australian welfare state from a state-based to market-based approach (cf. Yeatman, 1989). The historical and intellectual antecedents to this transition emerge from changes in the structures and processes that constitute 'citizenship' in English speaking welfare states.

In pre-capitalist societies the notion of a 'citizen' was someone who lived within the walls of the city and subjects lived outside the city. The citizen of the pre-modern city was entitled to the rights and benefits that the city offered under protection of a sovereign. Citizenship within the city made people 'civilised' and enabled them to more fully participate in public life. The boundaries of citizenship today extend to national territories and beyond nation-state interests. Twentieth century writers in the British social administration tradition such as T. H. Marshall and R. M. Titmuss promoted a societal model of citizenship that emphasised the provision of universal social welfare benefits to all citizens. In accordance with this tradition, to claim citizenship in advanced capitalist societies is, at least in part, to make claims for universal social rights. These included core social rights such as the right to work, the right to education and the right to a minimum standard of living.

According to Marshall's 1950 essay, welfare states structure their rights in a class system where citizenship rights challenge the accepted status hierarchy of market economies: 'citizenship is a status bestowed on those who are full members of the community' (1963:92–3). This positive view of citizenship is enshrined in the liberal egalitarian and socialist principles of reform of social democratic movements and parties. Marshall developed an evolutionary schema of citizenship that paralleled the rise of capitalist economies over the last two and half centuries. In his schema, the structure of modern social rights evolved from the establishment of basic civil and then political rights. Marshall's schema explained a basic contradiction within welfare capitalism between egalitarian socio-political rights and the persistence of social and economic inequality. Nevertheless, the development of citizenship differs across advanced welfare states and there is little unitary character across these countries (Turner, 1990:201). Recent empirical accounts suggest that Australia's welfare state might best fit between the passive democracy of England and the liberal pluralism of the United States (Esping-Andersen, 1990). The nation-specific histories and political cultures of citizenship indicate the status conferred on social groups by a group's access to social rights and privilege in a society. Citizenship is thus understood as the enhancement of social power across a range of status groups that include dimensions of gender, age and ethnicity.

Liberal political discourse on citizenship in pre-modern and modern society has always emphasised the exclusion and control of marginal groups. One key element of both classical and liberal interpretations of citizenship is the minimisation of social rights for the disadvantaged and dispossessed and maximisation of social rights for the affluent. Ancient Greek (Plato) to Lockian (Locke, 1965) interpretations of citizenship have emphasised that it is the well-off and not the dispossessed who are 'citizens' and, thus, have access to liberty and property rights. Modern democracies are founded on this exclusionist idea of citizenship.

The liberal idea of citizenship is viewed in this essay as justification for the pursuit of greater economic equity using social welfare institutions whether market or state oriented. The economic liberalism of political discourse on Australian welfare in the 1990s applies market principles to welfare provision to promote privileged access to social rights. It is only those with the privileged status of their education, inheritance and class that can claim to have attained social and civil citizenship in an unequal society such as Australia. In the Australian welfare state the marginal and dispossessed must claim social rights, such as the right to work or the right to a decent standard of living, from market, state or familial resources. For any group or class to make these claims is to argue and negotiate from within the politics of social policy conceived, as Titmuss (1974:31) did, as 'the command over resources through time'.

Certain questions about the way welfare policy rhetoric 'speaks' for these status claims is addressed in the next section. The arguments developed there focus on the significance of social justice rhetoric and the exclusionary nature of welfare policy in the 1990s. The review, later in this chapter, of social justice rhetoric evident in political–administrative and professional forms of community management, provides an insight into the agenda for social justice, social rights and welfare in the 1990s. Foucault's (1982) work reminds us that it is not so much what is said but what this discourse covers up and thus what is not said that excludes people from social participation. The control of the discourse on social justice and social rights in Australia in the 1990s excludes certain citizens from social politics.

Citizens' claims and welfare development

Recent literature tends to over-emphasise the theoretical and political significance of citizenship in Australian welfare politics (see for example MacIntyre, 1985). That the tradition has minor relevance in Australia's political past does not deny the strategic or theoretical value of citizenship theories in contemporary welfare debate. The literature indicates that citizenship in modern market economies has undergone transformation and evolution since Marshall's essay. Barbalett (1988:22–8), for example, argues that Marshall gave scant regard to the development of industrial citizenship in his evolutionary scheme. Barbalett's argument is that industrial citizenship has formed a cornerstone for the establishment and protection of social and industrial rights in many welfare states. The overlaps between industrial and social citizenship are particularly strong in the Australian welfare state with notions of social security tied heavily to industrial awards and adequate living standards for wage earners. One commentator has coined the term the 'wage-earners' welfare state' (Castles, 1985) to describe the development of Australian welfare this century and this term conveys the sense of industrial-welfare overlap.

Following Turner's framework (1990), Australia is a passive liberal democracy whose citizens en masse have remained a passive voice in the protection and promotion of their social rights and welfare needs. Australian citizens rely on the political-administrative system to process and structure their citizenship claims. In welfare terms this system includes, amongst others, government and non-government agencies, politicians, senior bureaucrats and other public servants, professionals and the media. Such a weak connection between civil wants and political life has required the representation of key actors of labour (unions) and capital (business interests) mediated by state agencies to judge citizenship claims in specific periods. Under Federal Labor's Accord agreements during the 1980s and early 1990s Australians were subject to consensus-building politics known in social science terms as neo-corporatism. These agreements effectively maintained the notion that social welfare in Australia was primarily for the wage earner in the form of social wage benefits such as superannuation and child care.

At the other end of the social scale in the social welfare system in Australia, low-income people were maintained through minimum income standards and more restricted social wage benefits mostly by way of state welfare such as social security payments. This restricted part of the welfare safety net caters for non-working people in the form of social security benefits and other social assistance payments in financial emergencies. The primary instrument for the protection and promotion of social rights outside the wage labour system in Australia has been state welfare provision. Historically, the state has also secured industrial rights such as the right to strike, whereby the state mediated between the claims of labour and the interests of business and employer groups.

Like the concept of need, the concept of rights can be seen as a central political idea of the modern welfare state. In the language of twentieth century citizenship, social rights such as the right to work or the right to social security are synonymous with 'welfare rights' arguments. Negative appraisals of the modern welfare state have broken this uncritical acceptance of social welfare institutions as foremost in the promotion of social and economic rights. These appraisals are evident in Left and Right critique and arguments on welfare (for a full discussion see Offe, 1984; King and Walden, 1988). King and Walden (1988) contend that the pursuit of universal rights of citizenship is only partly guaranteed by social welfare provisions. Several questions are raised by such criticisms for the Australian welfare state. First, does a liberal theory of citizenship best portray the political-strategic agenda of the Australian welfare state? Second, what theory of citizenship, if any, would preserve and encourage meaningful strategies of social justice, the political participation of marginal groups, and the pursuit of social equality? Finally, which social groups and social movements should or could promote an agenda of equality and social justice in the Australian welfare state? Some possible answers to these questions are suggested towards the end of this chapter.

Social citizenship, as one dimension of liberalism, is particularly vulnerable to ideological attack from the Right. This vulnerability was evident in the party political platforms of conservatism in Britain and the United States during the 1980s. These platforms have emphasised a 'law and order' welfare state and the 'privatisation' of welfare services (Ferris, 1986; King, 1987). Extensive use of administrative targeting and means-testing of poor people in the Australian welfare state during the 1980s under the Federal Labor Government narrowed welfare concerns to the targeting of marginal groups (Watts, 1989). If we accept the argument that universalist welfare provisions promote greater equality, the provision of these selective and residual benefits and services indicate that the strategy of equality via welfare is in demise in the 1990s.

The demise of social citizenship in Australia

The demise of social citizenship began bilaterally in mainstream Federal party politics in Australia during the Fraser Liberal-National Party Government (1975–83) and the Hawke Labor Government (1983–1991). This process of erosion has occurred despite selected adherence to the ideal of social citizenship at the administrative and research levels of social welfare in Australia. As chapter 4 in this book points out, the Whitlam Labor Government's (1972–75) rhetoric on welfare was only marginally more committed to collective and universal polices than those of the Fraser and Hawke era. The forces responsible for the transformation of Australian citizenship are linked to the higher echelons of the Federal Public Service who have embraced a paradigm for policy change based on the crude assumptions and ideology of classical economics and its modern counterpart, economic rationalism (Pusey, 1991). This 'new' economic paradigm for government can be counterposed to the dominant paradigm of the 1940s and 1950s of postwar Keynesian intervention (see chapter 3 in this book). During the 1980s state welfare policy was subject to harsh and mean-minded economic analysis with an emphasis on technical rationales for cost cutting in policies and programs.

TABLE 10.1

Gross household income 1974–75 to 1988–89, proportion of total income 1988–89 and proportion of household's family composition (Quintile – 20% shares), Australia

	Household Income Shares	
	Lowest 20%	Highest 20%
Proportion (%) of total income for:		
1974–75	5.5	39.2
1975–76	5.2	40.0
1983–84	5.1	42.2
1988–89	4.4	42.3
88–89 Proportion (%) of total income being:		
Wages and salaries	6.2	78.9
Own business	-3.8	11.4
Govt pension & benefits	83.5	1.4
Other	14.1	8.3
Total	100.0	100.0
88–89 proportion (%) of households with family composition of household being:		
Married couple only	24.4	20.9
With dependent children only	6.7	32.2
Other (includes non-dependent children)	0.8	31.5
Single parent one family household	9.8	0.7
Single person household	55.4	2.0
Other (includes multi-families)	2.9	12.7
Total	100.0	100.0

Source: Raskall (1991):14
    Australian Bureau of Statistics (1990) *Household Expenditure survey, Australia Detailed Expenditure items*: 4

TABLE 10.2

Average total weekly personal income (1) and private income (2) by area, occupational status, ethnicity and gender, 1988–89, Australia.

			Average total weekly pesonal income ($/individual)	Average total weekly private income ($/individual)
AREA (*)	1.	Capital city	247	225
	2.	Other urban	206	179
	3.	Rural	183	162
OCCUPATIONAL STATUS (*) (3)	1.	White collar	473	388
	2.	Blue collar	467	383
ETHNICITY (*)	1.	English speaking country of birth	307	277
	2.	Non-English speaking country of birth	280	249
GENDER (*)	1.	Female	137	–
	2.	Male	277	–

Key
1. 'Personal income' = gross income from all sources
2. 'Private income' = gross income minus government benefitrs
3. 'White collar' = summated categories:professionals, paraprofessionals, managers, clerks, salespersons and service personnel
   'Blue collar' = summated categories: labourers, plant operators, tradespersons

* All within group differences are significant (P<0.001)

Source: Australian Bureau of Statistics (1990), *1988–89 Household Expenditure Survey,* unit record file data

The changing structure of inequality can be illustrated using income distribution data. Tables 10.1 and 10.2 illustrate the income distribution in Australia during the 1970s and 1980s. Table 10.1 gives the changes from 1974–75 to 1988–9 in the proportion of total income for the lowest and highest quintile income groups in Australian households. Over this period, the household income share went up slightly for the highest income group while it went down for the lowest income group. The Federal Labor Government's policies of the 1980s are implicated in the creation of greater inequality in Australian society. This is perhaps a cruel irony given the traditional commitment of the Australian Labor Party (ALP) to principles of equity and equality. The major finding from this data is that income inequality has increased amongst households (defined as people sharing cooking facilities) during the 1980s (Raskall, 1991:12–14). Further, the quintile share of income for single parents and government beneficiaries and pensioners indicates the depth of income poverty these groups experienced by the end of the 1980s.

The evidence suggests that inequality has increased over this period partly as a result of the emphasis on selective programs and partly over a failure to attack those market mechanisms that restore and promote privilege to affluent groups and classes. An avowedly democratic socialist party, the Australian Labor Party, has not created policies that have promoted equality. During the longest period of Labor Party rule in Australia (1983–93), income inequality has increased substantially. Households with the lowest 20 per cent of income earners received only 5.1 per cent of total income in 1983–84 and 4.4 per cent of total income in 1988–9 (See table 10.1; Raskall, 1991:13). Other writers advance the view that is increasingly seen as political commonsense that the market should decide issues of public policy within both Liberal-National and Labor Party policy (Connell, 1991:131).

Table 10. 2 gives the average personal (individual income from all sources with no tax deducted) and private (income from all sources minus government benefits) weekly incomes of select social groupings in Australia in 1988–89. Several social and spatial factors are associated with the level of this income including area, occupational status, ethnicity and gender. These factors are major determinants of levels of income for individuals and households. The area variable shows significant differences in levels of weekly income across capital cities, other urban areas and rural areas. The variables of occupational status, ethnicity and gender further demonstrate that white-collar English speaking urban males are better off than other social groups in both personal and private income. Table 10.2 also shows that government cash benefits make little difference to the income disparities between groups.

What do these differences in socially produced income mean? Statistically, they illustrate the point that incomes as an indicator of social power are different for different socio-economic and status groups. Income is defined as an indicator of 'power of command over economic resources backed by property rights' (Raskall, 1991:6), a definition similar to that of Titmuss (1974: 31) of social policy as 'the command-over-resources through time'. This orientation towards a social understanding of income enables the development of the concept of welfare as socially produced. Income is produced by the mix of social groupings and social forces in society. The capacity of social groups to pay for and consume goods and services including welfare services (in Weber's terms their 'market capacity' or class position) is structured by social relations in the first instance. Levels of personal income in this sense are not simply a function of the economic value of an individual's skill or an individual's merits.

The distribution of status and assets in Australian society is partly shaped by the historical and political development of welfare policy as a key aspect of public policy. The differential access to and production of income by social groups in Australia illustrates the salience of forces of class, race and gender. Income and wealth distribution indicate the outcomes of class power and other status distributions. Recently, Bryson (1992) has indicated the significance of gender in the distribution of welfare in advanced welfare states arguing that the modern welfare state differentially advantages men over women (see also Bryson, chapter 11 in this book). Hammer (1990) has argued that in liberal democracies citizenship has allied with nationalism to exclude migrants and indigenous people from the political sovereignty of nation states. In other words, when national interests are used to exclude migrant groups then privileged access of the dominant racial group (e.g. Anglo-Saxon) to the distribution of citizenship is assured.

Economising the discourse on social justice

The following discussion outlines six distinct discourses or models on social justice extant in Australian welfare services. These models of social justice were articulated by government departments and non-government welfare bodies. In combination they provide a framework for understanding the possible directions of service policy in Australia during the 1990s. As formalised discourse, their conceptions are sometimes inconsistent and also make competing claims about the distributive imperatives for community services, and social rights of community service recipients. As Bryson (1992:30) points out discourses have the power to construct the reality of social welfare and service provision. In so doing, service provision discourse can obscure the political struggles of ordinary people for claims to social citizenship and an equitable share of welfare state resources.

These social justice models organise the way professionals and administrators think about issues of social justice such as equity, access and participation in Australian welfare services. Other writers (Offe, 1984:112–14) have described the social basis for such models as the 'scientization of politics'. In the implementation of services the models are rationalisation strategies that enable the management of service-dependent populations. Such models attempt to include or exclude social groups from citizenship, i.e. they disclaim citizenship through the legitimation of only certain specific and selective claims to welfare services. They are essentially 'managerial' in that their frames of meaning are both professionally and technocratically oriented towards the smooth functioning of a market economy. In this sense their discourse economises our views of social justice.

The first model economises national social justice, in that justice is contingent upon economic growth or economic decline and the nation's general economic performance. It is based on the Labor view that promotes the idea of social justice arising as an appendage to, or in the wake of, a nation's economy. The rhetoric of Federal Labor Party policy from the 1980s illustrates the economistic view of social justice:

> Social justice requires equal opportunities for all … [The Labor Party] is committed to making social justice both a primary goal of economic policy and an indispensable element in achieving economic objectives. As Australia enters the 1990s with economic policies starting to bear fruit, the Government is committed to continuing and sharpening its social justice strategy — drawing in particular on the findings of the Social Security Review.
>
> (Commonwealth of Australia, 1988: x–xi)

It was never made clear within these general statements on justice how further equality and opportunity would be pursued by Labor. The economic rationalist and economic liberal views of this Labor Government are well documented elsewhere (Pusey, 1992; Jamrozik, 1991; Battin, 1991; Beilharz et al, 1992). The 'new' Laborist doctrine of social justice subsumed social objectives under those of economic ones.

This national economistic discourse is continued in more recent statements by Federal Labor on urban infrastructure. The 1992 Federal Government Budget foreshadowed capital funding for urban infrastructure in a number of States including New South Wales. In 1992, four project grants totalling 240 million dollars were made to New South Wales for better roads, water supply and waterfront restoration. Even left-faction Federal Labor Ministers such as the Deputy Prime Minister Brian Howe have embraced the arguments of the economic rationalists:

> *It is impossible to address distributional issues within cities without addressing the need to enhance the productive capacity of those cities. After all cities only exist because they are the centre of economic activity [author's emphasis].*
>
> (Howe, 1991:37).

This rhetoric of equity and economic productivity conceals the political and economic reasons for Federal and State government sponsorship of 'Mega-Projects' for infrastructure development in urban regions. A key economic reason is that these projects are designed to pump prime urban economies left in a vacuum by the property investment busts of the late 1980s (Berry and Huxley, 1992:46–7). Another reason could be to place a 'human face' on the cost-cutting, running down and privatisation of Government infrastructure that occurred through the 1980s.

The second model of justice advances the idea that access, equity and participation in welfare services are determined by spatial density. The discourse is reflected in the current ideology of 'urban consolidation' in the planning of Australian cities. Urban consolidation as a major strategy of State and Federal Governments during the 1980s was designed to save costs on social infrastructure on the fringe of cities by utilising space and services in inner-city areas. A recent House of Representative Standing Committee Report has criticised the notion of the 'compact city' as not realising the true extent of socio-demographic and environmental changes in Australian cities. Nonetheless, the Report still emphasises the Labor view of social justice and a more limited acceptance of the urban density model:

> *Urban consolidation is a useful but limited program which must operate along with other policies and programs if governments are to reduce undesirable effects of urbanisation while retaining the benefits. The capacity of urban consolidation to save space and thus enhance economic, environmental and social benefits is limited …*

(The Parliament of the Commonwealth of Australia [TPCA], 1992:xii)

This more limited acceptance of the urban density model sets up a further strategy of reclaiming social welfare infrastructure as intrinsically of economic benefit:

Community Services like health, education and public transport can ... be seen as contributing to the productive capacity of the economy: a society which suffers excessive productivity losses through illness, lack of work force skills or absenteeism is not getting the most out of human resources.

(TPCA, 1992: xviii)

The strategy reiterates the Labor's social justice model of service provision as an appendage to the crucial goal of 'productivity' and economic growth.

The third model associates justice with the proper functioning of quasi-markets for minority or differentiated social groups. These markets, whether imagined or real, are the new audience for this discourse on service provision. Service users can expect to pay for the services if they have the resources in private wage or social wage income. In order for many service dependent groups to pay, they require integration (normalisation) into the labour market. This discourse makes social justice contingent upon a quasi-market, operationalised in political-administrative documentation. The discourse is illustrated by official rhetoric in the area of disability (see also Fulcher ,1989). A central component of the model is the idea of integration through community participation:

Community participation is also about integration. This involves having opportunities to have ordinary, everyday relationships with neighbours, friends and other members of the community ... It involves being a part of, and not set apart from the local community.

(NSW Dept. of Family and Community Services FACS, 1990:23)

This idea of integration commonly means the person with the disability is exposed to exploitation of their labour in non-unionised and lowly paid work (though official Commonwealth policy on people with disabilities asserts they are paid 'award' wages).

While the barriers to paid work for people with disabilities are acknowledged in this model, the imperative is towards competition with people without a disability:

Paid employment means having access to real work for real pay which recognises and rewards the skills we bring to bear; provides job security and opportunities for challenging jobs or moving onto more challenging work: develops the work to perform the tasks for which we are paid: and develops the social skills needed to establish and maintain work relationships.

(FACS, 1990:24–5)

People with disabilities are positioned by this discourse within a quasi-market whose operation relies on labour at a proportion of real wages and disciplines the person to comply with poor work conditions. This trend towards integration into the market economy through participation in the labour market is an emerging 'work ethic' for people with disabilities in English-speaking countries (Oliver, 1990).

The fourth model of social justice in service provision is a democratising view of 'community development'. This model is a form of community management that deals with access, equity and participation within a framework of participatory democracy for local communities and cultures in service programs. It is a model more associated with peak non-government welfare bodies and small government funded welfare agencies. A useful illustration of the model is in migrant services and the various programs and policies developed to promote social justice for migrants especially around issues of access to services:

> MAPS (*Migrant Access Projects Scheme — a Commonwealth funded scheme since 1989) incorporates a community development philosophy — local networks and local skills are developed and used to increase migrant access to general services. It is based on the very ambitious belief that by funding community organisations for a short period, enough commitment and work can be generated to initiate change for the better in terms of migrant access to services.*
>
> (Morehead, 1992: 32)

This model can be located in the more general one of local democratic politics based on the promotion of social rights:

> *Service providers should recognise the democratic rights to self determination for all residents, and their mutual interests in pluralist society, including the rights of minority groups and organisations to maintain and serve the special interests of their group.*
>
> (Mitchell, 1992:17)

Despite its intent, this democratising model neglects some of the exclusionist practices of its own making. These practices include the use of non-migrant labour in community development ignoring the adverse reaction migrant groups might have to professional (largely Anglo) service providers. The model constructs the other, in this case 'the migrant', as in need of governance by service providers. The need for access is a social construction that obscures the quality of the service delivered, the efficiency with which it is delivered and the cost of labour (professional or otherwise) involved.

The fifth model, related to the fourth, is the discourse on local/decentralised social justice. This model promotes the principles of access, equity and participation at a local level with services resourced by state welfare planning and funding. The discourse is a composite of the previous four and is grounded in specific strategies of urban planning for social policy. It includes discussion of issues of funding and management of programs and services as well as the values and principles that might underlie service delivery. This style of managerialist decentralisation has been a feature of Western European and Australian welfare development throughout the 1980s in areas such as health care, community care and education (Taylor-Gooby and Lawson, 1993).

Housing is a specific example of the impact of this kind of model on urban planning. Localised social justice includes the principle of housing equity and yet remains ignorant of the winners in the housing market (cf. Dalton, 1991, see also Mowbray, chapter 9 in this book). As with other areas of social policy, the focus on poverty neglects the localities of lived communities, the inequalities in housing and those who benefit from home ownership. Urban localities suffering hard financial times through recession are seen by state welfare planners as 'damaged' communities with the people of those suburbs needing work incentives (e.g. programs such as NEWSTART, for the long-term unemployed) and relocation to other localities if necessary.

These issues are illustrated in recent statements on urban social justice especially in the area of housing:

> It is possible. Indeed there is potential for much to be gained by the encouragement of more efficient management and pricing policies in urban planning and development.
>
> Inadequate accounting in the past has led to substantial subsidies to home buyers in new urban development, irrespective of their income, the value of their land, or the size of their block. Over the past few years these subsidies have been flowing to predominantly medium to high income households who are not first home buyers, and who are in no great need of assistance.
>
> (Lang, 1991:6–7)

These redistributive arguments for adjusting accounting procedures are laudable. Nevertheless, the use to which suggested financial gains might be put indicate a return to residualist and minimal social citizenship for renters;

> The use of this type of financing for social infrastructure should not be used to replace existing public funding which can be distributed more effectively to those in greatest need.
>
> (Lang, 1991:7)

The Labor discourse of social justice is reproduced in the language of a 'new' local politics and managerialism. Again, economic objectives subsume social objectives:

It ... is possible for social justice objectives to parallel efficiency objectives. If this does not occur, the social costs to individuals and families of poorly planned urban development and redevelopment will in the end be borne by the whole community as has been proven time and again in the past.

(Lang, 1991: 8)

This local justice strategy reflects current thinking, at a non-government and small agency level, on the local politics of service provision.

The final model relates the 'accountability' of access and equity in welfare services to social justice rhetoric at a Federal level. This model is located within a broader debate on the measurement of social justice outcomes in order to manage services more efficiently. The overriding aim of public service initiatives in the area is to develop an efficient management culture. The recent evaluation of Federal Labor's 1986–92 Access and Equity Strategy illustrate this managerialism:

The core of the Access and Equity Strategy has been a set of formal requirements to guide government departments in adjusting their programs and services to ensure that clients who may face barriers of language, culture, race or religion get equitable access to their entitlements. The strategy has also been about a way of thinking and managing - about a management culture.

(Dept of Prime Minister and Cabinet, 1992: ix)

This management culture is a new form of technocratic managerialism i.e. technical and professional experts are used to consult on the outcomes and effectiveness of programs implemented under the strategy.

Such forms of management in social welfare services mean that government and non-government welfare organisations adhere to particular frames of meaning on accountability and effectiveness issues within their management structures. Programs and policies are evaluated by those trained in scientific methods and, more specifically, in the social sciences (Spybey, 1984). Within the managerial frames of meaning imposed by these evaluations notions of access, equity and participation are commonly narrowed to their economic and legislative dimensions. Economic and legal reforms come to the fore when questions of social reform based on effectiveness and efficiency in welfare services are considered. The narrowness of these reforms ensures the selective gaze of the administration on target population groups in social policy. The administrative, bureaucratic and political definition of social policy is therefore narrowed from a social policy concerned with the welfare of all Australians to that of targeted dependent populations (cf. Bryson, 1992).

Certain questions about social justice and social welfare programs are raised by these models. What social change is effected by the political-administrative discourse of the models? How do these models or discourses manage the actions and behaviours of groups and classes in local communities? Does this set of discourses exclude poor people and other marginal people from social participation? A framework that can conceive answers to these questions would provide a critical understanding of the politics of welfare services. The models have been analysed from the perspective that their discourse is about the formal management of social groups and classes in Australia.

It is important to address what the nature of welfare politics will be within global or national strategies for social and economic change. There is a need to understand collective identity in urban and regional areas as part of a new international order where processes of localisation of services are subsumed under the global restructuring of capital and labour, and the erosion of self-determination for nation states. The core urban centres of Australia (such as Sydney, Melbourne, Brisbane, Perth and Adelaide) have uncoupled themselves from national development and are immersed in the 'competitive dynamics of deregulated environment in aviation, telecommunications and other areas' (Yeatman 1992:452). This shift from welfare state to the competitive 'urban' state has led writers on citizenship (Held, 1991; Lister 1991; Yeatman, 1992) to contend that local democratic politics should be neither state or market oriented. This local welfare politics should be 'open to organisations, associations and agencies pursuing their own projects, subject to the constraints of a common structure of action and democratic process' (Held, 1991:166).

Such a style of politics does not preclude several of the social justice models discussed above. However, this conception of local democratic politics divorces social welfare strategies from state or market-centred views of social policy. Once this divorce occurs, the reform of welfare policy can be separated out from the universal welfare values of the post Second World War period (Turner, 1990: 194–5). This revision of welfare politics suggests that a more selective approach to service delivery may be necessary with an emphasis on the promotion of equality and a respect for differential needs of social groups.

An initial strategic step towards new forms of social justice for differentiated groups would be to rethink the principles of equity, access and participation, that is, to rethink the basic principles of social justice especially as they enhance or maximise social citizenship for welfare recipients. Equity rather than equality could become, for example, the focus of identity politics in welfare services. According to Yeatman (1992:459), using the value of equity rather than that of equality as a principle for social justice would permit variations in what is justly due according to the needs of differentially positioned groups. Access to and participation in service delivery might then be contingent on the claims to citizenship and social justice that a group can articulate within a common identity. It should be borne in mind that this is not a 'just deserts' view of service provision where only the 'deserving' are provided for in residualist services. The view relies on the judgments of members of an identity group who are able to organise their citizenship claims with a degree of autonomy from state or market agencies.

Social struggles, social participation and citizens' rights

What theory of citizenship could encourage meaningful strategies of social justice, political participation and the pursuit of social equality? Some of the debate around this question will be addressed in the following section. Critics of the bureaucratic and class-based nature of the welfare state have highlighted anti-democratic elements in liberal citizenship theory. They have recast some of the debate on citizenship either arguing for the participatory space for oppressed groups created by New Social Movements (NSMs) between market and state (Habermas, 1981; MacIntyre, 1985; Keane, 1988, 1989; Oliver, 1990) or for the evolution of democratised spaces in struggles beyond class-based politics (Turner,1986; Pixley, 1993). Both sets of arguments develop more limited evolutionary views of citizenship than Marshall's and promote the dissident politics of NSMs of race, ecology and gender. The problem is that NSMs do not necessarily guarantee the social rights or welfare resources of heterogeneous social groups and populations. Further, 'democratisation' of social policies, say for women, do not guarantee citizenship for migrant or disabled women. In other words, democratic social spaces are not necessarily created equally in the formation of political projects of NSMs.

One reason for lack of social participation by social groups is the differential access to welfare/market benefits and services for select group membership. Difficult social questions are raised in the shaping of resource distribution in Australian welfare services when there is uncertainty over political identity. For example, does child care for 'middle class' welfare consumers — middle class women in particular — enable their participation in paid work over that of women and men in the working class? Does publicly funded tertiary education facilitate the access of Anglo-English speaking students at the expense of students with Non-English speaking and migrant backgrounds? The narrowness of much of the welfare debate, especially that on social justice as described above, means that definitions of policy are confined to single issue or benefit dependent groups such as single parents and the unemployed, with little comparison with the affluent and better off. The analysis of welfare issues in key social movements tend to base views on welfare policy within the narrow definitions of government policy. As a result, the values and ideas these movements articulate, exclude the interdependence of class, race and gender issues.

Evidence suggests that social movements do not have to be class-based or ethnically based to bring about historical change and social conflict (Pakulski, 1991: 179). Nonetheless, translating a NSMs' strategies into policy discourse cannot help excluding those who are not participants in or cannot identify with such movements. Feminists (Mitchell, 1986; Yeatman, 1990) and radical critiques of welfare provision based on the idea of citizenship (Taylor, 1989; Lister, 1990) have warned of the exclusionist and sometimes elitist nature of political thinking in NSMs on welfare policy. The political viability of NSMs is not at question here. The problem of exclusion in NSMs merely signals a warning against the neglect of socioeconomic and structural constraints placed on social activism and strategies of meaningful change in Australia.

Citizenship theory may be used as political argument in a number of ways. Commentators have used the term: to argue against market criteria in welfare (Marshall, 1963); as compatible with the emergence of the modern welfare rights of inclusion and social action (Turner, 1986); or as an argument for participation in public life (Yeatman, 1989). Only some of the processes of exclusion from social resources are conceived in these interpretations. A more fruitful strategic argument of NSMs and welfare activists in Australia would be to re-establish citizenship in their own terms and not those set by governments. As Lister (1991:69) demonstrates in her critique of the gender-blind nature of citizenship theory, only privileged social groups articulate or have access to major political and administrative decision-making arenas. In households, the informal and voluntary sectors, as in the rest of the welfare state, it is men (primarily Anglo-Saxon middle class men) who benefit the most from existing social and economic policies targeted at households.

Liberal citizenship theory has contributed through the ideas of social liberalism, albeit in a minor way, to Australia's social development especially around the most interventionist periods of government in the 1900s, 1930s and first half of the 1970s. At best, the broad framework of liberal citizenship in Australia is confined to formal political-legal systems. Even these systems divorce citizens from assuming public responsibility in activities such as compulsory voting, compulsory naturalisation or compulsory work schemes for poor people and the unemployed. The strategic point of departure from this liberal-conservative notion is for NSMs to reinvent social conceptions of citizenship that include the marginal and the dispossessed in policy discourse.

To promote equality in Australian society a number of alternate political strategies and action on welfare development will be necessary in the present decade. One strategy could harness the power of political votes behind the strong public support for universalist social welfare policies evident in this country since the 1940s (Smith and Wearing, 1987; Papadakis, 1990). A further strategy that extends from the first, could mobilise public and political support for more generous welfare provisions. This mobilisation could find its most progressive and reflective proponents in the NSMs. Such movements are centrally involved in the transformation of mainstream political life in Australia whilst autonomous enough from state agencies to provided a reflexive space from oppression and control (cf Melucci, 1988).

In keeping with the work of others (cf. Habermas, 1981; Ferris, 1986; Melucci, 1988; Oliver, 1989; Lister, 1991; Pixley, 1993), conceptions of social citizenship and social equality can be revitalised within movements of race, gender, ecology, unemployment and people with disabilities. The political potential of such movements is illustrated by the ability of some social groups to command some resources and direct policies towards their social needs during the 1980s in Australia. For example, people with disabilities and gays and lesbians have established a strong resource base to lobby for their social needs through the provision of specific services and funding. Further, that these groups have established more participatory claims on state welfare resources in Australia testifies to a breaking up of the old polity of rigid class-based politics. In recent years the industrial labour movement in Australia (arguably an 'Old' Social Movement) has moved with the political claims of NSMs (Jennet and Stewart, 1989).

Despite these new insights into the politics of citizenship, the possible collapse of social citizenship as an ideal of social welfare institutions raises strategic problems for theories of citizenship and their uses in social struggles. At a political level, more radical and strategic views of social citizenship may offer some respite from the destructive actions of market and state. Citizenship theory may have an important positive role in marshalling counter-arguments to the Right's critiques of welfare.

The real strategic value of citizenship theory is to effect argument against residualism and, in core social welfare areas, against selectivism (cf Alcock, 1989). For example, the strategic view of social citizenship offers a basis for attacks on cutbacks in social security arrangements and other residual policies in Australia. The recent introduction of university fees and more stringent means testing of social security benefits, especially the unemployment benefit, illustrate Federal Labor's commitment to a guarded selectivism in some areas of welfare delivery. Citizenship theory may also have a strategic role in the empowerment of undervalued and marginal social groups in capitalist societies. Restructuring of welfare arrangements towards more equitable outcomes could begin by giving increased economic value to women's labour including domestic labour and child care (Lister, 1991) as well as to migrant's cultural, economic and social contributions to a society.

CONCLUSION

This chapter has suggested that the transition to a new order of Australian welfare in the 1990s requires practitioners in welfare services to diversify their policy strategies and seek participation from new collective identities. The transition to market citizenship supported by a political-administrative system and driven by economic liberalism in the Australian welfare state in the 1990s ensures the persistence of a strong alliance between party politics (Labor or Coalition Governments) and 'market forces' (read business and the better off). The principles of a universalist Keynesian welfare state that promoted some of the ideals of social citizenship have all but been abandoned in Australia during the late 1970s and through the 1980s. This transformation of social citizenship to a market-based and an individualistic enterprise approach to social welfare appears to signal an end to the postwar politics and strategies of universalism and social equality. As a rejoinder to this demise, rather than suggest that the ideal of social citizenship has been asked to do too much in the recent history of the Australian welfare state, its strategic value needs to be reharnessed and recovered in a new collectivist politics of welfare for the current anti-collectivist climate.

REFERENCES

Alcock, P. (1989), 'Why citizenship and welfare rights offer new hope for new welfare in Britain' *Critical Social Policy*, (26), pp. 32–43.
Barbalet, J. M. (1988), *Citizenship: Rights, Struggle and Class Inequality*, Open University Press, Milton Keynes.
Battin, T. (1991), 'What is this thing called economic rationalism', *Australian Journal of Social Issues*, 26(4), pp. 294–302.
Beilharz, P. Considine, M. and Watts, R. (1992), *Arguing About the Welfare State*, Allen and Unwin, Sydney.

Berry, M. and Huxley, M. (1992), 'Big build: property capital, the state and urban change in Australia', *International Journal of Urban and Regional Research*, 16(1), pp. 35–55

Bryson, L. (1992), *Welfare and the State: Who Benefits?*, Macmillan, London,

Castles, F. (1985), *The Working Class and Welfare*, Allen and Unwin, Sydney.

Commonwealth of Australia (1988), *Towards a Fairer Australia: Social Justice Under Labor*, AGPS, Canberra.

Connell, R. W. (1991), 'The money measure: social inequality of wealth and income' in J. O'Leary and R. Sharpe, *Inequality in Australia*, William Heinemann, Melbourne, pp. 129–49.

Dalton, T. (1991), 'Moving away from welfarist housing' in R. Batten, W. Weeks and J. Wilson (eds), *Issues facing Australian Families: Human Services Respond*, Longman Cheshire, Melbourne, pp. 105–117.

Department of Prime Minister and Cabinet (1992), *Access and Equity: Evaluation Report*, AGPS, Canberra.

Esping-Andersen, G (1990), *The Three Worlds of Welfare Capitalism*, Polity Press, Cambridge.

Ferris, J. (1986), 'Citizenship and the crisis of the welfare state', in P. Bean, J. Ferris and D. Whynes (eds), *In Defence of Welfare*, Tavistock, London, pp. 46–73.

Foucault, M. (1982), *The Archaeology of Knowledge*, Tavistock, London.

Fulcher, J. (1989), 'Disability: a social construction' in G. M. Lupton and J. Najman (eds), *Sociology of Health and Illness*, Macmillan, Melbourne, pp. 42–67.

Habermas, J. (1981) 'New social movements', *Telos* (49), pp. 33–7.

Hammer, T. (1990), *Democracy and the Nation State: Aliens, Denizens and Citizens in a World of International Migration*, Avebury, Aldershot.

Held, D. (1991) 'Democracy, the nation-state and the global system' *Economy and Society*, 20(2), pp. 138–172.

Howe, B. (1991) 'Better cities, better communities - social justice in the 1990s' in P. Raskall and P. Saunders (eds), *Economic Inequality in Australia, Vol 1, Government and Redistribution*, SSEI Monograph, Social Policy Research Centre, University of New South Wales, Kensington, pp. 35–9.

Jamrozik, A. (1991), *Class, Inequality and the State*, Macmillan, Melbourne.

Jennet, C., and Stewart, R. G. (eds)(1989), *Politics of the Future: The Role of Social Movements*, Macmillan, Melbourne.

Keane, J. (1988), *Civil Society and the State*, Verso, London.

King, D. (1987), *The New Right: Politics, Markets and Citizenship*, Macmillan, London.

King, D. and Waldren, J. (1988) 'Citizenship, social citizenship and the defence of welfare provision', *British Journal of Political Science*, (18), pp. 415–43.

Lang, J. (1991), 'Social justice and urban and regional development' in New South Wales Council of Social Services (eds), *Urban Development and Social Justice*, NCOSS, Sydney, pp. 3–9.

Lister, R. (1991), 'Citizenship engendered', *Critical Social Policy* 11(2), pp. 65–71.

Locke, J. (1965), *Locke on Politics, Religion and Education*, Collier, New York.

MacIntyre, S. (1985), *Winners and Losers*, Allen and Unwin, Sydney.

Marshall, T. H. (1963), 'Citizenship and social class' in T.H. Marshall (ed) *Sociology at the Crossroads and Other Essays*, Heinemann, London, pp. 67–127.

Melucci, A. (1988), 'Social movements and the democratisation of everyday life', in D. Keane (ed.) *Civil Society and the State*, Verso, London, pp. 245–60.

Mitchell. M. (1992), 'Improving service delivery to migrants' in Australian Council of Social Service(ed), *Improving Service Delivery to Migrants: the Role of Community Development*, 1992 Conference Proceedings, ACOSS Sydney, pp. 12–17.

Morehead, A. (1992), ' Strategies to improve migrant access to services: findings from the ACOSS evaluation of MAPS' in Australian Council of Social Service(eds), *Improving Service Delivery to Migrants: the Role of Community Development*, 1992 Conference Proceedings, ACOSS Sydney, pp. 32–42.

New South Wales Department of Family and Community Services (1990), *Disability Services: A Focus On Outcomes*, FACS, Sydney.

Offe, C. (1984), *Contradictions of the Welfare State*, Hutchinson, London.

Oliver. M. (1990), *The Politics of Disablement*, Macmillan, London.

Pakulski, J. (1991), *Social Movements: The Politics of Moral Protest*, Longman Cheshire, Melbourne.

Papadakis, E. (1990), *Attitudes to State and Private Welfare: Analysis of Results From a National Survey* Social Policy Research Centre Reports and Proceedings, No 88, SPRC, University of New South Wales, Kensington.

Pixley, J. (1993), *Citizenship and Employment*, Cambridge University Press, Cambridge.

Raskall, P. (1991), 'Inequality in Australia — what we know and what we don't' in P. Raskall and P. Saunders (eds), *Economic Inequality in Australia, Vol 1, Government and Redistribution*, Social Policy Research Centre SSEI Monograph, University of New South Wales, Kensington pp. 1–34.

Pusey, M (1991), *Economic Rationalism in Canberra: a Nation-Building State Changes Its Mind*, Cambridge University Press, Cambridge.

Smith, R. and Wearing, M. (1987), 'Do Australians want the welfare state?' *Politics* (22), pp. 255–65.

Spybey, T. (1984), 'Traditional and professional frames of meaning in management', *Sociology* (18), pp. 550–62.

Taylor, D. (1989), Citizenship and Power, *Critical Social Policy* (26), pp. 19-31.

Taylor-Gooby, P., and Lawson, R. (eds)(1993), *Markets and Managers: New Issues in the Delivery of Welfare*, Open University Press, Milton Keynes.

The Parliament of the Commonwealth of Australia. (1992), *Patterns of Urban Settlement: Consolidating The Future*, AGPS, Canberra.

Titmuss, R. M. (1974), *Social Policy: An Introduction*, Allen and Unwin, London.

Turner , B. (1986), *Citizenship and Capitalism*, Allen and Unwin, London.

Turner, B. (1990), 'Outline of a theory of citizenship', *Sociology* (24), pp. 189–217.

Watts, R. (1989), 'In fractured times: the Accord and social policy under Hawke, 1983-87', in R. Kennedy (ed.), *Australian Welfare*, Macmillan, Melbourne, pp. 104-31.

Weber, M. (1978), *Economy and Society*, University of California Press, California.

Yeatman, A. (1989), *Femocrats, Bureaucrats and Technocrats*, Allen and Unwin, Sydney.

Yeatman, A. (1992), 'Women's citizenship claims, labour market policy and globalisation', *Australian Journal of Political Science*, (29), pp. 449–61.

CHAPTER ELEVEN

THE CHANGING SHAPE OF GENDER DIS/ADVANTAGE IN AUSTRALIA

LOIS BRYSON

INTRODUCTION

The pattern of women's lives has traditionally been different from that of men's and it is has been well documented that women have been disadvantaged, in terms of access to economic resources, social status and power. Nonetheless, over recent decades the demands of women for greater equality have been put into effect in a variety of ways and there are recognisable changes. These changes and their effects on gender equality within the contemporary welfare state are the focus of this chapter.

Setting the scene

When we come to consider social policies we find that most have had a clear gender sub-text so that in effect it can be claimed that there have been two intersecting welfare states, one relating to women and another to men (Bryson, 1992). Despite this obvious dualism within social policy and state activity, this is rarely given adequate recognition, and is frequently ignored, in academic analyses except for the work of feminist writers. A study by Anne Edwards (1992) of a range of apparently 'mainstream' texts on the welfare state, written over the last ten years or so, has demonstrated how little attention they pay to gender issues or even to women as a category of the population.

Of fundamental importance to the shape of the dual welfare states are the economic and employment systems which have been highly gendered and remain so despite signs of change. The labour movement's achievement of the regulation of employment through the setting of hours and conditions of work and rates of pay, has revolved around a male worker. Those active industrial relations processes, from both union and employer bodies have been almost entirely masculine. Also, as the work of Ryan and Conlon has graphically demonstrated, focus on the interests of male workers cannot be merely attributed to unreflective attitudes and behaviour, important though these factors have been. Male workers also acted in concert to preserve their advantages from the potential competition of female workers. Early this century, women were explicitly excluded from many occupations, particularly a range of trades. They were also restricted in their participation in others through, for example, bans on night work and a bar on the employment of married women, which in the Victorian Public Service was revoked only as recently as the early 1970s (Ryan and Conlon, 1988). As well as the employment system, the state's back-up to the labour market, the income security system, was also premised on a male breadwinner supporting a dependent wife and children.

Historically, women have been the subject of welfare state attention, but not in relation to their role in employment. Institutions specifically associated with women, have focused on their role in the family. For example, infant welfare services, income security for widows, and child welfare activities have all had women as their prime subject. Women's family work has nonetheless been under-valued, and remains so.

The history of dual welfare states is a history of associating women with domesticity and caring labour and men with the public world, particularly the economic world but also, other major institutions including politics, the military, religion, the law and sport. This dichotomisation of social life into two spheres, the private and the public, itself is ideologically gendered. The public sphere where men are traditionally located has much more social weight than the private sphere, which has been accepted as women's domain. Therefore an analysis which contemplates the changing shape of gender advantage and disadvantage in Australia must be centrally concerned with changes to this association of males with the public sphere and females with the private or domestic.

When we consider what has been happening over past decades, we find that women are increasingly in employment and recognised as workers. There are, however, some contradictions here and gendered elements of the welfare state may even be magnified by some recent developments. For example, greater emphasis on home care for the aged and those with disabilities, and community care programs more generally, are strongly underpinned by traditional approaches to women's work. As well, women's increasing employment is still concentrated in areas segregated by sex.

Ideally, a comprehensive assessment of gender advantage and disadvantage would consider each key state institution in turn to see what change has occurred. This would be appropriate because if we accept that the welfare state is essentially concerned with promoting equality, then focusing on narrowly defined social welfare issues is not sufficient. Such an analysis would also consider the private sector and look to economic benefits through, for example, occupational and fiscal welfare (Titmuss, 1974). However, to make the discussion manageable the chapter will be concerned with the explicit nexus between social policy, labour market and family. When we consider this complex and multi-faceted nexus it is clear that much change has occurred over the twentieth century. It is just as clear, however, that these changes have stopped far short of the production of gender equality. Details of the current situation will be discussed after a brief outline of some key points in the historical development of the gendered Australian welfare state.

The establishment of dual welfare states

To gain a broad historical perspective on changes in social policy as they relate to the nexus between labour market and family it is useful to draw on the concept 'decommodification', which Esping-Andersen uses in his much discussed book on the nature of modern welfare states, *The Three Worlds of Welfare Capitalism* (1990). At the same time, his usage of this concept exposes the widespread tendency for theorists of the welfare state to pay little attention to the gender axis.

Esping-Andersen sees the welfare state in terms of promoting social citizenship, with rights granted 'on the basis of citizenship rather than performance' (1990: 21). A key process involved in ensuring rights on the basis of citizenship, is the process of 'decommodification'. By this Esping-Andersen means the provision of rights to income support so that workers do not depend entirely on the income they gain from selling their labour as a 'commodity' in the labour market. Decommodified rights provide the basis of social security systems and offer alternative income support for times of, for example, unemployment, sickness, disability and in old age.

When we utilise this concept 'decommodification' to look at the history of the Australian welfare state, its gendered nature becomes very clear. Certainly, Federal social security policies did provide a meagre form of alternative support outside the open labour market, first, in 1908, for the aged and disabled, though not for all Australians because Aborigines and most Asians were excluded (Kewley, 1977: Chapter 3). In the 1940s, income support for the unemployed and temporarily sick was established. The situation of women in relation to these provisions was, however, quite different from that of men. These benefits were available for women who were employed, but this support was provided only where they did not have a spouse. Partnered women were accepted as in need of financial support only when their partner was not in the labour market. Women's rights were mediated by their partner's entitlement: each of the benefits had a wife's allowance attached to it. There was, and remains, provision for wives to receive the age pension at a younger age than their husbands so that where wives were younger, a husband's supporting role could be maintained. The unit for social security purposes was the family unit, with an expansive definition of a couple to include de facto as well as de jure relationship. This remains the case today.

The different treatment of women and men is most clearly seen in the provisions for widows: first, ex-service, after the First World War and then, civilian widows, in the 1940s. There were no equivalent pensions for widowers. Prime Minister Curtin's speech to parliament in support of the enactment of widows pensions in 1942 expressed a conviction that a woman who has been partnered 'has undergone not only a physiological revolution by marriage and child-bearing, but she has inevitably accomplished for herself a new relationship to the world at large' (Jordan, 1989:2).

The widow pension represents a 'decommodified right' based on marriage rather than child care since, for older widows, child care was not necessary for its receipt. The attitude that marriage removes women from the labour market and delivers them to a state of 'legitimate dependence' (Bryson, 1988) was embedded in the wages system as early as 1907 when a decision to establish a family wage, meant to cover a man, his wife and dependent children, was made by Justice Higgins. The family element of the minimum wage was not formally removed for the wages system until 1974. That men were officially paid a wage which covered their wives and children was taken into account when fixing wage rates for women. Their wages were assumed to apply only to a single woman, and hence were originally set at around half of the male rate. The official rate was set at 54 per cent of men's wages in 1912 and raised to 75 per cent in 1950. Formal equal pay came out of decisions made by the Conciliation and Arbitration Commission between 1969 and 1974 (ABS, 1993:x–xii). Actual equal pay remains to be achieved.

Changing gendered social policy

This brief history of the development of key social policies in Australia clearly shows that decommodification rights applied to males and single women as workers. In the case of partnered women, however, they were responded to largely as wives. It was not assumed that married women would be reliant on the sale of their labour power (i.e. their labour was not treated as commodified). However, over recent years we find a process of redefinition of women's labour within social policy. The reasons for this redefinition are multiple and are part of an international, rather than solely local trend. The trend is explained to a significant degree by increasing market demand for women's labour. A second element is a recent trend to reduce state expenditure on social security. Thirdly, and certainly very important, have been the demands made by a rejuvenated women's movement in the period since the 1960s.

Increasingly, as women are being responded to as workers, a process of commodification of their labour has been taking place. The formal duality of the welfare state is thus being lessened (Shaver, 1993). Policy has been redirected to facilitate women's involvement in the labour market on a more equal and independent basis, though there are still elements of dependency embedded in specific policies. For example, even though, since the early 1980s, partners of beneficiaries have received a 'spouse allowance' rather than a wife's allowance, all benefits still take the family unit into account. They do not deal with individuals and it is still usually the case that a spouse allowance is claimed in respect of a dependent female spouse. As well, in practice, women still carry out most of society's paid and unpaid caring work, which results in different and unequal profiles for women's labour in both the labour market and the family (Bittman, 1991).

Changes to the basis of social security provisions for widows exemplify the direction of change. Rather than the pension being based on a definition of a widow as not competent to compete on the labour market as a result of her previous dependency as a wife, the new sole parent pension has become a decommodified right based on the provision of care. Parental care of a child under sixteen is now a basis for a decommodified right for both men and women. The pension is still taken up by far more mothers than fathers, a point that is discussed later. Nonetheless, this does not alter the fact that there has been a reconstruction of the basis of this social security right on parenthood, rather than female dependency.

These changes have occurred since 1987. At that time, Class B widow pensions, which were available for older widows whether or not they had the care of children, were abolished, though they remained available to complete the entitlement period of earlier recipients. In 1989, Class A widow pensions, which required dependent children under 16 years, was gender neutralised and replaced by the Sole Parent Pension. At the same time, the third strand of the former entitlements, the Class C pension, which provides for a period of rehabilitation after the death of a spouse, became the Widowed Person's Allowance and equally available to men. The period of coverage was reduced from six months and is currently fourteen weeks (DSS, 1992:281).

The right to paternity leave, established in 1990 in wage awards, is the latest recognition of the caring role as not exclusive to mothers. This policy is, however, mainly symbolic. Because it is unpaid, paternity leave does not free workers from dependence on the market, that is, it does not represent a decommodified right. It is, therefore, unlikely to be taken up by many men. Maternity leave, on the other hand represents a new and genuinely decommodified right, when it is paid leave. This, however, is currently available to only a few women, mainly those working in the public sector. Unpaid maternity leave including rights to return to part-time employment does represent a new recognition in policy of the legitimacy of combining motherhood and employment. Nonetheless, it still implies dependence on another's income.

In March 1990, Australia ratified the International Labour Organisation Convention 156 'Equal opportunities and equal treatment for men and women workers: Workers with family responsibilities'. Ratification, among other things, commits the government to 'promoting and encouraging the sharing of domestic responsibilities between men and women'. Paternity leave was a small gesture towards honouring the Convention (Edgar, 1991:5). Another realm of symbolic equalisation relates to domestic labour. In 1991 the Office of the Status of Women initiated a publicity campaign to encourage increasing participation of men in domestic labour (see Commonwealth of Australia, 1992).

As well as these changes in the basis for support outside the labour market which make parenting gender neutral, social policy has also changed to specifically facilitate the commodification of women's labour. Strategies adopted range from the very specific to the very broad. Some specific strategies have been aimed at social security recipients, motivated by the potential for cost saving. For example, the government's active labour market program, the JET (jobs, education and training) program, is specifically targeted to encourage sole parent pensioners into the workforce. Other measures have been taken to reduce disincentives to taking paid work which were embedded in the form of means testing for pensions. There is now some provision for a period of transition into paid employment. The pensioner earnings credit scheme allows entitlements to be maintained for a time even though the pensioner may have earnings higher than the normally allowable rate (DSS, 1992: 289). As well, an employment entry payment of $100 is available to a single social security recipient to defray the cost of starting work (DSS, 1992:285).

The Child Support Scheme also incorporates the aim of facilitating women's engagement in paid employment or at least removing possible incentives to remain out of the workforce and reliant on a social security payment. One of the explicit aims of the scheme is: 'to ensure that neither parent is discouraged from participating in the workforce' (Child Support Advisory Group, 1992:1). The scheme directs to non-custodial parents some financial responsibility for their children. Earlier, maintenance payments were often paid at a low rate, or withheld, in order not to interfere with the custodial parent's (usually the mother's) right to a social security benefit.

The Child Support Agency was established in 1988 to collect maintenance through employers, along with pay as you earn taxation, and to oversee distribution by the Australian Taxation Office of the money to custodial parents. The extent of coverage of non-custodial parents by the scheme is still far from complete, though it is increasing. In the year 1981–82, only 19 per cent of custodial parents received child support. By 1989–90 this had increased to 28 per cent (ABS, 1993:178). The proportion is higher for those on social security. In 1990, 36 per cent of sole parent pensioners were receiving maintenance, up from 26 per cent before the scheme began (Child Support Evaluation Advisory Group, 1992:3).

The provision of child care and the fee relief offered to parents on low incomes represent another strand of policy which focuses on women as workers. The Whitlam government between 1972–75 established the basis of today's child care policies although there has been a variable rate of expansion of these services since. Prior to this there was some government provision but child care was available largely in respect of children perceived to be in some way at risk. Thus earlier policy is more usefully understood as part of a traditional approach to child welfare, rather than as aimed at facilitating women's paid employment.

The enthusiasm of the Federal government for providing resources for child care increased quite dramatically in 1988. This change of heart demonstrates the importance of revenue issues for determining government policies, though this is not to deny the importance of pressure from women themselves. In

1988, a research report was presented to government which established that the direct costs of child care to government would be more than offset by the release of women's labour into the market. These economic benefits were demonstrated to come through the increased taxation paid by the women joining the workforce, and from direct savings on the dependent spouse rebate and social security outlays (Ainstie, et al. 1988).

Between 1983 and 1991, there was an increase in the number of child care places from 70 000 to 250 000, a rise around 180 000 (Ross, 1991:2). In the run-up to the 1993 election Prime Minister Keating promised an extra 355 000 places over a four-year period and set the objective of meeting total work-related demand by the year 2001. Together with a promise for a national accreditation scheme and some other general support for improving quality, this objective suggests a solid commitment to child care. This is clearly a key element if women's labour power is to be commodified and, like men's, freely exposed to the labour market.

A broad, and relatively successful policy to increase employability has been that aimed at improving the education levels of girls and women. Other social policies have been aimed at improving the range of employment opportunities for women. However, this has proven more difficult after such a long period of institutionalised discrimination. Nonetheless, anti-discrimination measures, affirmative action policies and equal employment opportunity programs have all been part of a systematic attempt by governments, at both State and Federal levels, to focus on women as workers and thus to change the shape of gender disadvantage and advantage in Australia (Sawer, 1990).

The welfare state and community care

At the same time as decommodification rights for formerly partnered women have been honed to pivot around child care and the same rights extended to men, there has been a broadening of the basis on which state support can be claimed for providing informal care. Those caring for the frail, aged and people with disabilities can receive a carer pension, and there is an increasing take-up rate though the absolute number are small (DSS 1992:107, 126). This is a policy direction which can be seen to signal contradictory messages as far as women's employment is concerned. It is in some tension with other strands of recent policy which have been facilitating women's entry into the workforce. On the one hand the carer pension represents an appropriate recognition of unpaid caring labour and an extension of decommodified rights for men and women. On the other hand, it flags support of the privatisation of caring, that is shifting responsibility to individual families, or perhaps more accurately leaving responsibility with families. Moves away from collective solutions are likely to prevent carers from moving into, or remaining in the workforce. A survey of disabled and aged persons undertaken in 1988 found that the labour force participation rate for female carers was only 41 per cent compared with a rate of 59 per cent employment overall. The rate of employment for male carers was also lower than for all men, but the difference was not as great as for women (ABS, 1993:77).

The potential effects of carer policies may be magnified by the demographic projections which indicate a significant increase in the aged and disabled populations over coming decades. Nonetheless, it must be recognised that carer provisions do offer financial recompense for many carers who would feel compelled to do the caring anyway. Also it does directly locate caring, beyond child care, as a basis for decommodified rights.

The Home and Community Care Program (HACC) represents a similarly ambiguous development as far as gender equality is concerned. The architects of the HACC program (who were mainly women), did conceive of it as a program responsive to the needs of both clients and their carers (also mostly women), and sensitive to particular interests such as those of Aborigines and people of non-English speaking backgrounds (Yeatman, 1993). However, in a tightening economic climate, these aims seem unlikely to be achieved and greater burdens are likely to fall on families. As well, the program encourages the development of non-professional, low-paid and often part-time jobs — jobs which are usually filled by women (Steer, 1991:193). Residential and centralised services which the HACC program aims to replace have tended to be developed around the services of better paid and more powerful professional workers such as nurses, social workers, physiotherapists and doctors.

Women and the labour market

Having considered some key changes in the nature of social policy relating to the nexus between family and labour market, the next step is to consider how much the pattern of gender advantage has changed. This section takes a systematic look at the statistical profile of men's and women's position in the labour market today. There is unfortunately no single index which can tell us how women are faring overall, and in any case we find the trends are not all in the same direction.

As has happened world wide, women are increasingly being drawn into the labour force. In 1901, women officially made up 20 per cent of the labour force (Fischer, 1987:14), though had the informal economy been included the figure would have been higher (Ryan, 1986). By 1966 the official figure had risen to 30 per cent of the labour force, and by 1991 this proportion had risen to 42 per cent and it is still rising (ABS, 1993:123). The increase was almost entirely made up of married women whose proportion of the total workforce in 1966 was 16 per cent. By 1991 the figure was 26 per cent (Jamrozik and Boland, 1993:11).

In 1992, 52 per cent of all women were in the labour force, compared with 74 per cent of men and the rates for single and married women were similar. The projected increase for women is to a level of 60 per cent by the year 2005 and the rate for men is projected to continue the slow decline that has been evident over recent years (ABS, 1993:118–121). Even with this projected female rate of employment, Australia will remain among the middle ranking OECD countries. It is far behind the leader, Sweden, where over 80 per cent of women and an even higher proportion of men are in the labour force.

A trend to converging rates of men's and women's participation rates, however, should not blur the fact that there are still very distinctive features about women's employment. These still pivot around the nexus between the labour market and the family. The graph (Figure 11.1) for married women, with its M shaped pattern, illustrates this relationship in the fall away of employment between the early 20s and 30s as family responsibility for child-rearing affects women's labour market involvement.

There are many ways in which women's paid employment is constrained by their domestic situation. The most obvious effects show up in intermittent employment, with time out for caring for children or other relatives. A second element is expressed in more part-time employment. In 1992, 43 per cent of employed women were working part-time, compared with 11 per cent of men. Both figures are on the increase as employers shows a greater preference for part-time employees. Nonetheless, surveys show that the reason women give for taking part-time work is because this better allows for the accommodation of their dual commitments to family and work, whereas for men, part-time work accommodates study (ABS, 1993: 124). Women are also far more likely to be employed on a casual basis than men, though the gap here is also narrowing. In August 1992, only 16 per cent of males were employed on a casual basis compared with 31 per cent of females, however, the increase for males was greater. Between 1988 and 1992 the rate for men increased by 32 per cent compared with only a 17 per cent increase for women (ABS, 1993: 124).

FIGURE 11.1

Persons aged 15 years and over: Labour force participation rates

AUGUST 1966

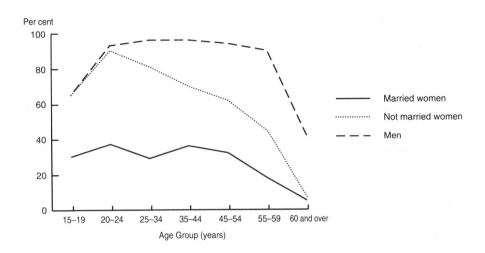

AUGUST 1992

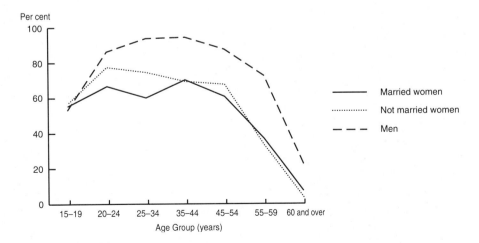

Source: Australian Bureau of Statistics, 1993: 119

A gradual moving together of female and male patterns in respect of part-time and casual employment is part of a world-wide trend towards workforce conditions that are less favourable to employees and more in line with employer interests, a process Wajcman and Rosewarne have referred to as the 'feminisation of work' (1986).

The effect that family responsibilities exert on patterns of labour market participation can be directly translated into loss of earnings potential. For a woman who raises two children and has an average level of education, the financial loss over a lifetime has been estimated to be around $384 000 at 1988 monetary values and with no allowance for interest on the money. For a woman with a high education level and two children, this reaches $537 000 or over $1.5m if interest is calculated at 5 per cent (Beggs and Chapman, 1988:40).

Another important connection between the two spheres of family and labour market is seen in the segregated nature of the labour force, with women increasingly working in public caring roles, in the education, health and community sectors. While the workforce in Australia has always been highly sex segregated, it is taking on new and distinctive characteristics as more women are absorbed into it.

In the industry category, community services, females significantly out-number males and this is the fastest growing industry. It covers workers in health, education, welfare and related services, with health and education representing two thirds of the category. Community services represented only 10 per cent of all Australian employment in 1966, well behind manufacturing (25 per cent) and wholesale and retail trade (21 per cent). By 1991, with 19 per cent of all employment, community services ran wholesale and retail trade a close second (still at 21 per cent) while manufacturing had dropped to 14 per cent of all employment (Jamrozik and Boland, 1993:11). Women workers made up 66 per cent of wage and salary earners in the community services industry, compared with their overall proportion in all industries of 42 per cent (Jamrozik and Boland, 1993: 11).

A key feature of the community services industry is the degree to which employment is in the public sector. Almost two-thirds of community services employees are public sector employees, compared with less than one-third of all workers. As well, even much of the private sector employment is wholly or at least partially dependent on government funding (Jamrozik and Boland, 1993:Chap 3). This phenomenon of women being over-represented in state employment is associated with the development of the welfare state generally. Esping-Andersen has pointed out that welfare states are no longer mere providers of services, in many countries they have become 'virtual employment machines', providing the services that allow for the commodification of women's labour such as child care, and relevant rights, such as paid maternity leave, but also providing the employment opportunities in health, education and welfare (1990:149). This concentration of women in public employment underpins the analysis of some feminist writers such as Hernes (1984) who see women as having moved from a state of private to public dependency. Such an insight highlights the fact that women are providing much of the broad social support for the community, which mirrors their family role. Also they are working in situations where women are not likely to be in control of the organisations. However, to speak in this way of a move away from private dependency tends to underplay the extent to which most women are still at least partially, financially dependent on their spouses, even when they are employed.

The data show that while women have been increasingly absorbed into the labour force, there has been a selective absorption. Women have moved into the caring roles in the community rather than being equally involved across the employment spectrum. Women, for example, make up only 23 per cent of workers in the group of industries concerned with material production (Jamrozik and Boland, 1993:25). This is not much more than half of the women's overall proportion of 42 per cent of the labour force. Yet even this appears a high figure when compared with the proportion of women in more powerful positions. In March 1992 for example, only 14 per cent of all members of Australian State and Federal parliaments were women (Sawer and Simms, 1993:139) and women are almost entirely absent from top jobs in the private sector.

A key feature of the community services industry is its high rate of professionalisation. Of all workers classified as professionals in August 1991, over half (52 per cent) were employed in the community services. The proportion of professionally trained women who were employed in this industry was even higher — 70 per cent compared with 39 per cent of all professionally trained men. The community services account for an even higher proportion of paraprofessionals (60 per cent over all), but with 86 per cent of paraprofessional women in the category compared with 38 per cent of men (Jamrozik and Boland, 1993: 1). The earnings of male and female paraprofessionals come closer together than they do in other occupational groups. Here females earn 85 per cent of the male rate (see Table 11.1).

TABLE 11 . 1

FULL-YEAR, FULL-TIME WORKERS: MEAN ANNUAL EARNINGS BY OCCUPATION, 1989-90

Occupation group	Mean earned income		Proportion of workers		Female/ male eamings ratio
	Women	Men	Women	Men	
	—$—		—percent—		
Managers and administrators	25,620	36,410	8.9	15.9	70.4
Specialist managers	38,590	47,580	1.7	4.6	81.1
Farmers and farm managers	18,150	19,800	2.2	3.8	91.7
Managing supefvisors (sales and service)	21,550	31,420	4.1	4.0	68.6
Professionals	32,850	42,500	16.0	14.0	77.3
Health diagnosis and treatment practitioners	37,800	67,260	1.1	1.3	56.2
School teachers	30,310	34,680	7.4	2.4	87.4
Otherteachers, instructors	33,860	37,980	1.3	1.0	89.2
Business professionals	35,050	42,840	2.9	4.1	81.8
Paraprofessionals	28,430	33,290	7.1	6.8	85.4
Registered nurses	30,070	28,880	4.5	0.2	104.1
Tradespersons	16,500	26,210	3.9	24.5	63.0
Clerks	22,630	29,330	36.2	7.4	77.2
Salespersons and personal services workers	19,820	29,540	16.1	7.0	67.1
Sales representatives	28,77	32,410	0.6		1.9
88.8					
Sales assistants	17,820	23,920	7.3	2.4	74.5
Tellers, cashiers and ticket salespersons	19,330	22,720	2.5	0.5	85.1
Plant and machine operators, and drivers	17,670	28,710	3.9	11.2	61.5
Labourers and related workers	18,130	24,410	7.9	13.1	74.3
Cleaners	16,890	24,210	1.8	1.0	69.8
Total	23,71 0	31,11 0	1 00.0	100.0	76.2

Source: Australian Bureau of Statistics, 1993: 183

Earnings of professionals come second in the equality stakes, with an overall women's earnings rate of 77 per cent of men's. As would be expected, however, there is considerable variation among sub-groups. For example, in 1989–90 in the professional category 'health diagnosis and treatment practitioners', women's rate of earnings amounted to only 56 per cent of men's. Different groups of teachers, on the other hand reached between 87 and 89 per cent. Registered nurses are classified as paraprofessionals and they are the one occupational group in which females earn more than males, with a ratio of 104 per cent. However, nurses' mean annual income of $30 070 in 1989–90 was less than half of the average for male 'health diagnosis and treatment practitioners' at $67 260 for full-year full-time earnings, which is the highest of all the earnings levels for any of the occupational groups (see Table 11.1).

An important group in terms of women's general social position are clerks, who make up 31 per cent of employed females and who, on average, earn 77 per cent of the rate earned by male clerks. Salespersons and personal service workers are the next largest group of employed females. They make up 24 per cent of all employed females and do very poorly in relation to men in the same category, earning only 67 per cent of the male full-year, full-time mean annual earnings (ABS, 1993:125). However, even this not very rosy picture of women's earnings overstates the general position because the comparisons are based on full-time, full-year earnings yet only 27 per cent of women, compared with 65 per cent of men, are in full-time, full-year employment (ABS, 1993:200).

This picture of income variation by occupational group raises the question of the role of education. An increase in the educational achievements of girls has been part of official government policy since the 1970s and this gives a clear indication of the deliberate facilitation, through social policy, of the commodification of women's labour. If the trend to higher levels of education for females is taken together with the picture of the higher levels of earnings for professionals and paraprofessionals, then this educational strategy does seem to offer possibilities for promoting greater equality. However, for women as a whole, this still leaves the wider gender gap in wage rates for those without higher educational qualifications, not to mention the very clear advantage of elite sub-groups of (largely) male workers.

Over the last 20 years the retention rate for girls at Year 12 level has increased from 27 to 77 per cent, whereas for boys the increase was from 34 to 66 per cent. This same increased emphasis on education for both males and females, but with a higher rate of increase for females, is evident in relation to post-school qualifications. In the decade between 1982 and 1992 the proportion of women with post-school qualification went up from 26 to 37 per cent. This remains a lower proportion than for men, at 47 per cent, but the rate of growth for women was much faster (42 per cent) than for men (26 per cent) (ABS, 1993:90–95).

Female students now outnumber male students in tertiary education, accounting for 56 per cent of completions of higher education awards in 1990, a rise of over 6 per cent since 1981 (DEET, 1992:1). At both secondary and tertiary levels, the patterns of subjects and choice of courses is becoming less gender distinctive, though the effect of traditional expectations are still evident.

An area in which little change has been achieved is in relation to trade qualifications. In 1992, only eight per cent of women with a post-school qualification had a trade qualification (predominantly in hairdressing), whereas the equivalent figure for men was 51 per cent. As has already been implied by the data on paraprofessional occupations, however, women predominate in the area of certificates and diplomas, with 72 per cent of women's post-school qualifications being of this kind, compared with only 26 per cent of men's. The relative advantage of female nurses (see Table 11.1) is borne out by a study carried out by the Australian Council for Educational Research which found that in 1989, while males with a degree earned on average $100 per week more than females, there was only a $10 gender difference in favour of males for those with a diploma (GCCA, 1992:7).

Women and family

It is clear that women still suffer economic disadvantage in the labour market because of their association with areas that are more lowly paid, but association with unpaid family work is even more basic to women's economic disadvantage. Income is important for a range of complex reasons which influence life choices. Income influences independence and dependence and therefore access to power both within the family unit and outside. The picture for all women's income is that it amounts on average to only about half that of men's ($14 000 compared to $26 000). This is accounted for partly because more women than men are in receipt of a government pension or benefit and partly, as we have seen, by women's patterns of employment. The situation is likely to be worsened by the current move to enterprise bargaining. This threatens to widen the gender gap in pay rates, because women are likely to be able to mobilise far less industrial muscle than men (Ryan, 1992).

Because of generally lower rates of pay, even where partnered women are employed full-time they usually are partly financially dependent. An international study by Hobson recently compared a number of countries on the degree of financial dependency of women on their male partners. The study emphasises the importance of economic independence to the exercise of power within marriage. It utilised data from the Luxembourg Income Study and Hobson plotted dependency ratios which effectively are the 'gap between the wife's and husband's proportion of family income' (Hobson, 1990:10). Dependency levels range from total, where the wife has no income, to no dependence where her income is not less than 9 per cent less than her husband's.

Hobson's data for Australia referred to 1985 and she found 40 per cent of partnered women were totally financially dependent and only 8 per cent had no dependence. This situation has improved since then because of an increase in the proportion of married women in employment (from 47 per cent in 1985 to 52 per cent in 1992 — ABS, 1993:120). As we have seen, there has also been an increase in the educational levels of women. The 1989–90 Survey of Income and Housing Costs and Amenities showed that of all married women in full-time, full-year work, only those in families with the youngest child over 10 years, and in those where wives were over 60 years of age, did the wife's income fail to reach 40 per cent of the income of the income unit (ABS, 1993: 197). However this figure must be viewed against the fact that only 27 per cent of employed women work full-year and full-time. Young married women without children, in full-time full-year work, came closest to contributing the same amount to the household budget as their spouses. Their income represented 42 per cent of the household income. Women with children between the ages of 5–9 years who worked part-time, contributed the smallest proportion at about 22 per cent (ABS, 1993:196–7).

When we look at proportions in receipt of government pensions and benefits, we find a very gendered picture except in the case of the age pension. In respect of other entitlements women are twenty times more likely to be in receipt of family allowance on behalf of their children than men as the allowance is normally directed to the mother. Women are approximately seven times as likely to be in receipt of a sole parent pension. On the other hand, women are only about a sixth as likely as men to be in receipt of an unemployment benefit and half as likely to be in receipt of Austudy (ABS, 1993:176). When we look at the data on men and active fathering we find, contrary to what might be expected, that the proportion of sole-parent families headed by men actually decreased between 1969 and 1991, though sole-parent families, as a percentage of all families rose from 6 to 9 per cent (ABS,

1992:44). The proportion of male-headed, sole-parent families peaked in 1979 at 17 per cent, (up from 13 per cent in 1969 — ABS, 1992:44). In August 1992, there were 340 000 single-parent families in Australia but only 31 000 (less than 10 per cent) headed by fathers (ABS, 1993: 18-19).

Despite changes towards the increased commodification of women's labour then, this gendered distribution of social security claims still follows the traditional pattern, discussed by Fraser in relation to USA, with men's entitlements essentially associated with their labour market status and women's with their traditional family status (1987). She suggests for the US that '... as clients, paid human service workers and unpaid caregivers, then, women are the principal subjects of the social welfare system' (Fraser, 1987: 92).

CONCLUSION

An overview of changes in the nexus between social policy, family and labour market, provides us with a mixed picture. There are undoubtedly some significant changes, the most important being the degree to which women have joined the labour force. Trends in the workforce are towards men's and women's situations drawing closer together. A major pressure towards change here has been exerted by economic forces including pressures on governments to reduce welfare spending. Women's involvement in the labour market is an important change however because this does provide economic and social resources, though women continue to receive less of these than do men. Nonetheless, access to economic resources is so fundamental to equality that this must be counted as a crucial axis of change.

When we look to social policy, we find equalisation in the formal characteristics of the social security system has occurred and the official duality of the welfare state has largely been removed. However, there is far less change on the ground. Women still make up the vast majority of sole parents and men are largely the recipients of unemployment benefits. Other policies aimed at improving women's position within the labour market have had differing degrees of effect. Child care and educational policies have been of obvious benefit. There has also been action on a wide front and the very breadth of the policies must itself be counted as fundamental to the achievement of change. A range of the disadvantages women suffer have been confronted, including the fundamental issue of violence against women. As well, there has been recognition that women cannot be treated as a homogeneous group. The distinctive circumstances of Aboriginal women, women from certain ethnic groups and women with disabilities, for example, have been acknowledged, though effective action for dealing with differing circumstances is yet to be achieved.

Changes are least identifiable in relation to the caring activities of society. It is assumed that women will take major responsibility for caring in the home and in the wider community and this shows up in the segregated nature of the workforce. The effect of this assumption that caring is women's work affects women whether they are single or married. Women's caring responsibilities translate into employment patterns which result in lower incomes. This means that even when married women are employed they retain a partial financial dependence. The provision of care in the community is also problematic because much of the work is not highly valued. The situation is becoming more problematic as community care programs are developed and cost-cutting is pursued.

The issue of caring has been and remains the most significant element which distinguishes men's welfare states from women's. Neglect of the issue of caring, and its gender component, must be understood as part of the general acceptance of the naturalness of the traditional sexual division of labour. This is compounded by the low status afforded much caring work, which renders it invisible to those who frame dominant discourses. Second wave feminism has, however, positioned caring labour as part of the debate about the nature of women's subordination and the sort of society that feminists strive to attain.

When we compare the situations of men and women today, even when there is formal equality, we find strong shadows of traditional patterns imprinted on the picture. It is clear that, in the absence of the achievement of a reconstruction of caring labour as a genuinely gender-shared task, and/or the elevation of caring labour to an appropriately valued activity, the effects of traditional notions of male and female tasks will continue to be imprinted on social life. Such a bifurcated welfare state is a continuing impediment to redressing gender disadvantage.

REFERENCES

Anstie, R., Gregory, R., Dowrick, S., and Pincus, J. (1988), Government Spending on Work-related Child Care: Some Economic Issues, Centre for Economic Policy Research, Australian National University, Discussion Paper, No. 191, Canberra.

Australian Bureau of Statistics (ABS) (1992), Social Indicators Australia 1992 No. 5, Catalogue No. 4101.0, Canberra.

Australian Bureau of Statistics (ABS) (1993), Women in Australia, Catalogue No. 4113.0, Canberra.

Beggs J. and B. Chapman (1988), 'The foregone earnings from child-rearinin Australia', Centre for Policy Research, Research School of Social Sciences, Australian National University, (mimeograph).

Bittman, M. (1991), *Juggling Time*, Canberra: Office of the Status of Women, Department of the Prime Minister and Cabinet, Canberra.

Bryson, L. (1988), 'Women as welfare recipients: women, poverty and the state', in C. Baldock and B. Cass (eds), *Women, Social Welfare and the State*, 2nd edn, Allen and Unwin, Sydney, pp. 134–49.

Bryson, L. (1992), *Welfare and the State: Who Benefits?* Macmillan, London.

Child Support Advisory Group. (1992), *Child Support in Australia*, Department of Social Security, Ref: 1552, Canberra.

Child Support Evaluation Advisory Group. (1992), *Child Support in Australia: Final Report of the Evaluation of the Child Support Scheme*, AGPS, Canberra, Cat. No. 92 14047.

Commonwealth of Australia (1992), *Another Tuesday Night* (video), Office of the Status of Women, Canberra.

Department of Employment, Education and Training (DEET) (1992), 'Higher Education Series - Female Students' *Update* No. 1, Canberra.

Department of Social Security (DSS) (1992), *Annual Report 1991-92*, AGPS, Canberra.

Edgar, D. (1991), 'Overview of ILO Conventions 156: Workers with Family Responsibilities' *Family Matters*, 28th April, p. 5.

Edwards, A. (1992), 'Feminism and male scholarship: the treatment of women and gender in social policy texts', *Australian Journal of Social Issues* 27 (1), pp. 31–58.

Esping-Andersen, G. (1990), *The Three Worlds of Welfare Capitalism*, Polity Press, Oxford.

Fisher, E. (1987), *Occupation: Unemployed Trends in Unemployment in Australia 1970 to 1986*, Social Security Review Research Paper No. 36, Department of Social Security, Canberra.

Fraser, N. (1987), 'Women, Welfare and the Politics of Need Interpretation', *Thesis Eleven*, (17), pp. 88–106.

Graduate Careers Council of Australia (GCCA) (1992), *Newsletter*, (55), August.

Hernes, H. (1984), 'Women and the welfare state: the transition from private to public dependence', in H. Holter (ed.), *Patriarchy in a Welfare Society*, Universitetsforlaget, Oslo, pp. 26–45.

Hobson, B. (1990), 'No exit, no voice: women's economic dependency and the welfare state', *Acta Sociologica*, 33(3), pp. 235–50.

Jamrozik, A., and Boland, C (1993), *Human Resources in Community Services: Conceptual Issues and Empirical Evidence*, SPRC Reports and Proceedings No. 104, Social Policy Research Centre, University of NSW, Kensington.

Jordan, A. (1989), *Lone Parent — And Wage-Earner: Employment Prospects of Sole-Parent Pensioners*, Social Security Review, Background Discussion Paper No. 31, Department of Social Security, Canberra.

Kewley, T. H. (1977), *Social Security in Australia,*2nd edn. Sydney UniversityPress, Sydney.

Ross R. (1991), 'Child Care for the 1990s', *Social Policy Research Centre Newsletter*, (40), p. 2.

Ryan, E. (1986), 'Women in production in Australia' in N. Grieve and A. Burns (eds), *Australian Women: New Feminist Perspectives*, Oxford University Press, Melbourne, pp. 258–72.

Ryan, E. (1992), 'Enterprise Bargaining' *Wel-Informed*, January, p. 4.

Ryan, E., and Conlon, A. (1988), *Gentle Invaders: Australian Women at Work*, Penguin, Ringwood.

Sawer, M. (1990), *Sisters in Suits: Women and Public Policy in Australia*, Allen and Unwin, Sydney.

Sawer, M., and Simms, M. (1993), *A Woman's Place: Women and Politics in Australia*, Allen and Unwin, Sydney.

Shaver, S. (1993), Women and the Australian Social Security System: *From Difference Towards Equality*, Discussion Paper No. 41, Social Policy Research Centre, University of New South Wales, Kensington.

Steer, M. (1991), 'Policy horizons for Victorians with disabilities: A Delphi Study', in P. Saunders and D. Encel (eds), *Social Policy in Australia:Options for the 1990s*, SPRC Report and Proceedings No. 98, Social Policy Research Centre, University of NSW, Kensington, pp. 181–194.

Titmuss, R. (1974), 'The social division of welfare: some reflections on the search for equity', in R. Titmuss (ed.), *Essays on The Welfare State*, Allen and Unwin, London, pp. 34–55.

Wajcman, J., and Rosewarne, S. (1986), 'The "Feminisation" of Work', *Australian Society*, 5(9), pp. 15–17.

Yeatman, A. (1993), 'Women and the State' in K. Pritchard (ed.), *Contemporary Australian Feminism*, Longman Cheshire, Melbourne (in press).

CHAPTER TWELVE

THE ECONOMIC CONTEXT OF SOCIAL POLICY

FRANK STILWELL

INTRODUCTION

Social policies reflect economic interests and conditions as well as prevailing social values and political processes. The relationship between these elements is not easily analysed. The proposition that the economic base determines the form of public policy and other elements of the social superstructure is overly mechanistic. On the other hand, seeing economic factors as merely a constraint upon the fulfilment of collective social goals understates the avenues through which economic influences operate. A balanced approach regards economic considerations as setting the context within which social policy operates. The form of social policy then 'feeds back' on the economy, impacting on how effectively the economy and economic policy operate. The size of the economic pie and how it is sliced are interdependent.

This interdependence is particularly evident in recent Australian circumstances. The last decade has seen a major shift in social policy from universalist to more selective principles, a shift which has been described as 'from entitlement to contract' (Weatherley, 1992). Prompted by the Social Security Review, there has been increased targeting of Federal government welfare and pension payments and more monitoring and scrutiny of applications for financial assistance. The public health service remains based on universalist principles despite the government toying with the idea of introducing direct charges for doctor consultations. However, higher education has been subject to the introduction of payments through the Higher Education Contribution Scheme (HECS). Public housing policies have come to be based even more on a residual welfare model rather than a general supplementation of the housing stock. There is a strong move towards 'privatisation' of pension arrangements through occupational superannuation schemes. All this has taken place in the context of mounting national economic difficulties and a seemingly persistent fiscal crisis of the state.

Of course, economising on the use of public funds is always seen as appropriate. The proponents of increased targeting of welfare expenditures also stress, quite properly, that the legitimacy of the welfare state depends upon it being widely perceived as efficient in meeting social needs. Axing 'middle-class welfare', tightening up on 'dole bludgers' and 'social security cheats' makes apparent sense in this context, although the widespread concern about these real or imagined rorts is partly the product of the politicians' own statements which often revive that old distinction between the deserving and undeserving poor.

What is notable is that this economising has been vigorously pursued by a Labor government, and that it has occurred in a period when the economy was moving into the deepest recession for over half a century. The political economy of this situation is at first sight perplexing. After all, the Hawke–Keating governments are the modern heirs to a political movement in which extension of the welfare state and collective provision of public goods has been an article of faith. To have pursued a programme of cutting back the size of the public sector and more selective provision of social security is a very significant feature of Labor in office in the 1980s. It is in some contrast to the commitments to an expanded 'social wage' which were embodied in the original 1983 Accord between the Australian Labor Party and the Australian Council of Trade Unions, and which was a key element in Labor's accession to office that year. Adding to the irony is the deepening recession in the early 1990s, itself partly a product of austerity in Federal government's fiscal and monetary policies, swelling the ranks of those excluded from the mainstream economy and therefore dependent on the social security system for their livelihood. Evidently there are some important contradictions to unravel here. Labor's role in paving the way for a more strident 'new right' programme is of particular importance in this context.

Looking further ahead, it is also important to ask what sort of social policies are likely to be compatible with economic conditions as we move to the year 2000 and beyond. It has been said that Australian social policy has been distinguished by a heavy focus on an employment-based approach to welfare (Castles, 1985). This has meant the pursuit of full employment, the relatively orderly determination of wage levels through a centralised arbitration system, supplemented by a social safety net for those falling outside the workforce. All this has taken place in the context of a system of controls over immigration, trade protection and income taxation designed to ensure some degree of socioeconomic stability and equity in the economy. It is a regulatory framework in the process of being dismantled (with the significant exception of the regulation of immigration). This is the main thrust of the 'economic rationalist' push which emphasises a greater reliance on market-driven outcomes. It is a change in the approach to economic management which will continue to have major implications for social policy.

In any case the assumptions underpinning previous social policies seem less sustainable in the contemporary context of structural economic changes which are rendering full employment unobtainable and increasing the extent of economic inequalities. Changes in technology, capital–labour relationships and the international organisation of production and trade make it unlikely that employment will fall below, around 6–8 per cent, even when the economy eventually comes out of recession. The traditional employment-based approach to welfare is difficult to sustain in these circumstances, particularly in conjunction with the overall ageing of the population and hence the growing proportion of people with claims to retirement incomes. The incomes of employed people constitute a shrinking economic basis relative to the growing share of people dependent on state expenditures which derive largely from taxes on those incomes from employment. This structural problem is exacerbated by a growing dualism among employed people, between those with secure and well-paid jobs and the growing ranks of those in the secondary labour market with casual and part-time jobs. A society featuring a permanent pool of unemployment and growing economic inequality is not one which can readily support a social policy developed on the assumption of full employment and the principle of comparative wage justice. Growing strains on the social safety net are inevitable. The whole question of the relationship between claims to work, income and social security will have to be rethought.

In these circumstances, an analysis of the changing economic context of social policy seems appropriate for the penultimate chapter of this book. It draws our attention to the structural economic changes, economic ideologies and economic policies which have to be taken into account if progressive social policy is to be relevant in contemporary conditions.

Structural economic changes

Following the terminology of J. K. Galbraith (1977) the period since the early 1970s can be characterised as an 'Age of Uncertainty', while one Australian political economist has more recently suggested that the 1990s mark a further slide into an 'Age of Upheaval' (Wheelwright ,1991). Certainly, the last twenty years have witnessed dramatic structural changes in the world economy, with important implications for Australia's position within it. Looking back, it is not difficult to see their origins. The long boom of the 1950s and 1960s rested on a historically-specific set of economic conditions and proved not to be as durable as the more optimistic Keynesian economists anticipated. The emergence in the 1970s of significant levels of unemployment, generated by the tendency towards a falling rate of profit and inflation fuelled by the OPEC oil price rises, proved difficult to resolve by conventional economic polices of demand management. It was evident that capitalist production would have to be restructured on a world scale if renewed conditions for capital accumulation were to be established.

The owners of capital pulled considerable investment out of productive industries and redirected it into real estate and other speculative ventures in pursuit of higher returns. However, this did nothing to arrest the slide towards lower overall rates of profit. More productively, other business enterprises were restructured, embodying new technology, a new international division of labour and new management practices. Changes in the organisation of business enterprises, including waves of mergers and takeovers, and more coherent orchestration of the world economy through the activities of transnational corporations and international banks, all contributed to the global restructuring. Then, in the late 1980s, the collapse of the 'communist state' regimes in Eastern Europe and then the USSR and the extension of capitalist market relationships there added further dimensions to the changed inter-national scene. It is little exaggeration to describe the whole period as an era of dramatic structural change, comparable in certain respects to other periods of upheaval like the industrial revolution, the age of imperialism, the years of the Great Depression and the Second World War. The casualties have not been so severe, but the extent of socioeconomic dislocation has been enormous.

The central element has been the tendency towards greater inter-nationalisation. This has not been uniform nor free of contradictions — witness the widespread continuation of diverse practices of trade protectionism, the formation of regional trading blocs and the resurgence of nationalist and regionalist political movements. Internationalism has not significantly affected the labour movement or the state, both of which remain fundamentally national in their constitutions and organisation. However, capital has become ever more international in character. In its *monetary* form it moves around the globe in response to instant commands transmitted by FAX messages, ISD phone calls or EMAIL instructions. In its *physical* form, capital investment in the means of production has become more geographically dispersed, as 'global factory' production for global markets has become increasingly commonplace. In its *social* form, capital as a class — comprising the most powerful owners and managers of capital — has become increasingly international in its composition, conduct and aspirations. It has become commonplace to note that, while Marx and Engels made the famous rallying call 'workers of the world unite', it is the capitalists who have implemented internationalisation in practice!

This internationalisation of capital has not eradicated conflict and competition in economic life, of course, nor has it been implemented as the result of any master plan, the earlier coordinating efforts of the Trilateral Commission notwithstanding (Bowles, 1978). However, it has had striking effects on the patterns of investment. In the formerly advanced industrial nations this has taken the form of a partial and selective 'deindustrialisation', as routine manufacturing industries have been relocated 'offshore' in cheaper labour countries. Superimposed on this has been a 'de-laborisation', as more capital-intensive technology has been introduced. A 'casualisation' of the workforce is a further tendency as the influence of trades unions is undermined and the share of jobs in the secondary labour market (affecting both manufacturing and service sector employment) has increased. These three tendencies have come together to create strikingly different patterns of employment and distributions of income. There are counter-tendencies, as always, reflected for example in the resurgence of some sectors of small business even within major regional metropolis such as New York, London and Sydney (Stilwell, 1993b). There are sweat shops even in the shadows of the skyscrapers in which the head offices of transnational corporations are located.

Overall, the dominant effect of these structural economic changes has been for economic internationalism to unleash the forces of economic instability and inequality. The conditions for global capital accumulation are secured at a very high price. This should hardly be surprising. Capitalism has a recurrent tendency towards spectacular but uneven development. The unevenness takes a temporal form as alternating booms and recessions, and a spatial form as unbalanced regional development. Concurrently, there is a persistent tendency towards increased inequality. This is the product of a system in which wealth is created collectively through the efforts of the people but appropriated privately according to property rights over the means of production. It has long been thus. What has kept the dominant tendencies towards unevenness and inequality in check has been the influences of the labour movement and of the state, to the extent that it has been oriented to stabilisation policies, welfare provision and redistribution. The significance of the increased inter-nationalisation of capital is that it undermines these countervailing tendencies.

Increased spatial competition for mobile capital even tends to lead the labour movement and the state into a complicit role in the process. Wage cutting, lower rates of corporate taxation, and other inducements to mobilise capital seem logical, albeit desperate, means to capture the investment needed for regional and national economic prosperity. The outcome is an impoverishing beggar-thy-neighbour process in which the relative economic power of capital is further enhanced. This is not to romanticise any earlier mythical 'golden age' of state-managed capitalist economic development. The role of the state in economic progress has always been constrained and contradictory, as is the role of trade unions in the pursuit of collective goals which transcend the interests of a geographically and sectorally divided workforce. The point is simply that increased spatial competition in an era of uncertainty and upheaval is not something external to labour and the state. It is a process in which they are participants but not generally beneficiaries.

The fiscal crisis of the state can be interpreted in this context, helping to clarify the limits on the state's capacity to finance the expenditures associated with social policy. It is a common observation that Australian governments, Federal, State and local, all have difficulties in financing the range of expenditures they are called on to make. In the last two decades, budgetary deficits have been persistent, temporarily relieved at the Federal level only in the late 1980s as the result of severe expenditure restraint before the recession plunged fiscal policy into the red again. It is a story of fiscal imbalance which has been evident in many other countries too. To describe it as a fiscal crisis of the state is to imply that its origins are structural rather than cyclical, that those origins are more profound than mere monetary mismanagement, and that the situation is not sustainable in the medium term.

The structural origins of this general tendency to fiscal imbalance were identified two decades ago by the American political economist James O'Connor (1973). The key element is the mismatching of the demands placed by business on the state for various expenditures (to underpin the capital accumulation process and to ensure the legitimacy of the existing socio-economic order) and its capacity to finance them through expanded taxation (to which businesses and upper-income groups in particular are strongly resilient). Since the 1970s the tendency has been further compounded by the internationalisation process and the beggar-thy-neighbour tendencies which we have already noted.

Internationally mobile capital has demanded state infrastructure expenditures (e.g. power stations to attract multinational aluminium smelting companies) but has minimised its tax contributions (e.g. through the use of tax havens and the practice of transfer pricing). On the domestic front, upper-income taxpayers have used diverse tax avoidance schemes, causing public finance analysts to comment wryly that taxation has become well nigh optional for the wealthy. As Australia's leading tax economist once observed 'the essential problem is not to make the rich pay high rates of tax or even to pay more tax: it is to make the rich pay any tax at all' (Mathews, 1980:106). A persistent fiscal imbalance is hardly surprising in these circumstances.

Privatisation (sometimes described as fire-sales of public assets) can help to defer such a fiscal crisis, but only at the expense of relinquishing long run revenue sources and the diverse public obligations which led to the establishment of public enterprises in the first place. In the social services the practices of corporatism and contracting out of service provision tends to reduce costs only at the expense of changing the quality of services and the intensity of labour, while often also throwing extra burdens onto the voluntary agencies. Alternatively, expanding public debt through borrowing, nationally or internationally, is a legitimate means of financing fiscal deficits, but adds, in the long run, to the burden of interest payments, which then compounds the general fiscal crisis. Such borrowing may also force up interest rates, leading to more inflow of foreign capital which locks the national economy even more into the vicissitudes of the international market place. It is not a context within which increases in expenditure on social security or more generally progressive social policies are readily deliverable.

Economic ideology

Alongside these structural economic changes, reinforcing them and legitimising the dominant political responses, have been significant ideological shifts. The ascendancy of the 'new right' and the influence of economic rationalism are its most obvious elements.

The 'new right' push has been subject to much scrutiny and concern (e.g. Sawer, 1982; Aarons, 1988). It has been well organised through numerous think-tanks and propaganda outlets (as described by Carey, 1987). It has been particularly influential in business organisations such as the Business Council of Australia (Dabscheck, 1990). It gets a prominent representation in the media through commentators such as Gerard Henderson and John Hyde. It has seen the dries triumph over the wets in the Liberal Party, symbolised in the ascendancy to the leadership by ex-Economics Professor John Hewson. Its key elements are heavily derivative from the ideas and practices underpinning

Thatcherism in the United Kingdom and Reaganomics in the United States in the 1980s but it has some distinctive local adaptations. It is a particular set of beliefs and interpretations of contemporary socioeconomic problems which has come to be widely held and which has pervaded the dominant institutions of Australian society. It has even pervaded the Labor Party, protestations by its leaders to the contrary notwithstanding. Its influence there is particularly linked to the doctrines of 'economic rationalism' which have been an important ingredient in Labor's claim to be a sound economic manager.

'Economic rationalism' is a particularly influential current within 'new right' ideology. Its distinguishing tenets are:

i   a primacy of economic over other social concerns, and

ii   a belief that market processes deliver better economic outcomes than the effects of government 'intervention'.

It is a set of beliefs which, as Michael Pusey (1991) has documented, has come to pervade the upper echelons of the public service. Among Labor politicians, its influence was evident in the policies implemented in the 1980s by Paul Keating, John Dawkins and Peter Walsh, among others. The term itself has come to be more unfashionable in the 1990s as bureaucrats and politicians distance themselves from the policy disappointments of the preceding decade, but the two basic tenets remain very influential, if not hegemonic, in public policy discussions. The effect has been to create a public policy environment where redistribution and progressive social reform is subordinated to a narrow concern with the pursuit of economic efficiency.

It is interesting to ask how and why this ideological shift has occurred in the last decade. What is its basis and whose interests does it serve? These are difficult questions, but it is important to ask how it is that particular economic ideas come to shape and constrain the possibilities for progressive social policy. Most obviously, the roots of 'economic rationalism' are in the dominant neoclassical economic theory which is at the core of economics teachings. Many of the bureaucrats who hold 'economic rationalist' views are economics graduates, as Pusey (1991) demonstrates. Thus, there is a clear link between educational institutions and the development of the Federal government's economic and social policies.

Neoclassical economics clearly embodies the two central tenets of economic rationalism. All the complexities of social behaviour are reduced to a model based on the rational calculations of 'economic man' (or the even more bizarre, 'economic person'); and the aggregation of such individual choices is held, subject to some distinctive conditions, to be conducive to an efficient overall outcome. But the concept of efficiency used here is very narrow, focussing on the allocation of resources at a point of time and asking whether any change in it could improve the well-being of some citizens without harming others. It is a static conception of efficiency which contrasts with a potentially richer notion of dynamic efficiency over time. Moreover, the restrictive conditions underlying the theory rule out the problems arising from monopoly and oligopoly, imperfect information, resource immobility, instability, unequal resource holdings, and so forth, all of which can cause divergence between market equilibrium and optimum outcomes. The better neoclassical economists acknowledge these problems. Indeed, depending on the stress placed on these conditions, (i.e. whether the divergence from the real world conditions is regarded as minor or major) the neoclassical theory can be used either for a glorification or a critique of market processes. In the latter case, it can be used to show that market processes will lead to outcomes which are inefficient, feature glaring imbalance between private wealth and public squalor, and foster environmental decay and social inequity (Stilwell 1975; Rees, Rodley and Stilwell, 1993). At best, the appeal to neoclassical economics to support policies of 'economic rationalism' involves a vulgarisation. At worst, it is a crude means of asserting sectional economic interests over broader social values.

Perhaps more insight into the influence of 'economic rationalism' on social policy can be gained through studying whose interests are served. There are many who suffer from this bias in public concerns. Those dependent on the state for income redistribution are obvious cases in point. In principle, 'economic rationalist' bureaucrats should also be casualties, since to be consistent they would be doing themselves out of their own jobs or finding short cuts the process by resigning. So who gains? Radicals might well respond by saying that it is the capitalist class. However, it is not clear that industrial capitalists do actually gain from the implementation of 'economic rationalism' in practice. On the contrary, many industrial capitalists depend on the state for the provision of infrastructure, for demand for their products, for subsidies or, more generally, for the orchestration of the economic and industrial relations conditions necessary for sustained profitability in the long run. The more obvious beneficiaries from 'economic rationalist' policies are financial institutions and speculators, who do not directly create wealth for the society but enjoy the market freedoms to re-deploy their capital in the pursuit of short-term financial gain. A similar generalisation can be made about the players in international capital and financial markets. Looked at from this perspective, the story of 'economic rationalism' is also a story of the changing balance between fractions of capital — industrial and financial, national and international.   Therein lies the link between the big structural economic changes and the changes in dominant ideologies which have taken place.

It is no coincidence that a neoclassical theory of markets which focuses on exchange relationships should fit in with these changing sectional interests. The neglect in that theory of production relationships, involving class and the labour process, sets it aside from the practical concerns of industrial capitalists. Likewise, the neglect of questions of distribution and redistribution puts it at odds with the interests of welfare recipients and, indeed, all who would favour the creation of a more equitable socioeconomic system. It is a dominant ideology which serves the interests of the least productive fraction of capital at great costs to the society at large.

Economic policy and social costs

The effects of structural economic change and the associated ideologies of 'economic rationalism' have flowed through to the experience of Australian economic policy. A series of policy experiments have produced disappointing, if not perverse, consequences. The social costs have been severe. An all too familiar listing is as follows:

- Financial deregulation created an economic milieu conducive to speculation rather than productive investment ushering in the era of corporate cowboys and paper entrepreneurs.

- Falls in the value of the currency failed to trigger off the promised 'J-curve' improvement in the nation's international trading position. The balance of payments current account deficit got larger and subsequent fluctuations in the value of the dollar seem to have had no consistent effect on nation's overseas indebtedness.

- Eliminating the government's own budgetary deficit in the later 1980s also failed to eliminate the nation's current account deficit, despite claims by the proponents of the 'twin deficits thesis' that reining in one deficit would also resolve the other.

- Tariff cuts have caused major job losses, in particular, industries like car production and textiles, clothing and footwear, while doing nothing to promote new industry development.

- Wage restraint has redistributed income from labour to capital but without any corresponding redirection of profits to productive purposes.

- Restrictive monetary policies caused high interest rates which added to the balance of payments problem by sucking in more capital from overseas. The interest payments on this capital are the biggest item in the balance of payments deficit which the high interest rates were ostensibly designed to reduce (Stilwell, 1993a).

Looking back over the last decade, we can see a struggle between two currents in public policy. One is expressed in the cooperative elements of the original 1983 Accord between the Labor government and the trade unions, continuing elements of regulation of the labour market, incipient elements of industry policy and a residual commitment to the 'social wage'. The other is expressed in the shift away from the original Accord to a narrower concern with wage restraint, privatisation, deregulation of finance, tariff cutting and so forth. For simplicity, these two currents may be labelled 'economic interventionist' and 'economic rationalist'. Over the decade, the effects of the latter have tended increasingly to swamp the former.

What have been the consequences for the economy and society? As always, one cannot know what would have been the situation if different policies had been pursued. However, the score card is pretty poor. Balance of payments problems have proved resilient to policies aimed at curtailing demand for imports and stimulating industrial competitiveness through exposure to international trade. The foreign debt burden has continued to grow. Employment problems have intensified, despite a quite impressive performance in terms of aggregate jobs growth in the 1980s. The economic recession of the early 1990s, the worst for over half a century, was the culmination of these difficulties, triggered by restrictive monetary policies designed to deal with the trade imbalance, but cutting deeply into capital investment. That has left a legacy of outdated capital stock in many sectors of industry and dried up the life-blood of economic expansion and renewal.

Paradoxically, such deteriorating national economic conditions generate more and more social casualties at precisely the time the state can least afford the expenditures necessary to provide an adequate social safety net. So, from the perspective of social policy, the problem of 'economic rationalism' is not only that it subordinates broad concerns with social justice to narrow concerns with economic efficiency. It is also that the 'economic rationalist' policies demonstrably fail to produce economically efficient outcomes, which adds to the strains on the existing social security system.

Unemployment is the most obvious expression of this paradox. Nothing could be more economically irrational than to leave human resources idle at the same time that there are major social needs unfulfilled. There is no shortage of social needs for better schools, hospitals, transport infrastructure, and so forth. Genuine economic rationality would involve the mobilisation of unemployed social resources for socially necessary production. Capitalism has never been a consistently rational system in this sense. The 'economic rationalist' policies which have led to over 11 per cent of the workforce being officially classified as unemployed (and others underemployed in part-time and casual jobs when they would often prefer more secure and full-time work) bring this feature of the system into sharp relief. An economy based on production for profit periodically leaves valuable resources idle whenever the conditions for profitability are not present. Social policy picks up the tab when it is least able to claim the necessary expenditure backing.

Growing economic inequality is the other principal expression of the paradox. The Australian evidence is clear — that there has been a polarisation of the income distribution, with a growing gulf between the economic conditions of the poor and the wealthy with a shrinking middle class in between (Raskall, 1993; Lombard, 1991; Gregory, 1992; Eaton and Stilwell, 1992). The attempt by the Federal Labor government to target welfare expenditures more effectively at the poor has apparently brought some relief at the bottom end (Harding and Landt, 1992; Bradbury and Doyle, 1991). However, this had been swamped by the effects of the Federal government's macro-economic policies (e.g. high interest rates in the late 1980s redistributing income to those with surplus capital) and the impact of the recession in expanding the economic underclass in the 1990s. It is a complex story but the broad implications are obvious — the economic rationalists' neglect of distributional issues has been counter-productive because the consequential widening of income disparities adds to the welfare burden. The concurrent lowering of the higher marginal rates of income tax further undermines the capacity to finance such expenditures and thereby compounds the fiscal crisis of the state.

Further insights into these processes can be gained by studying the impact of the Accord on the distribution of income and on the government's fiscal position. Three points are particularly notable. First, the focus of the Accord on wage restraint unmatched by comparable restrictions on non-wage incomes (e.g. from interest, dividends, rents, professional fees and executive salaries) was bound to lead to widening income disparities unless other mechanisms were established to cream off the resulting surplus. Second, the successive re-negotiations of the Accord in the 1980s and early 1990s not only brought about greater wage restraint but they also involved wage-tax trade-offs. The Australian Council of Trade Unions (ACTU) agreed to reduced real wage rises in exchange for general reductions in income taxes, on the grounds that this would preserve workers' after-tax income levels. This simultaneously lowered the Federal government's tax revenue and hence its capacity to deliver the 'social wage' expenditures which were a key component of the original Accord. Third, the subsequent move towards award-restructuring and enterprise bargaining tends to accentuate income inequalities among wage earners, as those in stronger unions are able to strike better agreements than other workers whose capacity to demonstrate productivity improvements and/or apply industrial strength in pursuit of wage claims is more limited. The development of the Accord has come to be a three-part story — a general redistribution of income from labour to capital, a depletion of the government's capacity to finance the 'social wage' and a redistribution within labour's share which has the effect of further widening economic inequalities.

Finally, what of the impact of these economic changes on social cohesion? All these various policies, designed ostensibly to improve aggregate economic performance, rest on the assumption that economic inequality is no impediment to this objective, or that it may enhance it. This is what is sometimes called the 'trickle-down' or 'incentivation' view of economic progress. It can be countered by a quite contrary view that a more egalitarian society is one in which there is more likely to be the cooperative spirit necessary for sustained economic progress. As Robert Kuttner (1984) argues, on the basis of a review of comparative international experience, it seems that, in practice, better macro-economic performance has been notched up by the countries with the more developed welfare states and more egalitarian income distributions. There is no general efficiency-equity trade-off.

Meanwhile, the social costs of economic restructuring and 'economic rationalist' policies continue to escalate. In addition to the direct personal hardships and social opportunity costs of unemployment, there are the costs of policing an increasingly unequal society. It is pertinent to note, by way of comparison, that the item of public expenditure which expanded most rapidly during the years of Thatcherism in the United Kingdom was expenditure on the police. Expenditure on the jails and the legal system can also be expected to rise with a growing incidence of poverty-related crime. So too, there are well-established statistical and casual links between economic inequality, health problems and health costs. It is not only that the poor and unemployed are particularly prone to ill-health, but there is now growing evidence of more general links with the overall extent of economic inequality (Wilkinson, 1992). These social costs arising from current economic trends further compound the fiscal crisis of the state. As progressive social policy becomes more and more necessary it becomes more and more circumscribed by economic circumstances and prevailing economic orthodoxies.

Towards an agenda for radical reform?

Contemporary structural economic changes, the internationalisation of capital and 'economic rationalist' policies take us along a road which leads to no solution for contemporary socioeconomic problems. It follows from this reasoning that a reform agenda must be more than marginal, seeking to ameliorate the adverse social consequences of the dominant economic trends. On the contrary, it evidently needs to be radical, literally tackling the issues at their roots. This means confronting the structural economic changes, economic ideologies and economic policies which obstruct more progressive social policy. Unless each of these interacting elements is addressed, there is the tendency for proposals to shade into a non-operational utopianism. Even then that tendency is ever present, since the political processes necessary to turn the situation around are hard to identify. These issues can be illustrated by looking at each element in turn.

First, there is the issue of structural economic change. Responding to the dominant tendencies towards the internationalisation of capital, labour-displacing technological change and growing polarisation in the distribution of income is a tall order! However, there is some scope for alternative directions within a nation like Australia, with important implications for social policy. Internationalism is a case in point. It is a set of beliefs and practices which has potentially progressive elements, involving the potential to transcend parochialism and conflicts based on nationalist prejudices. However, those are not the dominant features of the internationalisation of capital which, as we have seen, intensifies particular class divisions and impedes democratic processes. In those circumstances it seems less sensible to embrace an open-door policy to international trade and investment than to manage international economic relations more selectively with judicious combinations of trade policy, industry policy and the regulation of financial flows. Labour training and retraining programmes also have an important place in that alternative approach as means of ensuing that the social costs and economic opportunity costs of structural economic change are minimised. The myth of the 'level playing field' can be replaced by a program of managing human and natural resources in pursuit of a more rounded set of social and economic objectives.

Likewise, dealing with the effects of technological change can involve the reassertion of a public interest rather than a capitulation to technological determinism. The benefits of advances in technology can be captured without the polarising and socially-costly effects of the currently fashionable market-induced changes. Andre Gorz's (1985) proposals for more flexible work-leisure relationships are relevant in this context. Recognising that only, say, 35 000 hours need be worked by each person over their lifetime in a technologically advanced society, individuals could choose how to balance those hours against leisure e.g. by working full-time for 20 years straight, by working 40 years half-time, by mixing work with periods of education or leisure, and so forth. The key point is that this flexibility would require the replacement of the fixed work/wage nexus which currently prevails. In other words, the timing of claims to income would need to be independent of the timing of periods to work. Much social policy concerned with redistribution of income over time (e.g. temporary unemployment benefits, aged pensions) could be redundant in such a context.

As an interim step towards such a radical restructuring of income distribution processes, the introduction of a guaranteed minimum income system is warranted. This would require a significant restructuring of the tax scale, effectively involving a negative income tax below a particular level set to ensure the avoidance of poverty. It is not a new proposal, and it has its advocates on the political right (seeing it as a replacement for more complex and intrusive welfare provisions for those with low incomes) as well as those on the left (who stress its role in extending the rights of all citizens to a decent livelihood irrespective of their capacity to sell their labour in the capitalist economy). It is a system which would significantly re-shape social policy. Among other things, it would relieve the state of many of the problems of the existing tax and social security system, such as the 'poverty traps' which arise when low-income earners lose benefit entitlements when they earn a little more income.

Changing the dominant economic ideologies is a yet harder task, but this cannot be separated from the policy initiatives just discussed. Ideologies such as 'economic rationalism' thrive in particular political and policy contexts. They can be challenged and reversed, particularly where the policies derived from those ideologies fail to work effectively in practice, as has been demonstrably the case in Australia in the last decade. Of course, there are always some politicians calling for yet bigger doses of the failing medicine to deal with persistent economic problems; but policy failures create ripe conditions for alternatives to get a hearing. In the current context there is no shortage of proposals for alternatives to 'economic rationalism' which integrate economic policy more with the principles of social justice, ecological sustainability and participatory democracy (e.g. Flew, 1992; Rees, Rodley and Stilwell, 1993).

Ultimately, however, it is the capacity of the political processes to respond and implement these changes of direction which are at issue. This chapter has stressed the structural constraints on economic and social policy, but this is not to deny the importance of political choices. It is in this respect that the character of the political process and the major political parties comes into the spotlight. Evidently the principle of democracy is severely restricted in modern capitalist societies, despite its official status as the hallmark of a free society. The principle does not operate in the daily lives of ordinary working people or welfare recipients. Its operation in the political sphere is effectively limited to periodic choices between the major political parties who offer policy menus which tend to converge in practice. The Labor Party, the traditional party of reform, is now quite conservative in economic management, whereas the traditional conservative parties — the Liberal-National Coalition — offer a rather more explicitly 'new right' variant. The policy principles set out in the preceding paragraphs are difficult to get on the political agenda in these circumstances, especially given the generally conservative character of the mainstream media and the lack of a strong tradition of involvement of intellectuals in public life. Recent attempts to break the mould through the formation of new progressive political parties and coalitions have proved to be an uphill struggle (Stilwell, 1992; Frankel, 1992).

However, the dramatic changes in economic conditions in the current era are unlikely to leave political conditions stable. Looking to the longer term, for example, the next ten to twenty years, it is possible to envisage both dangerous and exciting possibilities opening. The impacts of the spatially homogenising capital, as described by David Harvey (1989), will certainly throw up new conflicts and contradictions. Regionalist and localist sentiments are political expressions of these conflicts and can have a potentially progressive role. Growing polarisation in the distribution of income and the economic dualism between those in primary and secondary labour markets creates new sources of economic and social tension and greater pressures on the state for social security and redistribution. The intensifying environmental crisis can be expected to strengthen environmental social movements and the potential influence of Green parties. Coalitions between the various disaffected groups can be a particularly potent force for progressive economic and social change.

Economic, social and political conditions are in a continual state of flux. What this chapter has sought to demonstrate is that social policy cannot properly be divorced from these broader conditions. Changing economic conditions, in particular, throw up new demands on the system of social security, service provision and income redistribution, while changing economic ideologies influence the policy responses of the state. It follows that a progressive reformulation of social policy needs to be integrated with an alternative economic strategy and a programme of political change. This is a tall order, but anything less involves a capitulation to the forces responsible for generating the instability, inequality and social costs with which social policy has had to cope. Put this way, social policy may be regarded as a key ingredient in the process of radical reform. This is also a political-economic context in which social work can provide empowerment (Rees, 1991) rather than 'band-aids' for the victims of the economic system.

REFERENCES

Aarons, L. (1988), *Here Come the Uglies*, Red Pen Publications, Sydney.

Bowles, S. (1978), 'Can the Trilateral Commission make democracy safe for Capitalism?', *The Journal of Australian Political Economy* (2), pp. 69–75.

Bradbury, B and Doyle, J. (1991), 'Family incomes and economic growth in the 1980s', in P. Raskall and P. Saunders (eds), *Economic Inequality in Australia Vol 2, Some Factors Causing Inequality*, Social Policy Research Centre SSEI Monograph, University of New South Wales, Kensington.

Carey, A. (1987), 'The ideological management industry', in E.L. Wheelwright and K. Buckley (eds), *Communications and the Media in Australia*, Allen and Unwin, Sydney, pp. 156–179.

Castles, F. G. (1985), *The Working Class and Welfare: Reflections on the Political Development of the Welfare State in Australia and New Zealand*, Allen and Unwin, Sydney.

Dabscheck, B. (1990), 'The BCA's plan to Americanise Australian industrial relations', *Journal of Australian Political Economy* , (27), pp. 1–15.

Eaton, M. and Stilwell, F. (1992), 'The super-rich in Australia', *Journal of Australian Political Economy*, (30), pp. 140–147.

Flew, T. (ed.) (1992), *Australia Can Work: An Alternative to Recession*, Left Book Club, Sydney.

Frankel, B. (1992), 'Social movements and the political crisis in Australia', *Arena*, (2), pp. 11–14.

Galbraith, J. K. (1977), *The Age of Uncertainty*, Houghton Mifflin, Boston.

Gorz, A. (1985), *Paths to Paradise: On The Liberation from Work*, Pluto Press, London.

Gregory, R. G., (1992), 'Aspects of Australian labour force living standards: the disappointing decades 1970–1990', The Copland Oration, 21st Conference of Economists, University of Melbourne.

Harding, A. and Landt, J. (1992),'Poverty and policy: trends in disposable incomes', *The Australian Quarterly*, 64 (1), pp. 19–48.

Harvey, D. (1989), *The Urban Experience*, Basil Blackwell, Oxford.

Kuttner, R. (1984), *The Economic Illusion: False Choices between Prosperity and Social Justice*, Houghton Mifflin, Boston.

Lombard, M. (1991), *An Examination of Income Distribution in Australia 1983-1989*, Research Paper No. 340, School of Economic and Fiscal Studies, Macquarie University, Ryde (NSW).

Mathews, R. (1980), 'The Structure of Taxation' in Australian Institute of Political Science (ed), *The Politics of Taxation*, Hodder & Stoughton, Sydney, pp. 82–118.

O'Connor, J.(1973), *The Fiscal Crisis of the State*, St. Martins Press, New York.

Pusey, M. (1991), *Economic Rationalism in Canberra*, Cambridge University Press, Cambridge.

Raskall, P. (1993), 'Widening income disparities in Australia', in S. Rees,
    G. Rodley, and F. Stilwell (eds), *Beyond the Market: Alternatives to Economic Rationalism*,
    Pluto Press, Sydney, pp. 38–52.
Rees, S. (1991), *Achieving Power: Practice and Policy in Social Welfare*, Allen and Unwin,
    Sydney.
Rees, S., Rodley, G. and Stilwell, F. (eds.) (1993), *Beyond the Market: Alternatives to Economic
    Rationalism*, Pluto Press, Sydney.
Sawer, M. (ed) (1982), *Australia and the New Right*, Allen & Unwin, Sydney.
Stilwell, F. (1975), *Normative Economics*, Pergamon Press, Sydney.
Stilwell, F. (1992), 'New life on the left?' *Current Affairs Bulletin*, 69 (5), pp. 10– 16.
Stilwell, F., (1993a), 'Economic rationalism: sound foundation for policy?', in S. Rees,
    S. Rodley, and F. Stilwell (eds), *Beyond the Market: Alternatives to Economic Rationalism*,
    Pluto Press, Sydney, pp. 27–37.
Stilwell, F. (1993b), *Reshaping Australia: Urban Problems and Policies*, Pluto Press, Sydney.
Weatherley, R., (1992), *From Entitlement to Contract: Reshaping The Welfare State in Australia*,
    Working Paper No. 7, Administration, Compliance and Governability Program, Research
    School of Social Sciences, Australian National University, Canberra.
Wheelwright, E. L., (1991), 'Global capitalism now: Depression in the 1990s', *Arena*, (94),
    pp. 63–75.
Wilkinson, R. G., (1992),'Income distribution and life expectancy', *British Medical Journal*,
    (304), pp. 165–8.

CONCLUSION

REINVENTING WELFARE?

The political future of the Australian welfare state

MICHAEL WEARING AND ROSEMARY BERREEN

The debates contained in the foregoing chapters emphasise the contested and contradictory nature of social policy discourse and welfare development in Australia since white settlement. In this two-hundred-year-period, Australian welfare has developed as both innovator and reactor, as both 'social laboratory' for welfare capitalism and the 'lean and mean' oppressor of the marginal and dispossessed. The Australian welfare state is now facing a major period of transition and structural reshaping more in tune with the economic liberal doctrines of laissez-faire and individualism than the collective and, thus, social production and consumption of welfare in a market economy. We are in a process of reinvention and innovation that will fashion social welfare arrangements anew and perhaps break completely with cherished post-Second-World-War notions of universalism, full employment and a bureaucratic state as providers of citizens' welfare.

The objective of this book has been to enable segments of the intellectual discourse on Australian welfare and social policy to open up the reader's historical and political imagination. In coming to the end of the text it is hoped that readers will interpret the prospects for Australian welfare as neither bleak nor overly optimistic. There are political possibilities and political choices within the historical, economic and social trajectories of our current welfare development. These possibilities and choices about welfare may lead, as Tawney (1952) once hoped, to a more equal and free society however contradictory these principles may appear in the making and shaping of social policy arrangements. We concluded part one of the book with a chapter on the concept of social justice as both central to normative debate on welfare and as opening up possibilities for a collective sense of what is valued amongst groups with a socially shared identity. The linking of social justice to social welfare, like the link between citizenship and welfare, is one strategic alliance which may bear meaningful change in Australia. It is not, however, the only alliance that could bring new strategic possibilities.

The conclusion to a book of this type is never a sum of the parts. It is more a place to look for direction beyond the parts. Although a reiteration of some themes is inevitable, what follows is not a summary of the value of each chapter. In accord with previous chapters the Australian welfare state may be conceived as locked within contest about principles that guarantee the social welfare of Australians including, amongst others, questions about how to maximise and minimise freedom and equality in our society. These principles relate to the outcomes of resource distribution and the social goals of welfare; they also relate to the conditions and policies that are practiced in social policy domains such as health, housing, education, transport, child and family policy, among others. Nonetheless, out of concern for all social groups and classes of Australians, social policy must also deal with issues of production and the degree to which labour is 'commodified' through the consumption of goods and services in welfare capitalism (Esping-Andersen, 1990).

In this conclusion we reflect again on some of the major challenges, concepts, oppositions and questions raised by the book. We discuss more closely general developments in advanced welfare states and Australia's place within these developments. We also discuss the future of welfare politics in Australia with the focus on a discourse of economic liberalism and the disconnection of social citizenship from welfare development in this country.

Contesting the basis for welfare

Rudolf Klein has recently considered the impact of Thatcherism on the British welfare state and, more specifically, the National Health Service (NHS) during the 1980s. He asks whether the NHS will 'continue to evolve within the existing institutional framework in order to adapt to the new environment or will the marble crack as the stresses get too much?' (Klein, 1989:xi–x). Australian social welfare institutions are also at a point of stress and transition having experienced both the economic failure of the more general universalist model of 'welfare for all' in the mid 1970s and the social limitations of a residualist and highly targeted model of the 1980s. The Labor and Liberal Federal and State governments of the eighties are not entirely to blame for the stress. Unlike the strong ideological attack on state welfare in Thatcher's Britain, significant changes in Australia's material circumstances since the

Second World War and a lack of sensible industry policy during the 1950s and 1960s has made the 1970s and 1980s harder for Australians than they might have been. The social and economic limits of universalist arrangements and targeted benefits are evident in the 1990s. What kind of programs and polices will emerge from these limits remains to be seen. One prominent social theorist has argued that the utopian energies of the welfare state are 'exhausted' in advanced societies (Habermas, 1989) and people must reconceive their social goals under stress from the worst hardships caused by the exercise of power and money in capitalist economies.

One question that is posed by the exhaustion of a universal vision of welfare is 'Will the welfare state always be with us?' This question arises from the decline, in the last two decades in Australia, of social liberalism (see. Beilharz, Considine and Watts, 1992:Chapter 2). The social liberalism of Australian welfare is based partly on the liberal Keynes-Beveridge postwar settlement amongst business, state agencies and labour interests, which secured a stable and economically productive society based on full employment (Kemp, 1988). The possibility of radical change to Australian welfare resulting from the New Right and conservative pressure exercised during the 1980s and early 1990s has moved the liberal-left politics of Australian welfare to compromise with the Right or, at the very least, a struggle to maintain things as they are. What would a transition to and compromise over a new order of welfare bring to Australian society? Who would benefit and who would lose from the new order? It seems that Australians can no longer rely on an inherited post-Second-World-War view that public welfare will evolve into a universalism for all citizens from 'cradle to grave'.

A second question, that arises from the first, is posed, *What will the direction of the Australian welfare state in the 1990s be?* Signs of this direction are already evident in the political contests and conflicts of Australia's major parties. The Australian welfare state was to face major structural upheaval if the Liberal National Party Coalition had been elected to Federal government in March 1993. The centrepiece of the Right's social and economic policies, a goods and services tax (GST) of 15 per cent, was announced in November 1991. As part of their GST programme the conservative Parties revealed that they intended to cut the Social Security budget by a staggering (by Australian public spending standards) $2.5 thousand million, and use the savings to compensate the remaining welfare recipients for the effects of the GST. Its effect on Australian welfare policy, social welfare services and the numbers eligible for welfare benefits would have been substantial. Under the conservatives, policies were likely to be more 'residual' and meanly targeted in nature, although there was little in the policy rhetoric to suggest that their economic strategies would be more equitable or reduce inequalities. The Right's intentions to 'meanness' were disguised in a more punitive justice of delivering benefits to the genuinely needy and the deserving poor.

The Australian Labor Party won the March 1993 election on a platform of promises of $8 billion in budget cuts and the maintenance or increase in areas of social spending. By July 1993, however, the Keating Labor Government — burdened with the prospect of much less optimistic economic expectations than envisaged a year before — made plans to dramatically reduce their Keynesian styled answer to the country's poor economic performance. For most of the 1992–3 period unemployment was steady at a high rate of 11 per cent and the future prospects for the long-term unemployed and other marginalised groups remain uncertain. One factor most analysts are agreed upon is that high unemployment rates and the numbers of long-term unemployed will remain a central feature of the Australian economy. It would appear that the scarce resource of paid work remains simultaneously a symptom and perhaps a cause of economic scarcity. Nonetheless, on economic indicators there is only relative scarcity in Australia today; economic growth is around 2.7 per cent, underlying inflation 2 per cent, and interest rates are low. On the other hand, Australia's debt problem does produce scarcity and internationally low demand for exports which means that high unemployment could be a problem throughout the next decade.

The models of citizenship suggested by the conservative Federal Opposition, under Hewson's guidance, and to a slightly lesser extent that of the Keating's Labor Government, are market-based. These models are contrary in several respects to the liberal model of social citizenship that has dominated postwar social theories of welfare and the welfare strategies of social democrats. Positive appraisals of the welfare state in the 1980s anticipated the re-emergence of a critical social democratic defence of welfare arrangements. (see e.g. Bean, Ferris and Whynes (eds), 1986). As with earlier debates on welfare development in advanced societies (Offe, 1984:147–61), there are parallels in the rhetoric of Left and Right between the critical defence of welfare and the neo-conservative criticisms of welfare arrangements. A brief sketch is possible of some of these parallels.

First, both Right and Left are concerned to demonstrate the administrative ineffectiveness and economic inefficiencies of social welfare services especially where such services have either directly or indirectly benefited the middle class. Second, both are concerned with the possible repressive nature of much service delivery in the welfare state — the Right talk of state coercion of welfare consumers and the withdrawal of their liberty by state intervention (James, 1989), the Left of surveillance and 'normalisation' of welfare claimants.

Finally, both want to develop a normative model that proffers a defence of their respective positions on the welfare state. The neo-conservatives and conservatives want to minimise the degree of welfare state interventions in civil life and create significant roles for 'market forces' and non-government organisations in welfare arrangements (Hayek, 1944; Hendrie and Porter, 1987). There is also the less sophisticated positivist economic liberalism that imposes the gloss of libertarian 'facts' on a country's economic performance as somehow neutral in political terms (Battin, 1991). The critical social democrats want to defend the ideal of citizenship, a contributory welfare state, and a more guarded pursuit of universalist policies (Esping-Andersen, 1985, 1990; MacIntyre, 1985).

Critics of the social democratic model of welfare development have undermined what they see as a reworking of the 'irreversibility thesis' on the welfare state. Simply put, the thesis contends that government cannot wind back the social welfare state. Three major criticisms of this thesis are proffered by commentators. First, they have questioned the capacity of trade union power or social democratic governments alone to develop more generous welfare provisions given the emasculation of unions and labour parties in OECD welfare states (Mishra 1985: 16). Second, they emphasise the need for distinction between the reformist measures of social democratic welfare policy — 'the struggle for improving capitalism' - and the quest for socialism — 'a society free of alienation' (Przeworski, 1986:239–48). For socialists, improving capitalism requires a much stronger emphasis on socialisation of production that creates personal freedoms through more equal material circumstances. Finally, this model has been questioned in light of recent evidence on the demise of social spending and social support for universalism in Scandinavian welfare states (Marklund, 1988; Baldwin, 1990; Kangas, 1991) and, in particular, Sweden (Vandenberg and Dow, 1991).

Whilst these criticisms highlight certain problems with the older versions of Right and Left debate on the welfare state, they do not unravel the economic mythology that underpins much of the old and new political debates over welfare. The weaknesses of the debate and criticism are exemplified in Australian public discourse on the proper role of economy and state.

The myth of an economic soul

A great deal of public debate on social policy and welfare during the last decade has concerned itself with the myth that the Australian polity has primarily an economic core largely divorced from social and political forces.

The public discourse on welfare in Australian society has been forced into a narrow and limited agenda based on this myth. Technical, bureaucratic and economic perspectives on social policy concerning international comparisons, the growth of poverty, dependency ratios, the adequacy of income maintenance provisions or the levels of income and wealth inequality in Australian society tend to deny that they are premised on both political decisions about the directions of policy change and value-positions on these policies. Further, these interpretations of Australian welfare development exclude more far-reaching concerns about the production and distribution of welfare to the whole population, including questions such as: Who shapes policy, who makes it, who benefits, and when and why?

The myth of an economic soul to Australian life has reasserted itself in public discourse on numerous occasions despite the significant impact of, and change induced by, the social and cultural transformation of the Australian state and economy since the postwar years. Some of these changes include: a move from a homogeneous view of social life to a more cosmopolitan view based on an increasingly culturally diverse labour force; a growing recognition of the rights of indigenous people, children, women and migrants; a movement towards more liberal and permissive attitudes on a range of social and moral issues; and a more accurate intellectual view of Australia's place in the South-East Asian region and the global order. The economistic views of social policy have dominated much of the policy debate since the early 1980s. As if to reflect the changing climate, and for good sociological reasons, social policy analysis has moved away from social explanation to the less politically controversial areas of empirical and technical investigation (cf. Jamrozik, 1991). Even Keynes took the view that social policy for all a nation's population was as much a part of the organisation of production as it was about reinvigorating consumption. Today, however, the predominant view of 'welfare' is as residual measures designed to take up failures in the market.

Residualism in practice does not mean, however, that certain key issues and controversies should not be addressed in public debate. Many of these issues are crucial to public discourse if Australia is to move beyond the highly selective and 'targeted' reality of much welfare provision. For example, the social wage as the interplay of public and private benefits to social groups and classes cannot be narrowed to include only social security payments or benefits provided by a narrowly defined public sector. Neither can false oppositions continue to be rehearsed by policy analysts to obscure the rich interplay of forms of provision in the practice of service delivery. Claiming exclusive categorical divisions such as between professional and bureaucratic power, decentralisation and centralisation, community care and institutional care, expert paternalism and consumerism, old management practices and new managerialism, or individualism and collective enterprise, can in the end only highlight issues not offer strategic intervention to change the distributive prerequisites of the social welfare system.

An explicitly democratic public culture should find representation of broad welfare issues in political organisations and political parties as they do in industrial, religious and social agencies in Australian society. Liberal democracies allow a certain amount of public criticism of the status quo and in the current climate this appears to come from agencies and organisations usually guarded in their direct criticism of governments. For example, the Australian Catholic Bishops Conference released a statement on the distribution of Wealth in Australia in 1992. They claimed that:

> ... the idea of a commonwealth refers to a society founded on its common wealth, where wealth is broadly understood. It includes notions of our common possession or heritage and the general welfare and well being of the whole population ... Increasingly in Australian culture, the measure of worth and well-being has been reduced to an economic calculation, and then a bank balance, with a consequent impoverishment for everybody.
>
> (Australian Catholic Bishop's Conference, 1992: xi)

It is the particular nature of white Australia's history that the Church as both oppressor and liberator of the weak and marginal within the community has made statements contrary to Government thinking on social welfare policy.

In the Catholic Bishops' statement the economic soul of Australia clearly has morally dangerous outcomes which rest upon 'anti-Christian' doctrines of greed, injustice, selfishness and deceit. Other non-church commentators have included similar moral arguments against the tide of economic liberalism that has swept over the last decade (Pusey, 1991; Battin, 1991; Rees, Rodley and Stilwell (eds), 1993). Some have also engaged political moralism (whatever its rhetorical merit) to counteract the assumptions of economic rationalism:

> The doctrine derives from one distinctive branch of economic theory, based on a host of assumptions about competitive markets which seldom apply to the real world. It subordinates broader social values to free market economics.
>
> (From a letter to all leading newspapers in Australia in December 1991; cited in Rees, Rodley and Stilwell (eds), 1993: 305).

What such criticism of 'the market' neglects is that economies are nearly always competitive in complex societies unless administered outside a multi-party society or monopolised by trans/multi-national companies. Further, these criticisms obscure, on moral and/or political-ideological grounds, the consequences of diverse and multiple markets. To see markets as theoretically homogenous and containing a generalised structure is an essentialist view of their workings (Hindess, 1987 147–55). Such essentialism serves to perpetuate the myth of a unified economic 'soul' driving policy development in Australia.

To these critics, the economy consists of dark unconstrained forces that could be tamed with substantial public intervention and the ensuing socialisation of production. A more positive approach to economic activity would analyse the consequences of markets for productivity and the allocation of resources on an equitable basis. This analysis could include the so-called unproductive markets such as those who perform domestic labour (mostly women) and markets that operate for socially different people such as people with disabilities. It could equally be argued that through their unpaid activities these people enhance social capital through socialisation for employment, social responsibility, and respect for all citizens. Like the officially unemployed, they also form part of the surplus (unpaid) labour force who contribute as either consumers or producers of goods to more marginal or 'black' economies that are not assessable in national accounting figures.

In the current policy climate the only economically productive and efficient work force is seen to be characterised by the affluent and well-educated middle class. Unfortunately, it is at least partially true that policies of deregulation appear to set market forces in key economic domains, such as housing and education, against those who are at the mercy of powerful commercial interests. Nonetheless, the notion of an 'economy' can have different meanings within policy frameworks and policy development. If policy analysts and community practitioners investigate the soul of economic essentialism they might better understand the limitations and historical bankruptcy of much of economic thought in the neo-classical, liberal and radical traditions (Myers, 1983). They might further understand that much conservative thought is based on quaint nineteenth century English ideas, that under capitalism good citizens are those who pursue their own ends in a spirit of entrepreneurship and charitable philanthropy to others. It is with this tradition of thought in mind that we turn to a peculiar hybrid of liberal conservatism implemented in the welfare policy of the current Federal Labor Government.

What is the character of policy culture in an age of economically liberal political agendas? The preceding brief discussion of the essentialism evident in Left-liberal arguments against the market economy can also be applied to the

New Right and emerging forms of economic liberalism in the public discourse on Australian welfare. The origins of the active society lie in the blueprints for change developed during the 1980s. Despite the influence of New Right thinking on conservative politics in Australia in the 1980s and early 1990s, the Federal Labour Government has also employed much of the rhetoric of conservatism and, in some instances, radical conservatism to justify policy developments. The rhetoric of the two major parties on welfare since 1972 have had greater similarity in this regard than might be imagined.

One example of the influence of conservative thinking on policy occurs in the Social Security Review set up by the now Deputy Prime Minister of the Federal Labor Government, Brian Howe, in February 1986. In the 1988 Issues Paper of the Review, entitled 'Income Support for the Unemployed in Australia: towards a More Active System', the argument and policy direction is put that unemployed people should be more embodied with a work ethic through closer integration between 'income support programs and labour market training programs' (Cass 1988:276). This Issues Paper clarified one of the objectives, for the Federal Labor Government, of income support for the unemployed:

> *... as a payment to support active job search, particularly in the early period of unemployment when enthusiasm for active job search and the likelihood of its success are at their highest and when the majority of youth and significant proportion of prime-age adults find jobs. This is the job search function of unemployment assistance.*

(Cass, 1988:274)

It is remarkable how much similarity there is between the Australian Social Security Review and Norman Fowler's Social Security Review under Britain's conservative Thatcher Government in 1984. Under the British review unemployed people were caught in what was known then as 'a social security trap' (commonly termed a poverty trap) between a government's low wages policy and levels of social security payment (Esam, Good and Middleton, 1985: 142). The Social Security Review represents an extension of the entrepreneurial culture of the 1980s that encouraged people to be active in the market economy whether as consumers or producers.

What is an active society? We characterise an active society within the shell of welfare capitalism as oriented towards high market activity that encourages unequal and individual reward in the population. Australia is rapidly approaching the ideal of an active society on the basis of party rhetoric and economic policy of the nineties. This active society requires a passive citizenship and high levels of cooperation between a compliant workforce and business. In order for the workforce and marginal groups to resist compliance to business and state agencies a strong political culture of activism over social rights is necessary. This is usually achieved through the politicisation of citizenship. Nonetheless, Australia's liberal state and economy are relatively unresponsive to the needs and wants of ordinary people when compared to other OECD countries such as Sweden or even the United States. Current policy directions in Australia towards an active society maintain a political impasse between the twin goals of social citizenship and collective welfare. In order for these goals to coalesce (or, at least, become clearer) a reinvention of welfare politics is required.

Beyond welfare and passive citizenship

The Australian welfare state has particular economic and political structures and sets of socio-administrative practice in relation to most advanced welfare states. Australia has been described as a social assistance or liberal welfare state 'with its mainsprings in the poor-law tradition' and is 'characterised by a means test or income-test with varying degrees of stringency' (Esping-Andersen, 1990: 48). The historical legacy for our social assistance system is found in the nineteenth century establishment of charitable and welfare programs (for examples see chapters one and two). As mentioned in the Introduction, this nineteenth century legacy is repeated in current media and political discourse in Australia that searches for an 'underclass' and genuine poor to raise the problem of the extent of poverty as morally abhorrent. Such politically motivated morality sits comfortably with the Federal Government's current social security policy direction to better target welfare payments.

The poverty discourse from experts sends a symbolic message to Australian society that poverty is a harsh social and economic 'prison' from which one can only escape in a free-market economy through diligence, honest hard work and individual entrepreneurship. The politicisation of phrases such as 'the cycle of poverty', 'the underclass', 'the unemployed' or even 'welfare beneficiary' all connote, in our current welfare culture, a lack of personal freedoms and access to an equitable share of resources. We would suggest that the symbolic power of party, media and research discourse that focuses on poverty and 'the poor' in contemporary Australian debate is to obscure the nature of inequalities and create a climate of opinion that social rights belong only to the included and active wage-earning citizen. Dean (1991) has recently argued that the genealogy of these forms of discourse originate in a 'liberal mode of governance' that permeates the social relations of English speaking welfare capitalism. The social technologies of this governance are exercised in the micropolitics of discursive sites that include the family, hospital, asylum, factory, community locality and welfare agency. The processes of this micro-governance reiterate a civil life in Australia of passive citizenship i.e. where labour is largely commodified by the market and people play out their everyday lives in the midst of a consumer culture.

Over and against this kind of discursive control and commodification of life it can be argued that strategies of welfare have, since the 1940s and 1950s, allied with arguments for social rights and citizenship for all (cf Marshall, 1950; Beilharz, Considine and Watts, 1992). In the current Australian climate these strategies of citizenship are increasingly disconnected from those of welfare and the promotion of political and moral equality. Questions such as what is the nature of 'new welfare politics' are being asked to reassess fundamental problems in the distribution and redistribution of resources. Arguably the shift away from rigid class-based politics to a kind of critical pluralism and flexible identity politics within welfare capitalism based on class, sex, race and other fundamental categories and divisions in society tells us something about the character of this new social order. Some political theorists have reconceived social justice and forms of oppression within societies which seem to feature such pluralism (Walzer 1983, 1993; Laclau and Mouffe, 1985; Lasch and Urry, 1987). Walzer (1993) has linked these conceptions to the multiple social spaces within the polity that exclude and create spheres of injustice for differentiated and oppressed groupings. Although the new politics is tentative and uncertain it does create an idea of what the distribution of advantage for certain socially identifiable groups and classes might mean in the future.

The smooth transition to a free-market economy and active entrepreneurial society of exclusion during the 1990s appears almost assured under the guidance of economic liberalism's narrow definitions of social justice, social rights and social policy. It is conceivable that during this decade Australians will pay more for less social welfare services and this will strengthen the market individualism of various policy domains. The demise in Australia of what little is left of social citizenship and its political cousin, social liberalism, looks imminent in the 1990s. Under pressure from this new market order, a more restricted and minimal social and industrial citizenship will have difficulties challenging inequalities created by market mechanisms and economic management structures. If we are not to engage an analysis that sets markets up as essentialist, Australian policy analysts will need to use what they know about more equitable and just allocation mechanisms in their own domains of policy to counter conservative market essentialism.

The development of alternative political and economic strategies on citizenship and links with collective forms of welfare are required to counter some of the detrimental effects of the transition to market-based welfare provision in Australia and keep pace with managing diverse social identities. Strategic solutions to this transition to an active society are uneasy and necessarily hesitant in their ability to disrupt the political will of conservatism in this country. Some commentators (Evatt Research Centre, 1989; Coombs, 1990, 1993) have suggested that more control over the economy by Australians would be achieved if democratic social criteria were considered in making national investments. They suggest that instead of having the bulk of investment in low employment industries an investment plan would make the economy larger and provide considerable employment. This 'investment citizenship' would be decided upon democratically with industry planning done according to social criteria and the kind of economy people want. Whatever the value of such solutions, a restructuring of Australian welfare which brings greater equality and social justice for excluded citizens will depend on sustained resistance to conservatism and significant political action from social movements including the industrial labour movement and welfare lobby groups.

REFERENCES

Australian Catholic Bishops' Conference (1992), *A Statement on the Distribution of Wealth in Australia: common wealth for the common good*, Collins Dove, Melbourne.

Australian Council of Social Service (ACOSS) (1992), 'The Economic Statement: Keating's Cautious Kick-Start', *Impact*, 22(2), pp. 10–11.

Baldwin, P.(1990), *The Politics of Social Solidarity: Class Bases of the European Welfare State 1875-1975*, Cambridge University Press, Cambridge.

Battin, T. (1991),' What is this thing called economic rationalism?', *Australian Journal of Social Issues*, 26(4), pp. 294–302.

Bean, P., Ferris, J., and Whynes, D. (eds) (1986), *In Defence of Welfare*, Tavistock, London.

Beilharz, P. Considine, M. and Watts, R. (1992), *Arguing About the Welfare State*, Allen and Unwin, Sydney.

Castles, F. (1988), *Australian Public Policy and Economic Vulnerability: a comparative and historical perspective*, Allen and Unwin, Sydney.

Cass, B. (1988), *Income Support for the Unemployed in Australia: towards a more active system*, AGPS, Canberra.

Coombs H.C. (1990), *The Return of Scarcity: strategies for an economic future*, Cambridge University Press, Cambridge.

Coombs, H.C. (1993), 'Independence or Bust', *Australian Business Monthly*, January, pp. 60–63.

Dean, M. (1991), *The Constitution of Poverty: Towards a genealogy of liberal governance*, Routledge, London.

Esping-Andersen, G. (1985), *Politics Against Markets: the social democratic road to power*, Princeton University Press, New Jersey.

Esping-Andersen, G. (1990), *The Three Worlds of Welfare Capitalism*, Polity Press, Cambridge.

Esram, E. Good T., and Middleton, P. (1985), *A Radical Review of Social Security*, Verso, London.

Evatt Research Centre (1989), *State of Siege: Renewal or Privatisation for Australian State Public Services?*, Allen and Unwin, Sydney.

Grampp, W.D. (1965), *Economic Liberalism Vol 1: The Beginnings*, Random House, New York.

Green, D.G. (1987) *The New Right*, Wheatsheaf, Brighton.

Habermas, J. (1989), 'The crisis of the welfare state and the exhaustion of utopian energies' in S. Seidman (ed.), *Jurgen Habermas on Society and Politics: A Reader*, Beacon Press, Boston, pp. 284–322.

Hayek, F.A. (1944), *The Road to Serfdom*, Dymocks, Sydney.

Hendrie, D and Porter, M.G. (1987), 'The capture of the welfare state', *Canberra Bulletin of Public Administration*, 51, pp. 20-30.

Hindess, B. (1987), *Freedom, Equality and the Market*, Tavistock, London.

James, M. (1989), 'Welfare, coercion and reciprocity' in M. James (ed.), *The Welfare State: foundations and alternatives*, Centre for Independent Studies, St Leonards, NSW.

Jamrozik, A. (1991), *Class, Inequality and the State*, Macmillan, Melbourne.

Kangas, O. (1991), 'The bigger the better? On the dimensions of welfare state development: social expenditure versus social rights', *Acta Sociologica* 34(1), pp. 1–68.

Kemp, D. (1988),' Liberalism and conservatism in Australia since 1944' in B. Head and J. Walter (eds), *Intellectual Movements and Australian Society*, Oxford University Press, Melbourne, pp. 322–362.

King, D. (1987) *The New Right: Politics, Markets and Citizenship*, Macmillan, London.

Klein, R. (1989), *The Politics of NHS* 2nd edn, Longman Cheshire, London.

Lasch, C. and Urry, J. (1987), *The End of Organised Capitalism*, Polity, Cambridge.

Laclau, E., and Mouffe, C. (1985), *Hegemony and Socialist Strategy*, Verso, London.

Liberal and National Parties (1991),*Fightback! Taxation and Expenditure Reform for Jobs*, Fyshwick, ACT.

MacIntyre, S. (1985), *Winners and Losers*, Allen and Unwin, Sydney

Markland, S. (1988), *Paradise Lost? Nordic Welfare States and the Recession 1975–1985*, Arkiv forlag, Lund, Sweden.

Marshall, T.H. (1950), 'Citizenship and social class' in T.H. Marshall (ed.), *Sociology at the Crossroads and other essays*, Heinemann, London, pp. 67–127.

Mishra, R. (1985), 'The Left and the welfare state: a critical analysis', *Critical Social Policy* 15(5), pp. 4-19.

Myers, N.L. (1983) *The Soul of Economic Man: Ideas of Self-Interest — Thomas Hobbes to Adam Smith*, Chicago University Press, Chicago.

Offe, C. (1984), *Contradictions of the Welfare State*, Hutchinson, London.

Pierson, C. (1991), *Beyond the Welfare State?: The New Political Economy of Welfare*, Polity Press, Cambridge.

Przeworski, A. (1985), *Capitalism and Social Democracy*, Cambridge University Press, Cambridge.

Pusey, M. (1991), *Economic Rationalism in Canberra: A Nation-Building State Changes Its Mind*, Cambridge University Press, Cambridge.

Rees, S. Rodley, G., and Stilwell, F. (1993), *Beyond the Market: Alternatives to Economic Rationalism*, Pluto Press, Sydney.

Smith, R., and Wearing, M. (1987), 'Do Australians want the welfare state?', *Politics*, 22(2), pp. 55–65.

Tawney, R.H. (1953), *Equality*, Allen and Unwin, London.

Vandenberg, J., and Dow, G. (1991), 'Farewell to the Swedish model', *Australian Left Review*, (126), pp. 26–30.

Walzer, M. (1983), *Spheres of Justice: a defence of pluralism and equality*, Basic Books, New York.

Walzer, M. (1993), 'Exclusion, injustice and the democratic state', *Dissent*, (40), pp. 55–64.

Watts, R. (1989), ' "In fractured times": the Accord and social policy under Hawke, 1983-87', in R. Kennedy (ed.) *Australian Welfare*, Macmillan, Melbourne, pp. 104–131.

Yeatman, A. (1990), *Bureaucrats Technocrats and Femocrats*, Allen and Unwin, Sydney.

INDEX

4 5 6 7 8 9 0 1 2
A B C D E F G H I J

TO THE OWNER OF THIS BOOK

We are interested in your reaction to *Welfare and social policy in Australia: the distribution of advantage*, edited by Wearing and Berreen.

1. What was your reason for using this book?

_____ university course   _____ continuing education course

_____ college course   _____ personal interest

_____ TAFE course   _____ other (specify)

2. In which school are you enrolled?_____

3. Approximately how much of the book did you use?

_____ 1/4   _____ 1/2   _____ 3/4   _____ all

4. What is the best aspect of the book?

5. Have you any suggestions for improvement?

6. Would more illustrations/diagrams help?

7. Is there any topic that should be added?

Fold here

(Tape shut)

REPLY PAID 5
Managing Editor, College Division
Harcourt Brace & Company, Australia
Locked Bag 16
MARRICKVILLE, NSW 2204